Praise for *W*

Bravo for Paul Freiberger! *When Can You Start?* is exactly what job-seekers need in today's competitive market. This book is the bible for finding and landing the job and career of your dreams. Logical, step-by-step, and packed with insight from experience, Freiberger's work clearly demonstrates he is the thought leader in the field. His advice is priceless. Five stars!

—LARRY JACOBSON, SIX-TIME AWARD-WINNING
AUTHOR OF *THE BOY BEHIND THE GATE*

An invaluable treasure trove of ideas, tools, tips, and advice that will help job seekers at any level prepare for and manage the maddening and stressful hiring process.

—ANDREW GIANGOLA, AUTHOR OF
THE WEEKEND STARTS ON WEDNESDAY

The most exhaustive, best researched book about job interviewing, filled with insights and research.

—JEAN-LOUIS GASSÉE, GENERAL PARTNER, ALLEGIS CAPITAL

Highly useful to anyone facing an important job interview, especially if they haven't been practicing for a while. Practical and well-researched, with extensive and realistic examples. This will stand the test of time.

—MARC SINGER, DIRECTOR, MCKINSEY & COMPANY

No one knows the job search process better than Paul Freiberger. In *When Can You Start?* he cuts through all the rigmarole to truly help the job seeker and captures what everyone needs to know in a positive way.

—RICHARD MORAN, CEO, ACCRETIVE SOLUTIONS

Freiberger delivers a fun and informative read. You will get a job a lot sooner if you read this book. Perfect for new grads at the beginning of their careers and powerful ammunition for the rest of us.

—GUY KAWASAKI, AUTHOR OF *APE: AUTHOR, PUBLISHER, ENTREPRENEUR*
AND FORMER CHIEF EVANGELIST OF APPLE

This book is powerful and expertly researched. Packed with interview advice you need to get your next job. Learn the right way to network and do informational interviews, how to handle "ambush" interviews, what to do with your phone during an interview, the right and wrong answers to "What are your weaknesses?" and how to negotiate salary. And who knew that, not unlike dating, it turns out there's some pretty good advice on when you should or shouldn't make a follow-up call after an interview and when you can send a thank-you note. A fun read, this book both tastes good and *is* good for you.

—LARRY KRAMER, PRESIDENT AND PUBLISHER, *USA TODAY*

This is an excellent guide to a pivotal event in the hiring process—the interview. Paul has delivered an effective and pragmatic guide that should be read by anyone preparing for an interview.

—AVERY LYFORD, CHAIRMAN, THE CHURCHILL CLUB

Noted technologist Alan Kay said, "Perspective is worth 80 IQ points." Freiberger brings just such perspective with this fresh, highly engaging book. Ranging from millennia past to the latest in social media, the text draws from Freiberger's experiences as celebrated Silicon Valley historian, journalist, researcher, and consultant to large companies and individuals alike. Whether the reader is 18, 38, or 58, you will finish all the wiser from Freiberger's counsel.

—BRYGG ULLMER, ASSOCIATE PROFESSOR, LSU

I've seen a lot of career advice books in my three decades as corporate recruiter and career coach, but none of them were such fun to read. *When Can You Start?* is chock-a-block with great tips weaved into a narrative that is engaging and enlightening. Freiberger covers everything a job seeker needs to know to be a successful job candidate in clear, shimmering prose. He demystifies the interview process and reveals the thinking behind newer interview techniques, such as the so-called Google-type interview, that have unnerved job seekers recently. If you're looking to successfully navigate today's competitive job market, you need this book.

—TOM BALLANTYNE, CAREER COUNSELOR, SANTA CLARA UNIVERSITY

Informative and insightful, Paul Freiberger's *When Can You Start?* is an essential resource for any job seeker.

—LISA THOMPSON, HUMAN RESOURCES EXECUTIVE,
SAN FRANCISCO 49ERS

WHEN CAN YOU START?

The Only
Job Search Guide
You'll Ever Need

PAUL FREIBERGER

CAREER
UPSHIFT
PRODUCTIONS

SAN MATEO, CA

When Can You Start? *The Only Job Search Guide You'll Ever Need*
By Paul Freiberger

Career Uplift Productions
801 E. 16th Ave.
San Mateo, CA 94402

Book and Cover Design: 1106 Design, www.1106Design.com
Editor and Project Manager: Marla Markman, www.MarlaMarkman.com

Publisher's Cataloging-In-Publication Data:

Names: Freiberger, Paul, author.
Title: When can you start? : the only job search guide you'll ever need / Paul
  Freiberger.
Series: When can you start?
Description: Includes index. | San Mateo, CA: Career Upshift
  Productions, 2017.
Identifiers: ISBN 978-0-9887028-6-8 | LCCN 2016963471
Subjects: LCSH Job hunting. | Career development. | Career changes. | Vocational
  guidance. | BISAC BUSINESS & ECONOMICS / Careers / Job Hunting
Classification: LCC HF5382.7 .F735 2017 | DDC 650.14--dc23

978-0-9887028-6-8 (Print)
978-0-9887028-7-5 (e-Books)

Printed in the United States of America

23 22 21 20 19 18 17   10 9 8 7 6 5 4 3 2 1

To anyone who has searched for a job, changed careers,
written a cover letter or a resume, and survived
an interview. And to Mel, who never gave
up on this book becoming a reality.

Also by Paul Freiberger

When Can You Start? Ace the Job Interview and Get Hired

Fire in the Valley: The Making of the Personal Computer (with Michael Swaine)

Fuzzy Logic: The Revolutionary Computer Technology That Is Changing Our World (with Daniel McNeill)

Computer Sense (with Daniel McNeill)

The Apple IIc (with Daniel McNeil)

Contents

Introduction:
Another Jobs Book?

Tʜᴇʀᴇ ᴍᴜsᴛ ʙᴇ *some people* who enjoy the job search. After all, there are people who wait with gleeful anticipation for the chance to dive into their income taxes every year. We may not understand them, but we acknowledge their existence. They neither want nor need a streamlined approach to Form 1040. In the job market, they're not really looking for a simple path to an offer. Why take all the fun out of tax season? Why take all the mystery out of the hiring process?

This book is not for them.

It's for the rest of us, the people who see the job search as, at best, a necessary evil—the people who would rather be doing just about anything other than fighting their way through resumes, applications and interviews. This book is for those people who soldier through the mess that is the hiring process, knowing it's the only game in town.

Is hiring really such a mess? We think so, especially for the applicant. The process is maddening. It's stressful. It's mysterious, subject to arbitrary rules. It's a place where decisions are made and never explained. It's a system that can deliver hit after hit to your self-esteem, especially if things are going badly and the search drags on. It's a process that can leave you feeling just as lost on the eve of an interview as you were when you typed out the first draft of your resume. You don't know what you're doing right. You don't know what you're doing wrong.

In the end, though, you don't have to love the search. You *do*, however, have to be good at it. That's our one and only goal.

In these pages, we're not going to fix the hiring process. We know our limits. We'll discuss some of its flaws, especially the ones that affect an applicant's strategy, and we'll even talk about history and theory when it helps you to understand what's happening and leads to better choices. So while we can't fix the hiring process, we can make it comprehensible.

You'd think, though, that with so much at stake in this inscrutable process, someone must have found a way to give applicants the help they really need. There must be some readily available source of expert guidance. There must be some book that clears things up or some reference that illuminates it all, some reliable advisor who pulls back the curtain, exposes the hidden machinery, and sets applicants on the right path.

Yes, you'd think so, but you'd soon learn that the help you really need is awfully hard to find. It turns out that the search for a truly worthwhile book about the job search is almost as daunting as the job search itself.

The problem is not a lack of options. In a sense, it's quite the opposite.

Here's one example: As of this writing, an Amazon search for books about job hunting delivers more than 13,000 results. A search for books about jobs in general delivers more than 34,000, a number that's inflated a tad by the inevitable inclusion of books about a Jobs named "Steve." Once you get past the first page of results, though, Steve pretty much disappears, yet you're still left with some 33,990 choices.

Why, then, launch another job-related book into the world? Aren't 34,000 enough? Is there some compelling reason to make that smaller pile of 13,000 a little higher? Wouldn't 100 books do just as well, and wouldn't they hit just about every topic imaginable? They might neglect careers in artisanal pickle making in Namibia, but they wouldn't neglect much else.

Why, then, add one more volume to the already teetering pile?

To ask the question another way, what does this book do that the other 34,000 don't?

The answer is that the state of the art is not encouraging. We can't claim to have read each and every one of those books, but we've seen more than enough to draw some conclusions:

- Some job books are better than others, but "better" does not necessarily mean "good."

- Some of the better books offer one particularly good idea, but one good idea is not enough.

- Some books, lacking even one good idea, are happy to rehash every stale tip that's out there. As a result, some books are filled with great advice for the 2008 job market.

In the end, it's enough to say that none of them, even the best of the breed, do it all. And if they don't do it all, they don't do enough.

Nothing out there gives you the comprehensive help it takes to get you from the very beginnings of the search—the time when you're still wondering what you should be looking for—to its happy conclusion.

Nothing gives you the practical approach that is dedicated, every single step of the way, to the simple proposition that the only thing that matters is getting you hired.

Practical advice matters. If you're simply looking for a job, you haven't studied the job market. And that unfamiliarity leaves you at a disadvantage. When it comes to advice, you have no way of knowing who's telling you the truth and who's not, and it doesn't help that there are enough conflicting theories out there to make your head spin. Which advice works? Which is utter nonsense? To make things worse, a lot of advice can sound pretty good from the outside. It may seem like a particular tactic should work. It certainly *sounds* like good advice. However, reality is another story, and advice does not magically become useful just because it has a nice ring to it.

In fact, there's a lot of good-sounding advice that can actually hurt your chances. How can you tell fact from fiction? The hiring process, with its tightfisted approach to feedback, won't help you learn from your mistakes. It won't reveal clues about a hiring manager's rationale. It won't highlight a critical omission from your resume. It won't call attention to an interview misstep. On the contrary, many people learn one frustrating fact about the market very early on: For their own reasons, employers rarely, if ever, tell you why you didn't get the job. Without feedback, you risk repeating the same mistakes again and again.

How do we get beyond this impasse?

We think the answer is quite simple. In this guide, we don't care how things sound or whether some particular strategy is part of the entrenched wisdom of the job search. We only have one criterion: Does it work?

If it works, we'll tell you how and why. We'll also talk about mistakes, the things you shouldn't do, especially when those mistakes are less than obvious. We'll look objectively at conventional wisdom, and we'll tell you when it's just plain wrong. From time to time, we'll look at some research, but we'll stick to the sort that explains how hiring decisions actually get made. We'll even consider theory, but only when it's borne out in the real world and only when its consequences help you do the job search better.

Our theme, then, is clear as can be. Faced with the existing mountains of guides for job seekers, we became increasingly frustrated. Nothing covered the subject from beginning to end. Nothing told the truth, the whole truth, and nothing but the truth. In a world of rapid change, one in which your 2012 strategy won't quite work today, nothing was sufficiently current.

You might ask, though, how we know what works for a job seeker in today's market. Again, the answer is not complicated.

We begin with the premise that the real world is all that matters. It's what shaped this guide. Our conclusions come from years of experience with hiring managers and recruiters. They're conclusions drawn from years of helping applicants—at every level and in many different industries—make their way success-fully through the hiring gauntlet. At heart, this guide is a report from the trenches, filled with hard-won lessons that all speak to one goal: Everything here—every strategy, every tactic, and every bit of advice—is about what it takes to get hired, nothing more and nothing less.

FIVE PRINCIPLES

In drawing those conclusions and sharing them with you, we wanted to do something different and better. To achieve that, we focused on five key principles:

- **Significance:** The only lessons here are the ones that matter, the ones tied to consistent success in the job market. We give them lots of space. We don't waste space on things that don't matter, even if those things get a lot of coverage elsewhere.

- **Simplicity:** "Business-speak" has its place, but this is not that place. Admittedly, there are times you need to know the jargon. Rightly or wrongly, it can convince people that you're one of them because you speak the same language, and sometimes that matters. However, many job books use business-speak to camouflage a lack of good, practical ideas. What's worse, a gloss of trendy jargon can make bad ideas sound good. The focus here is on plain steps explained in plain language.

- **Small steps:** The job search is a series of steps. That's very much our focus. We like small steps, where each one is completely manageable and gets you a little closer to your goal. There's nothing dramatic, nothing intimidating, and nothing that requires you to reinvent yourself or to drop everything you're doing. We don't think that's necessary or effective. The steps we recommend are simple. They're clear. They work.

- **Synthesis:** We have no interest in reinventing the wheel. We're not too proud to take a good idea that's out there and use it—*if it still works.* We don't care who thought of it first. We don't care if it's old or new. We do care, however, if it's five years out of date and no longer helps. At that point, we move on to something that's still effective. Our goal is to ensure that you have every possible tool at your disposal, regardless of source. You don't have to use them all, but you have to know your options. We'll see to it that you do. That's a big part of *our* job.

- **Pragmatism:** We're pragmatists. We're not wedded to a philosophy; we're only attached to what works. We don't care if we lack some unique insight never before considered by mortal man. If a timeworn approach works, you need to know about it. We don't even care if something we recommend smacks of "gaming" the system. While we won't counsel you to lie, we think the job search is one place where the end can justify the means. We're not purists. We synthesize everything we've learned, and we're more than happy to include old ideas, new ideas, our ideas, and others' ideas. If it gets people hired, we're on it.

FRESHMAN ORIENTATION

We promise to take you from beginning to end, and we mean it. We'll track the job search chronologically. We freely admit there's nothing earthshaking about that approach. Plenty of other books use it.

The similarity ends there. We have definite ideas—very definite ideas—about what each step should be, the order of those steps, and the best places to invest your energy and time.

To understand what that means, let's take a very brief tour of what's to come. We'll preview some of the chronological milestones, but we'll add a bit of annotation to introduce our way of thinking. We'll alternate between the typical approach, the one used by many job seekers and recommended by too many guides, and a contrasting approach, the one we believe in. Of course, we'll cover things in detail once we really get started. Consider this a pregame warmup for the main event.

Typical: Most job guides are happy to assume that you've chosen your career. The truth is that many of us are unsettled, and we can be unsettled even in the midst of the job search. We know that you haven't necessarily settled on a career just because you're out there looking for work. Wouldn't it be nice, though, to conduct your job search in the field that's right for you? And wouldn't it be infinitely easier if the search grew out of genuine interest and enthusiasm?

Our way: Choosing a career is not necessarily a matter of waiting for lightning to strike, nor is it always a question of "living your dream." Lightning and dreams may not follow your schedule, and it can be dangerous to treat career choice as something that depends on a sort of mystical enlightenment. There are big decisions to be made here. We'll help you identify your options, weed out the also-rans, and focus on what works for you; and we'll do that with some straightforward tools that anyone can use.

Typical: With some sense of a career path, you could, of course, put your resume together, and you could start letting the world know that you're available.

Our way: That's not the path we take. Instead, we look at two different ways to start things moving in the right direction. First, we introduce the idea of the "rough resume," a very broad, rather informal approach to a version of your resume that makes it much easier to achieve resume perfection when you really need it. Second, we're going to talk about people. We don't know exactly where we'd put the relative importance of what you know versus the importance of whom you know. We do know that the importance of the people you know, the people you can get to know, who you can talk to, and who's willing to talk to you cannot be overstated. If you'd like to think you're dealing with a meritocracy, a job market in which your contacts and connections are secondary to your competence, we won't argue, but we'll urge you to try something a little different.

Typical: Some people would say that the easiest path to getting hired is reserved for the boss's daughter and the hiring manager's boyfriend. We won't argue. They'd go on to say that, for those of us without the right relatives, the best course is to keep applying, answering ads, and searching job postings everywhere. We can't create the connections that would give us an inside track out of nothing.

Our way: While that may be true, we're going to stick with the people theme and use it to give you an edge in your search. As part of that, we're going to convince you to take advantage of the underused gem of the job search: the informational interview.

We'll explain what it is, and we'll show you who to ask, how to ask, and what to say when you get there. We'll give you a long list of ways to find and connect with people who can help you. We'll tell you what to expect and how to use the opportunity to your best advantage. As you'll see, we put enormous faith in the power of getting a foot in the door. We'll try to make you a believer, too, and you'll know how to make sure your foot is in a door that actually matters to you.

Typical: When it comes to resumes, the best approach is to list your qualifications, your education, and your employment history. Keep it simple, correct any mistakes, and you're good to go. It's a piece of paper that pretty much speaks for itself.

Our way: Resumes have changed along with the job market. We'll explain how to create a resume that works in today's market. For starters, you'll need a resume that gets through all the automated screening you're likely to face these days. You need a resume that tells your story as forcefully and convincingly as possible. It should, in effect, sell your candidacy to a prospective employer. Most resumes don't do that job very well, but we have some simple ways to create the kind of resume that makes employers happy. Some of our advice relates to content, some to style, and some of it falls under the heading of tips and tricks. Once we share those tips and show you the tricks, you'll be in a position to deliver a resume that works as hard as it possibly can on your behalf.

Typical: Aren't cover letters old hat? They seem like relics of a bygone age when penmanship mattered, visiting cards were *de rigueur*, and French was still the language of diplomacy. Do you really need one today, when you can't even be sure that your resume will be seen by a human being? Why waste your time on something so insignificant?

Our way: Cover letters may not always be required, but we don't advise ditching them entirely. For one thing, a cover letter doesn't call for an enormous investment of time. Don't begrudge a mere 20 minutes of your time, especially if it's meant to get you a job you really want or, for that matter, one you really need. That's not all. In many situations—you're overqualified, you're underqualified, you're changing fields, your job history is a problem—a cover letter is your best friend. We'll deal with those situations and show you how to write a cover letter that solves problems and answers questions, especially the ones that can't be managed by your resume alone.

Typical: An interview is always scary. It's a tough, unnatural situation, and there's nothing you can do to make it better or easier. The best you can do is to equip yourself with a list of potential questions and think of some decent answers. At least you won't be taken completely by surprise.

Our way: We'll cover interviews in-depth. We know they're tough, but we don't think they have to be as tough as they seem. You'll find everything you need in terms of interview styles, typical questions, interview formats, best answers to difficult questions, and much more. We'll also look long and hard at the interview through the eyes of the interviewer so that you'll understand what the interviewer is really looking for, both good and bad, no matter what he might be saying. We won't neglect the practical choices that make big differences, from what to wear to what message your body language is sending. We'll walk you through the right way to prepare, using a method that leaves you cool, calm, and collected, ready to be at your best. You may not end up loving the interview experience—there's a limit to our powers—but by the time we're done, you certainly won't be dreading it.

As they say, but wait, there's more, a lot more—from finding the right openings to managing social media, from big questions to small details. Should I handle paper and electronic resumes differently? What's the right salutation for a cover letter? What should I do after an informational interview? What should I do after a real interview? What should I be doing on the web? (*Hint:* Join LinkedIn, a site we'll explore in detail.) What if I get a job offer? How should I handle crazy interview questions?

Although we'll hit all the nitty-gritty details, we're really trying to answer only two questions: What should I do now, and what should I do next? No matter where you stand in the job search, whether you're still deciding on a career or you're negotiating an offer, those are always the pertinent questions. The way we see it, the answers can't be vague, general, or discouragingly difficult. Instead, the answers have to be concrete, specific, and eminently manageable. The answers must appear as a series of small, clear, virtually painless steps that each makes a contribution. Those are the answers you'll find in this guide, every step of the way.

Let's get started!

Part 1

BIG-PICTURE
THINKING

Chapter 1

Who Are You—and Where Do You Want to Go? *Finding Your Place in the Career World*

"Never forget what you are, for surely the world will not. Make it your strength."

—George R.R. Martin, author of *A Game of Thrones*

Are you having a terrible time finding career advice? Unsure about who moved your parachute? Still deciding on the color of your cheese?

A scarcity of advice is certainly not the problem. If anything, the problem is information overload, with a twist. We have an overload of information of dubious utility yet a shortage of good, practical advice that actually stands a chance of getting you where you want to go.

But here's the twist: There's another problem, one that all the good, practical advice in the world—although we'll get to that—can't solve.

How can you use that good advice unless you've answered the one question that looms over the whole enterprise: When all is said and done, where exactly is it you want to go?

Do you know? Are you a new graduate without a clear sense of what the future holds? Are you unsure about the field you thought you'd like? If you've been working for a while, did you know where you wanted to go once upon a time? Are you a lot less sure now? Have you soured on what you've been doing? Is it time for a change?

These are big questions—perhaps *the* big questions. They're not so far removed from asking what it all means, and the answers won't arrive fully formed like Athena from the head of Zeus. They won't be delivered by a man on a flaming pie the way John Lennon mused the Beatles got their name. Get used to the fact that there won't be a bolt of lightning and a clap of thunder.

So how do the answers arrive? For all but the lucky few who found their callings in kindergarten, it's a journey.

If you're just starting out and haven't found your calling, or if you want to change a working life already in progress, don't be deceived into waiting for the big moment of inspiration. This is no mystical quest. It's a trip and, like any trip, it must be taken one step at a time. The first step always has to come before the second, the second before the third, and so on.

If you haven't noticed, this is actually very good news. Reaching your destination only requires a series of small steps. You may have trouble taking that first step, but you can take comfort in the fact that it is, after all, only a small step, and that other small, manageable steps will follow.

To make any journey, whether you're taking the first step or the fifth, you need the right map. Thankfully, we specialize in career cartography, and we're going to unfold that map and walk you through it right now. The journey will include five distinct steps:

- **Step 1: Decide to Decide.** No journey can begin until you decide to get out of your seat and walk through your front door and out into the world.

- **Step 2: Who Are You?** We're not going to go all meta-physical on you here, but there are a lot of simple, concrete questions you can ask yourself that will guide you to the right career decisions.

- **Step 3: What Big Eyes You Have!** No matter how you answered those questions, and no matter how clear you are now about your ultimate goals, there's a very good chance that you won't reach those goals in one big leap. Forget the big picture for a moment. What you need is a system that makes it easy to take one specific, simple, small step at a time.

- **Step 4: Learn Everywhere.** In addition to learning something about yourself, there are a lot of ways to learn about the field that interests you. With that done, you can put those two kinds of knowledge together in a way that moves you closer to your goal.

- **Step 5: The 7 Pillars of Career Wisdom.** Finally, it's time to synthesize everything you've learned. There's no magic involved, only a series of questions that will focus your decision-making on what matters most to you, even if you hadn't quite identified the most important personal criteria before.

STEP 1: DECIDE TO DECIDE

Before you make any first step, you make the decision to move your foot. The same thing happens here. You can spend a lot of time dreaming about your dream job, but that gets you nowhere. Or you can decide to take the first step toward that dream job, and that gets you a little closer to your goal. Yes, just a little, but that's all a first step can do.

If you're not ready to start walking down this road, stop. The fact that it's a journey of small steps doesn't make it an easy journey, and it's no crime to decide that, for now, it's better to wait. Do, however, think about the following list and what it tells you about the urgency of the decision. If you disagree with most of the statements, something needs to change.

- You get paid to do what you like to do.

- You get paid to do what you're good at.

- You can be yourself at work.

- You look forward to going to work—not necessarily always, but a lot of the time.

- You don't feel burned out at the end of the day—most of the time.

- You don't see work as an intrusion on what you want to be doing.

- You don't have separate work and non-work identities.

- Your job brings out the best in you.

- You enjoy your work environment, and you like most of the people you work with.

- You don't have to pretend to be someone you're not at work.

- Your work doesn't drain you; it gives you energy.

- Your work rewards you in ways that matter to you.

- You tell people about your work and feel good doing so.

- Your work may be hard and it may be challenging, but, most of the time, it's fun.

- Your job allows you to maintain what feels like the right work-life balance.

If you're on the fence, unsure of what direction to choose, remember this: People tend to underestimate what they can accomplish. They fear failure from attempting feats that may be beyond them, but that kind of thinking may be the biggest failure of all.

Aim high and you may miss, but when you hit, you'll achieve things that lowballers never do. No one ranks success in life by the percentage of goals you reach. Imagine a minor leaguer who's hitting .357 but refuses to move up to the big leagues because his batting average could drop.

Of course, don't be unrealistic. Don't strive for a Nobel Prize in physics if you have trouble understanding quadratic equations. But aim higher than you think you can reach. You'll find your quest feels sweeter and your life more energized—and you may even succeed.

Ask yourself:

- What should I strive for long term? What do I believe I can achieve, and what lies a level or two above that?

- What can I do now to build toward my long-term goals?

- What am I good at? What professional skills—such as finance—do I have right now? Am I better at originating programs, implementing them, or maintaining them?

- What skills would I like to have? Do I need new skills to reach my goals and, if so, what am I doing to obtain them?

STEP 2: WHO ARE YOU?

The better you know yourself, the easier it will be to figure out what's right for you.

A useful piece of advice comes from a man who managed to make a successful career in theater and never had to resort to waiting tables: This above all, to thine own self be true, Shakespeare told his many readers. This advice is great, except he left out one step.

The first order of business is to find out what your "own self" is. How can you be true to something if you don't quite know what that something is?

To find the answer, you have to ask some questions. What are you really like? What do you hate? What do you really like? Where have you been happy? Where have you been miserable, bored, or stressed? Where have you dreaded going into work or couldn't wait to leave?

Give some thought to those questions. You might start with a bit of personal history, a look at the places you've been and what they've meant to you. This is not just about past jobs. If you're still in school, consider classes you've taken and projects you've done. We want to figure out the characteristics that have made one situation good and another bad. We want to understand what the good ones had in common and what made the bad ones bad.

This Job Is Killing Me!

You spend at least a third of your time at work.

Add in the time spent thinking about it, the time getting to and from your job, and the time it takes to get ready in the morning, plus the time it takes to decompress at night, and it adds up to half your life—and an even bigger fraction of your waking life.

In the past, you could have some expectation that once you left the office, your time was your own. That's less and less true now that we're all connected 24/7. In many jobs, there's an expectation, spoken or not, that you should be constantly available.

Is it any wonder that your work can affect your health? There are reams of studies confirming this. The notion of "effort-reward imbalance" (ERI) is one scale on which working life is weighed. In general, it refers simply to the effort it takes to reap whatever rewards may be available at work.

In one recent study, people with high ERI, where a lot of effort led to little reward, were 40 percent more likely to have a variety of lifestyle risk factors like smoking, heavy drinking, obesity, and no physical activity. Another study found that high ERI more than doubled the risk of dying from cardiovascular disease.

These kinds of studies raise the question of where all that effort is coming from. Perhaps these people are internally driven. They're "overcommitted" to the job, to any job, and the problem would occur no matter what these people did. A review of 45 studies found little support for this proposal. What mattered was "extrinsic" ERI, the simple combination of high effort with low reward.

In other words, you're not the problem. It's not as if you'd be happy and healthy if you didn't overcommit or if you weren't so driven. Instead, you'd be happy and healthy, regardless of your personality type, in the environment that was right for you. The challenge is finding your niche.

A Matter of Choice

Questions to ask yourself range from the mundane—yes, small things can be important—to relatively abstract "big-picture" items that can be hard to pin down but that matter nonetheless. You can apply the following questions to jobs you've liked and disliked. But don't stop there. Ask these questions about your ideal job, too, the one you've yet to experience. Don't hesitate to let your imagination run wild. Everything you learn here can help you with your choice.

Environment

- What was the physical space like?

- Was it open or not?

- Was it noisy or quiet?

- What sort of area was it in: urban, suburban, or rural?

People

- What were the people like?

- What were your co-workers like?

- How many were there?

- Did you work in a team or alone?

- How closely did you work with colleagues?

- How much interaction was there?

- What was your supervisor like, and your supervisor's supervisor?

- How closely did you work with your supervisor?

Activities

- How did you spend your time?

- How much routine was involved? Was every day the same?

- Who set your priorities, and how much independence were you afforded?

- What was a typical day like?

- What sorts of deadlines were involved in your work?

- Were you mainly at your desk or moving from place to place?

- Were you working alone or with others?

- Were you mainly working on a computer, on the phone, or face-to-face?

- How much of your work took you out of the office and into the field?

Engagement

- What tasks attracted and maintained your interest?

- What tasks bored you?

- Which ones made the day seem longer or shorter?

- Which ones were fun?

- What did you look forward to doing?

- What did you dread?

Big Picture

- When it was time to head off to work, how did you feel?

- When it was time to go home, how did you feel?

- What is your best memory of the experience? What's your worst?

- In what situation did you feel that you did your best work?

- In what situation did you receive the most positive feedback from others?

- Where were you able to express yourself as fully as possible?

As you can see, these are not the kind of questions that call for years of isolated contemplation in a mountain cave. We're looking within, but without leaving the real world of jobs and salaries and daily life. We don't need to uncover universal truths, only those truths that apply to you and your career.

As we stated earlier, you can even ask these questions about a career that you've yet to experience. You need to know something about the reality of that career—and we'll get to that—but your answers can provide insight.

Answer the questions truthfully, then step back and look for commonalities. Fantasy has its place, but a dream job, if it's to be more than a dream, has to be grounded in reality. Your answers can be a first step toward seeing your dream in a real context, either in opposition to that context or in harmony with it.

STEP 3: WHAT BIG EYES YOU HAVE!

When the wolf ate grandma, he swallowed her whole. Only then could the Brothers Grimm end the tale with a happy reunion of Little Red Riding Hood and her grandmother. The earliest versions of the story, which predate the Grimm's retelling by hundreds of years, take a more practical approach. Grandma is consumed in pieces, and sometimes the appetizing steaks and chops are used to lure the girl to her appointment with destiny at grandma's house.

We're not advocating cannibalism, but the oldest stories have a point: When you're faced with a big project, whether you're a wolf preparing dinner or a person deciding on a lifetime career, break things into smaller steps. Otherwise, the size of the project is itself an obstacle, likely to remain on the back burner because of its intimidating scale.

Focusing on the big picture alone is a wonderful way to nurture procrastination. To get past that obstacle, analyze the big picture with the aim of finding the steps you'll need to take along the way. They should all fit the criteria of a simple system: S.T.A.I.R. (Small steps, Time-sensitive, Actionable, Individual, Realistic.)

Small steps: No matter where you are in the process, each step should be a small one. *Example:* A big step would be finding a relevant internship. A smaller one would involve finding internships that are offered in your area.

Time-sensitive: You should be able to accomplish each step within a short time frame. *Example:* "Get Master's degree" is only doable in a short time if you've done everything but collect your diploma. You can, however, find out what programs offer degrees in your field with a little research.

Actionable: Each of those small steps should be something that can actually be accomplished in a limited time frame. *Example:* "Find the right career" is not that kind of step. A better option would be finding out what qualifications you may need.

Individual: No step should have multiple parts. Think of each of those parts as its own step. *Example:* If you want to have an informational interview with someone in your field, the step is not "set up informational interview." Instead, it could involve a little research on LinkedIn, for example, to find interview candidates.

Realistic: Each step has to be something realistic that can actually be done in the time you've set. *Example:* If you're leaning toward an investment career, grabbing lunch with Warren Buffett might be a very good idea. However, the odds of dining with The Sage of Omaha may not be in your favor. The odds of coffee with someone local, someone with whom you're even tenuously connected, are much better.

STEP 4: LEARN EVERYWHERE

You've already asked questions about your past experience, and perhaps you've started to get an inkling of what makes your working life a pleasure and what can make it an ordeal.

Don't stop questioning. This time, though, consider two separate areas of inquiry: the nature of the career you're considering and the nature of your own unique self.

With respect to the first, the nature of a given career, you need to know as much as you can to make educated decisions.

- *What's the latest news in your potential field?* Look at newspapers, magazines, and trade publications, online and off.

- *Get an insider's view.* Look to friends, family, colleagues (if you're willing to let them know), and former colleagues. See who you might be connected to on the web, whether it's through a career-oriented site like LinkedIn or a social free-for-all like Facebook.

- *Get even more of an insider's view by going inside.* Look for chances to volunteer and for internship opportunities. Everyone can benefit from some hands-on experience. For new grads especially, it's not only a chance to learn, it's an opportunity to add something concrete to your resume.

- *Pay particular attention to your alumni network.* These are people with whom you have a built-in connection. It's a resource that is often forgotten, but it can be a very rich source of potential contacts. Remember, too, that there are frequently virtual networks that allow you to interact with fellow alumni.

- *Find industry-specific websites that provide input from people in the field, even if that input is from anonymous commentators.* By all means, take it with a grain of salt, but it can be well worth a look for an insider's view.

- *Check out the Bureau of Labor Statistics' website at bls.gov.* The site is crammed with data about almost every imaginable field, broken down by geography and demographics.

With respect to the second area of inquiry, the nature of your own unique self, you really are looking within—and there are a multitude of questions worth asking:

- What matters to you?

- What are your career goals?

- Where would you like to be in five years? In 10? In 20?

- What do you want to contribute?

- What do you see as your place in the world?

- What aspects of your life are most important?

- What values do you hold most dear?

- How do you like to spend your time?

- What are your hobbies and interests?

- What are the things you do even when you're not being paid to do them?

- How much money do you need?

- How much money do you want?

- How important is salary to you?

- What other types of rewards do you find meaningful?

- What kinds of people do you like to work with?

- What kinds of people do you like to work for?

- What are your feelings about managing others?

- Do you feel more at home in a formal or an informal setting?

- Are you more at home in a hierarchical setting or in something more free-flowing?

- What skills are you proud of?

- In what areas are you especially knowledgeable?

You don't have to answer every question, but you have to be sure that you're not avoiding any of them. Is there something important to you that doesn't square with your self-image? It's time to get those inconsistencies out of the way. If you don't take an honest look, you run the risk of being a square peg struggling to fit into a round hole.

That's not the same as saying that a job should fulfill each and every one of your wishes. Life's not like that. At least arm yourself with an understanding of what really matters to you. Know what's at your core. Then, if compromises must be made, you'll know where you might be willing to make them—and, even more to the point, where you draw the line.

While one career imperative is making sure that your career is a natural fit, a place where you can express your true self, there is a further inquiry that can be enlightening. How do others see you? What would your colleagues say about you? What about your supervisors? What would they say are your strengths and weaknesses? How would they describe your skills? How would they characterize your work style? You may not have received feedback that explicitly answers those questions, but you undoubtedly have impressions of how they would respond. The idea here is not to base your decisions on what others think—what you think is what really matters—but answering these questions can help you take a step back and get a different, possibly more objective, perspective.

STEP 5: THE 7 PILLARS OF CAREER WISDOM

With a long look at where you've been, an informed sense of what's happening in your field of interest, and an understanding of your own inner workings, you can start combining those three inquiries into a coherent approach.

Before starting to look at what this synthesis means, there are two pitfalls to bear in mind:

- *First, some people have a tendency to become stuck in the data-collection stage.* Admittedly, there's a lot to know, but resist the temptation to use research and inquiry as tools to postpone taking the next step. There is always something else you can investigate, one more bit of data that you believe would really make the picture complete. Don't let paralysis set in.

- *Second, the result we're looking for does not entail a breathtaking moment in which you renounce everything and, with as much drama as you can muster, take up the sword of a new career.* Joan of Arc could make that work, but, for most of us, a meaningful change comes about because of a series of small decisions. Your career takes shape one piece at a time. Don't postpone decisions until you're ready to take the dramatic plunge. Start wading into the water, moving in the direction you want to go.

Looking within and without, you should be able to start filling in the blanks in seven areas:

- *Where do you want to be?* Would you prefer a big city or a small town? Up north or down south? The mountains or the coast? Are you willing to relocate?

- *What kind of people do you want to work with?* What's felt good in the past? Who are your ideal colleagues?

- *What should your working environment be like?* Do you need flexible time? Do you want direct contact with the public?

Do you do best when things are predictable, or can you manage uncertainty?

- *What are your values?* How does your career fit those values? How does it fit with your goals in a broader sense?

- *What kind of compensation do you need, both in terms of salary and other rewards?* How does this fit with your other criteria?

- *What are your real interests?* What would you be doing if pay were not an issue?

- *And, finally, what do you bring to the table?* What are the skills that set you apart? What are you good at? What do you know?

When you've answered all these questions, you may find yourself in an uncomfortable place. Your answers may be telling you that you'll have to leave the comfort of a familiar world for one that involves risk and uncertainty. The change may be painful, but any change can involve discomfort—even a change for the better.

Get Cooking!

When you're mid-career, making a change can be intimidating. If you decide to change course, though, take comfort that you have plenty of company—in fact, plenty of famous company.

Julia Child started her working life as a copywriter for a furniture store. She then worked for the government as a clerk, ultimately joining the Office of Strategic Services, the precursor to the CIA. That job sent her travelling, first to Sri Lanka and then, after marrying Paul Child some years later, to France.

In the time between the two trips, Julia had returned to her home in California, where she took some cooking classes. When she arrived in France, she fell in love with French cuisine and attended cooking school again, this time at the renowned Cordon Bleu. After graduating, she started her own cooking school aimed at visiting Americans. It was not terribly profitable.

Julia had certainly found an interest, but she didn't launch herself at mass media all at once. One of her partners in the cooking school was writing a cookbook, and Julia got involved. It was Julia who managed to get a sample chapter into the hands of a willing publisher. The book's success led to an appearance on a morning TV show, which, in turn, led to *The French Chef,* which ran for more than 100 episodes.

The show did not debut until 1963, almost 20 years after Julia had attended her first cooking classes. The progression was gradual. In retrospect, however, it seems almost inevitable and the most natural outgrowth of her various interests.

She had a mission. Since she put great stock in the systems that the French applied to their kitchens, she wanted to introduce Americans to those systems.

She brought certain relevant strengths to the table. Her attention to detail, nourished, perhaps, by her years as a government clerk, made her recipes accurate and complete.

She had a destination in mind. Her goal was to educate, to raise the level of American home cooking, and all of her endeavors aimed at that goal.

Did Julia Child ever make a decision to become a famous TV personality? No. She took a cooking course, then another, helped write a book, and gave some lessons.

> Each of those decisions were small, but, in the end, they
> added up to a career that was larger than life.

The good news, however, is that nothing will serve your job search better than your own passion. No tool will do more to advance your career than the sense that this is where you really belong. If you let it, that attitude will invariably express itself, whether in resumes, cover letters, or interviews.

True passion is a hard thing to fake. When it's real, however, and you're truly passionate and legitimately engaged, people notice. Once they notice, they respond. Your next task is to find ways to make sure that the response you want is the one you get.

 Fantasy or Reality?

Isn't the idea of a "dream job" more fantasy than reality?

Not at all. Finding the career that fits the real you is not a luxury. It's a necessity.

Bronnie Ware started out in banking, left that field for a series of stopgap jobs, and ended up as a caregiver for the elderly. There, she found what she called her "heartfelt" niche in palliative medicine, caring for people who had returned home to die. Her history is an example of changing direction to find what's right for you, but Ware also has something specific to contribute, something she gleaned from her work with the dying. She learned what ultimately mattered to people, and she tackled that subject in her book *The Top Five Regrets of the Dying*.

What was single biggest regret people shared? "I wish I'd had the courage to live a life true to myself, not the life others expected of me."

Obviously, that sentiment can apply to areas other than a career, but it's hard to imagine a more ringing endorsement of the fundamental value of finding your own heartfelt niche. We all have different dreams, but too many of us ignore our desires until it's too late, when we can only regret what might have been.

Key Lessons

+ Find your place in the career world by embarking on a journey to answer the all-important question: Where exactly do you want to go?

+ Take the first step toward your dream job by evaluating your current work-life satisfaction and long-term goals.

+ Analyze both your previous work experiences and your ideal job to help better understand yourself and what's important to you.

+ Break down bigger projects and goals into simple steps that are time-sensitive, actionable, and realistic, to make them less intimidating and easier for you to achieve.

+ Learn as much as you can about the career you're considering through networking, online research, and other resources so you can make educated and objective career decisions.

+ Focus your career decision-making by synthesizing what you've learned about your past work experiences, your desired field of interest, and your own inner nature.

Chapter 2

Weathering the Job Market Storm: *Keeping Your Spirits High and Your Ship from Sinking*

"The fishermen know that the sea is dangerous and the storm terrible, but they have never found these dangers sufficient reason for remaining ashore."
—Vincent Van Gogh

We're all different. We think differently, we feel differently, and we respond to the world differently. Despite the differences between us, there are some things almost all of us agree on.

One of those things is the job search. Almost all of us agree that the job market is a stressful place, and most of us think "stressful" is a bit of an understatement. For some of us, it's a confusing, discouraging, maddening, nerve-wracking, confidence-destroying, and even soul-crushing place. If you pick a gloomy adjective, there's a good chance it will describe the job market many of us see.

It's not the same for everyone, of course. We bring our own inner natures to the search, and some of us are more naturally resilient or optimistic than others. We find ourselves in different situations, too, and that matters. Some of us have jobs and want something better. Others are unemployed. Some of us are older, with problems that are not the same as those faced by the new grad. Some of us are changing careers. Others are overqualified. Your place in the job market certainly affects your experience.

If we find the market difficult, though, let's make one thing clear immediately: The difficulty here is not the product of personal failings or some unique inability to handle adversity. The fault here is in the process, not in ourselves. If you're discouraged or depressed, with your motivation slipping away inch by inch, that's not a sign of weakness, despite the fact that some rare people don't seem to suffer through the process. Those people are part of a minority so small as to be barely countable. In reality, the job search is tough, and if it drags on, it only gets tougher.

If you've been living with the job market for any length of time, you'd be excused for thinking that the point of the whole diabolical system was to make you as miserable as possible.

How can the process fail you? Let us count the ways:

- You encounter rejection on a regular basis.

- It's a special kind of rejection, one that's particularly painful if you equate your career with "who you are."

- To make matters worse, the market is not responding to your strongest efforts to put your best foot forward.

- Feedback is minimal at best. You launch your application into a black hole, and you can consider yourself lucky if you hear anything at all.

- Since you hear nothing, you don't know what to change.

- You may well be doing this completely on your own, without any personal interaction or any of the support that can help you through tough times.

- You may also be reluctant to reach out to other people or to share what you're going through.

- You have no structure to fall back on. There's no schedule to meet and no immediate financial reward to keep you going from one week to the next.

- If you're unemployed, you can feel an enormous, alienating gulf between you and people with jobs. You can end up isolating yourself from the very people who might help you carry on.

The list is not by any means complete, but you get the point—maybe too well. The job search can be psychologically brutal, and it has nothing to do with your personality, your coping mechanisms, or your ability to thrive in the working world itself. The hiring process is a meat grinder that can get the best of the best of us.

This guide is meant to make the hiring process manageable. It gives you a clear idea of what you can and should do at any given time and in any situation. We know that a system can itself become a burden, and we've kept that in mind. That's why, instead of calling for heroic undertakings, we simply ask for small, easy steps, each with a very practical focus. Even with the best system in place, however, we know full well that the search can wear you down.

If that's happening, there are ways to cope. Once again, we focus on what's practical, what's doable, and what actually helps. You do have to soldier on. We won't pretend that telling you to soldier on is anything like a useful piece of advice. Here, then, are a few possibilities.

GET UP AND GET OUT

For many of us, there's a real temptation to pull the covers over our heads and hide. If we're out of bed, we're home and likely to be in sweatpants-and-slippers mode. Clothes may or may not make the man—or woman—but there's no doubt that what you wear has an effect on how you see yourself and, as a result, how you feel about yourself. Get out into the world on a regular basis. It doesn't have to involve some job-specific activity. Go out for coffee. Grab a bite to eat. If nothing else, take your laptop to the coffee shop or the library, and work on your resume there. The whole enterprise will make you feel part of the wider world.

KEEP IN TOUCH

Don't be a hermit. It's too easy to become isolated. Make time for friends and family. Talk to people on the phone. This is another activity that doesn't need a direct payoff in the job market. It's enough that it maintains connections with other people, no matter who they are.

STAY UP-TO-DATE

Keep in touch with what's happening in your field. This will actually serve you very well in the job search, but that's not what makes it valuable as a coping mechanism. It's also another way to remind yourself that you're still part of something, that you still have a place in a community of people with similar interests. If there's a seminar or conference that's relevant, go. If not, stay in touch via the web. Participate in an online forum or take an online course. It's all evidence that you're in the picture, to others and, of even greater importance, to yourself.

REMIND YOURSELF OF THE POSITIVES

If you're unemployed and counting the days until you find a job, the fact that you're not tied to the daily grind has a good side, hard as it is to see that side right now. Your time is your own. You can do things you never could do while working. Take advantage of those hours. Go to a museum. Take in a movie. Head out to the ballpark on a weekday afternoon when everyone else is stuck in the office. If you have kids, bring them along. Trust us: If you don't take advantage of your freedom, unwanted though it may be, you'll regret it when you're back at work.

ADD STRUCTURE

If the lack of structure is a problem, add some yourself. Set aside specific hours for specific tasks. Set limits. Looking for a job does not have to be a full-time job, especially when you approach the search systematically. We know, however, that any task has the potential to fill whatever time is available. When your available time is effectively limitless, you can find yourself spending a day on something that should take an hour. A schedule, with its built-in limits, can actually make you more productive. It can also give you a sense of accomplishment: You've stuck to the schedule and put in the time, and you can cross a task off today's to-do list.

FACE YOUR FEARS

The job search is an environment in which worry thrives, and that's not necessarily a sign of trouble. It's natural, for example, to be anxious before an interview, but sometimes a little anxiety actually helps by keeping us motivated and focused. "Free-floating" anxiety is different. It's the kind of pervasive anxiety that's not tied to a specific event. When it gets out of hand, anxiety is everywhere, and that can be paralyzing, not just unpleasant. For starters, put a name to what's worrying you, whether it's finances, the fear that you won't find a job that compares to the one you've lost, worries about what others think, or any other concern. At least, then, you'll have a target to aim for, and you can direct your energies at specific problems. For more general help, consider meditation or yoga. The payoff isn't instantaneous, but give one of those tried-and-true methods a chance.

GET MOVING

You're probably not just a brain in a jar, although that would make for some interesting interviews. Your physical self is important, if only because the physical and emotional are closely linked, and this is not the time to put exercise on the back burner. If you've had a regular routine, stick to it. If not, and you now have the time, get started. Caring for your physical side is worth it on its own, but endorphins, the mood-altering chemicals your body naturally produces in response to exertion, are a real thing. Get moving, and give your body a chance to do its bit to lift your spirits.

DON'T COMPARE YOURSELF

You know someone who found a great job in a week. But you've been looking for the last six months. What's wrong with you? Chances are, nothing. It's entirely possible that your strategy needs help, but that's why we're here. Before you start comparing yourself to anyone, though, remember that the job search is affected by a thousand things that none of us can control. Luck, timing, and the market itself all play their parts. Your friend's success is, for all intents and purposes, irrelevant. All you can do is put yourself in a position where those external factors have the best chance to work for you. Again, that's why we're here and, presumably, why you're here too.

REMEMBER THE TRUTH

Millions of people have looked for jobs before you. Somehow, they all coped. Why are you having such a hard time? It's easy to see yourself as the source of the problem, but it's not accurate. We've listed some of the things that make the hiring process miserable, and many of those can be direct hits on your confidence and self-esteem. If you find yourself thinking that it can't possibly be so bad and that you should be handling it better, stop. The truth is that you're doing what you can to cope with a process that has brought many a strong man or woman to tears.

GET HELP

There may come a time when you need help to make it through. If so, don't hesitate to seek it out. Help can come in the form of a group of fellow searchers, a place to get support, some tips, and the opportunity to share your experiences with people in the same boat. Professional help is also an option. It can come from a therapist or, for practical advice, from a career counselor who, brave soul, deals with the job market every day and knows what works. Any of these things can take some of the load off your shoulders, but you have to seek them out. None of the resources will magically appear when you need them.

In the end, it's no surprise that people suffer in the face of a terribly flawed hiring process, but many of us leave it at that. If you don't take an affirmative step or two, you can end up stewing over the whole mess by yourself while the job market does its best to beat you to a pulp. Its best, of course, is very, very good. It doesn't have to come to that. Do the practical things you need to do. The right practical choices will make the process easier and make your efforts more effective. At the same time, take care of yourself in all the other ways that have nothing to do with the job market. Do those things that aren't all about career and work. Don't become a hermit. Your psyche will thank you, and, if you need more incentive, your job search will actually benefit from some of those "irrelevant" things as well.

Key Lessons

+ The job search is grueling for almost everyone, but the fault lies in the process and has nothing to do with you personally.

✦ Getting out into the world on a regular basis and maintaining connections with friends and family will help you cope with the stress of the hiring process.

✦ Stay up-to-date with what's happening in your field via the web or by attending seminars to remind yourself and others that you're still part of the community.

✦ Take advantage of your current weekday free time to do the fun activities you couldn't while working.

✦ Setting a schedule with specific hours for specific tasks will make you more productive and give you a sense of accomplishment.

✦ Identify the source of any anxiety you are experiencing, and then direct your energies toward solving those problems.

✦ Maintain or implement an exercise routine to support your physical health and gain the benefits of mood-boosting endorphins.

✦ Don't compare yourself to others. The job search is affected by a thousand things you can't control, and your friend's success is irrelevant.

✦ When you get discouraged, remember you're dealing with a process that has brought many strong men and women before you to tears.

✦ Seek out help when you need it, whether from fellow job searchers or professionals.

Part 2

PREPARATION STATION

Chapter 3

From the Dream World to the Real World: *Building Your Resume*

"How many legs does a dog have if you call the tail a leg? Four. Calling a tail a leg doesn't make it a leg."
—Abraham Lincoln

Having identified your place in the sun, you have to find a way to get there. It won't happen by itself. You have to transform ambition into reality, and that means learning to communicate with the job market. At this point, you know yourself, but we want employers to know you, too—not haphazardly but as you want to be known. To top it off, we want to make employers' lives easier. When we're done, it should be the simplest thing in the world for them to see you as the right candidate—even, or especially, if you're a single face in a very large crowd.

This can be a difficult proposition, hardest, perhaps, if you're just starting out or changing careers. Your resume can seem like a big, imposing blank that you can't fill in, but there's hope. Stay the course. Believe it or not, you have a lot to say, and you may be surprised to find that your biggest job is editing what you do have so that it makes the strongest impression.

Before we touch on specifics, there are two principles to enshrine as job search axioms. Everything revolves around these two ideas:

1. *You are marketing yourself.* Period. End of story. Your resume is, in every meaningful sense, an ad. Everything you do is meant to sell your candidacy to the people who matter. If you don't feel like you're a natural salesperson, don't despair. We have a plan.

2. *You have to keep employers interested.* Always remember that you're answering a single question: What can you show employers that will make them want to find out more? Keep that crucial question in mind. There are stories of exceptions, but it is a vanishingly small percentage of applicants who are hired on the basis of resumes alone. At every stage of the process, your goal is to reach the next stage, whatever that is. Your resume, for example, does its job if it gets you an interview. A screening interview is a success if it gets you to a follow-up.

No matter where you are in your search, keep those axioms in mind. Whenever you're in doubt or faced with a difficult choice, remind yourself that each action you take should serve the two principles that make up your real agenda.

Are You Ready for Some Job Search Football?

No book of advice would be complete without at least one sports analogy. Here's one about getting to the next stage that's too perfect to resist. If you're Peyton Manning, or Joe Montana, or Andrew Luck—or any NFL quarterback who plays the position well—you understand that your job is not to go long on every play. Unless you're down four touchdowns and desperate, you're not supposed to be throwing a 50-yard pass every chance you get, hoping one of them winds up in the end zone. The professional approach is all about efficiency. It involves getting ahead in chunks, 10 yards at a time, and with a fresh set of downs. Your play is tailored to this approach above all.

That's the job search. It's not about the Hail Mary. It's about methodical progress, where success is defined as "keeping the drive alive." Just as it's easier to score from 12 yards out than it is to score from your own end zone, you want to get closer and closer to a job offer one step at a time. That's our goal, and the strategy is built to keep your drive alive. Desperation never enters the picture.

THE SHOEBOX APPROACH

In the beginning was . . . the shoebox?

You've probably heard of those people who, facing April 15 every year, arrive at the accountant's office with a shoebox overflowing with a year's worth of receipts. You may even be one of them. Accountants don't come cheap, so the shoebox may not be the best approach to taxes, but a similar method can provide a starting point for your resume, especially if you're a new graduate or if you don't have a long history in the field you're targeting.

Start with everything, including coursework, jobs, volunteering, internships, extracurricular activities, continuing education, hobbies, and interests. There are a lot of resume-worthy skills and accomplishments you can pull from here.

- *If you took courses in the field you're aiming for, list them individually.* If there was a relevant project or presentation, make note of it. If you did especially well in courses that are really relevant, make note of your grades. We're looking for all the things that stand out. It doesn't have to be a Nobel Prize. If you were a research assistant to a professor, include that in your list.

- *For all those activities, consider the skills you had to employ and the results you reached.* Perhaps you gave a presentation that was very well received. It was that presentation that led to your research assistantship. That's worthy of note.

- *List your special skills, including fluency in a foreign language and competence in any area of technology.* Make note of any certifications you've earned.

- *For anything even vaguely resembling a job, list your responsibilities in detail.* Make special note of accomplishments and results. Apply those same criteria to volunteer work and to extracurricular activities. What did you do? What skills did you use? What results did you obtain? What did you accomplish?

- *For those just starting out, those job-like activities don't have to be in your chosen field and they don't have to be innately impressive.* If you waited tables twice a week, you put some skills into play. Perhaps the skills were organizational. Perhaps you developed customer service skills. Maybe your job helped pay for your schooling. You probably learned to juggle competing demands on your time and energy.

In other words, this is the all-inclusive list. The idea is to fill your shoebox to overflowing with lists of skills, responsibilities, and accomplishments, with all the things you did and all the things you learned.

You may be surprised at some of the things your inventory reveals. You may be reminded of skills you'd forgotten you had, or you may uncover skills that weren't on your radar—simply because you took them for granted since you must have had those skills to perform in a given setting.

What we have so far is not, of course, a resume. It's not even a rough draft. Much of what you've included will end up on the cutting-room floor once you begin to tailor your efforts to specific job descriptions, but we're not editing yet.

THE REAL RULES OF THE REAL GAME

Before we dig down into the details of resume building, a bit of context is in order. An applicant needs to know how the process really works to gauge a resume's chance of success.

Let's open with a quick quiz.

True or false?

1. *Your resume will get a careful look.*
   False: Your resume will get a quick glance. Some estimates put the average time spent on each resume in an initial screening at around six seconds.

2. *Your resume will be reviewed by someone who makes hiring decisions.*
   False: If you're applying for work at a three-person operation, a decision-maker may well be on the front lines. Otherwise, your resume will be screened by a member of the support staff or by a contracted third party. While those people can't decide to hire, they act as gatekeepers, determining which resumes move forward and which ones don't. They often decide who not to hire.

3. *At least your resume will be reviewed by a human being.*
   False: Especially at larger companies, the blessings of automation often play a big part. Machines can screen resumes,

looking for keywords. You don't have the right keywords?
Your resume joins the discards.

4. *Your resume allows the reviewer to find the best candidate.*
False: This is a fundamental disconnect between the candidate's assumption and the employer's process. "Best candidates" may emerge further down the line, but the first order of business is discarding resumes, finding the ones that are easy to reject.

5. *If your resume is good enough, it will land you a job.*
False: As we'll see, a great resume is not enough. Finding a job is about research and networking and putting yourself out there in a multitude of ways. It's about interviews and follow-up. You need a great resume as part of the search, and it will always be asked for, but it's only one piece of the puzzle.

The overriding theme of this little quiz is that reviewing resumes, especially in the early stages, is not about deciding who to hire. It's about culling the herd, about getting numbers down to a manageable size so that the rest of the hiring process can continue. Do employers lose some potentially great hires in the process? Yes, but they're willing to live with that. They're not about to commit more resources to hiring or to spend more time reviewing applicants. If what they're doing works "well enough," they'll leave it alone.

From this perspective, your job is to stay out of the discard pile or, harking back to our football analogy, to get 10 yards closer to the goal with a fresh set of downs. You can't score a touchdown at this point. Your goal is to try to stay in the game.

A Necessary Evil

For the moment, pretend you're not you. You're not combing the want ads, polishing your resume, or practicing for interviews. In fact, the shoe is on the other foot. Suddenly, you find that you're a hiring manager trying to fill a position. Strangely enough, it's the very position in the very industry the old you was applying for. You posted the opening on the company site 15 minutes ago, and you already have 100 applicants. If those applicants only knew how hard your job was, they'd surely sympathize.

Perhaps not, but you still have to get the job done. What do you want to see? In the job posting, you listed some specific qualifications, so you surely want to see evidence of those. You described what you needed, so you hope that a few of these applicants paid attention to that.

What else do you want? What can an applicant tell you that will make you want to take a second look? Are there certain accomplishments that would make your eyes light up? Is there something that tells you that a candidate can do the job? Do any of these applicants understand that all you care about is what they can do for you and your company? Do they know that it's not about fulfilling their dreams or making them happy?

Now you, the applicant, can return from this out-of-body experience and consider your own strategy from a different perspective. Plan your approach by focusing on the things you know must matter to the person on the other side of the fence. Always try to cover those points and hit them as hard as you can. You'd be amazed at the number of people who forget that this is all about showing employers what you can do for them. It's never about what they can do for you.

MAKING THE RIGHT IMPRESSION

Now that you know what employers are looking for in general, and you have some sense of how they go about finding whatever that is, you can start thinking about a resume in context. Your resume is not some platonic ideal. It has a very definite job to do, and it has to be custom made for its particular circumstance. For one thing, each resume is aimed at a specific employer and a specific job, and, as a result, each one should be different.

The same can be said of your specific situation. You have unique skills, a unique education, and a unique history. Resumes can and should be constructed to accommodate individual situations and individual jobs. Before getting down to individual cases, though, there are some guidelines that apply to all resumes, and they're worth knowing. These are rules that every resume should follow, and they govern both form and content.

3 Rules of Form

Fail to heed these three rules and you can say, "Goodbye, job!"

1. *This rule should be self-evident, but it's worth repeating: Even small mistakes can kill you.* Don't give screeners a reason to say "no" with barely a glance. Review your resume thoroughly for mistakes of all kinds: typos, misspellings, formatting errors, and inconsistencies. The screener's job, you will recall, is to get rid of the losers, not to pick the winners. Make a mistake, and you've all but volunteered for the discard pile.

2. *Pay strict attention to employers' formatting requirements.* They will frequently ask for resumes in a specific format, often .doc or .pdf, sometimes plain text. If you've created the resume in one format and you're asked for a different format, make sure the resume displays and prints properly before you submit it. If you're nuts for fonts, especially for

crazy fonts, rein in your enthusiasm. You don't know that your beloved but exotic font is installed at the receiving end. When it's not there, the system is likely to replace your special font with its own close approximation, and that tiny substitution can be enough to make a radical change in your formatting.

3. *Looks count!* There's no one look that's right for every situation. An investment bank needs a different resume from one that will work at a software startup, but, within the bounds of situational appropriateness, both resumes have to look great. We'd like to think that great content will rule the day, but the real world says otherwise. Great content is useless if it doesn't grab the reader's attention immediately. If you're not much of a graphic designer, get help.

 5 Simple Design Tips

When it comes to resume design, nothing should be extreme, except for adherence to the mantra: Moderation is always the best path.

1. **White space:** You may have a lot of content you'd like to include, but dense text can be uninviting and difficult to read. White space can help draw the eye to the things you want seen, and it's sometimes worth trimming some fat if the result is a more readable resume.

2. **Length:** Ignore the warning that a resume should never exceed two pages or that a one-page resume is a necessity. These are endlessly circulated falsehoods, like the idea that the Great Wall of China is the only human creation visible from space. Employers (usually) don't demand one-pagers, and the attempt to pack all your achievements onto a single sheet can

force omission of highlights and make the document look like a text compactor.

3. **Bullets and lists:** Use them. They organize things for the reader. As a result, you look organized. They call attention to specific items that you want to emphasize.

4. **Fonts, sizes, and styles:** You can use different fonts within the same documents, but limit yourself to two relatively standard fonts, perhaps one serif and one sans serif. The latter tends to work well in headings and the former in text, and there's some truth to the idea that serif fonts are especially suited to printed documents, while their sans serif cousins look better on the screen. Different sizes, or bold and italic variations, are also acceptable. Text boxes have a place, used, for instance, as a way to call attention to an opening summary that leads into the resume. But again, don't overdo it.

5. **Physical specifications:** Although the Internet plays a huge and growing role in the job market, there are still occasions when paper makes an appearance. If you're submitting your resume on paper, use good quality paper stock that is relatively heavy, not the paper you'd load into the copier. For all but the artiest situations, paper should be white or off-white. Color ink can easily look amateurish, so think twice before departing from basic black. Use a good printer at high resolution so that everything is crisp and clear. If there's an envelope involved, don't use one that only seems to match if you don't look too hard. People notice.

To see some sample resumes, go to my website at www.shimmeringcareers.com.

5 Rules of Content: B.R.A.T.S.

No, we're not referring to sausages; these are fives rules of content, or conduct.

1. **Brand:** So it's come to this: We're all our own brands. In reality, the notion of personal branding is not so new. At one time, you had an image. Now, you have a brand. The real difference is the multiplicity of places, many of them online, in which your brand reveals itself to the world. Your resume is part of that brand, and it should do its part to enhance the whole picture. Part of that is form and part is content. Emphasize the substantive matters that add to that brand, and that will bring value to an employer.

2. **Results:** Employers only care about your history, your skills, and your abilities for one reason: Will those qualities help us to achieve the results we want? That's the question a good resume answers. It's the resume's inherent theme: Hire me because I will do good things for this organization. Think of all your skills and qualifications in that context, and frame them accordingly. When describing your experience, always ask yourself if the employer will make the connection between that experience and the organization's needs.

3. **Accomplishments:** To that end, nothing says "I will get results" better than a history of getting results. The essence of your resume is not the responsibilities you had; the essence is what you achieved. Consider departing from the standard format—a reverse chronology of experience followed by education—and opening with a short summary of the value you bring, and a bulleted list of four or five achievements. Each one should be something that speaks to the company in question.

4. **Track:** Employers don't keep their needs secret. They shout them from the rooftops in the form of job postings. They tell you what they want, whether it's a certain amount of experience, a specific qualification, a particular skill, or a more general quality they're seeking. Pay attention. Your resume should track the posting. If they want someone who has managed sales teams, highlight that experience in your resume. If they tell you that the job will involve addressing groups of potential clients, be sure that your resume clearly points to relevant experience you've had. As long as your resume responds to the very explicit needs that the employer deems important, you stand a very good chance of hitting any keywords that may be in use. In other words, don't ignore the very valuable information that employers put right in front of you.

5. **Specific:** Of the five rules that govern resume content, one wins the prizes for most important and, at the same time, most often overlooked: Be specific. Those two simple words cover so much ground that they're worth an extended visit.

   - *Be specific about your achievements.* If you led a successful sales team, that's very nice. If the team you led was given sole responsibility for the company's most important product line or the company's most important customer, and your work led to record-breaking volume, that's an achievement that will resonate.

   - *Be specific with the help of numbers.* Few things speak as loudly as figures. Your team's sales of widgets led the company, and that's good. Your team met its annual quota of widget sales within seven months and exceeded that quota by 40 percent for the year? That's better.

- *Be specific about the job you want.* It can be awfully tempting to cram a resume with as many skills as possible, perhaps on the off chance that if you don't get the job that's posted, some screener will notice that you're qualified for something else. Employers, however, are looking for focus, for the candidate who best fits the very specific opening they've decided to fill. That's your target. You're not a jack-of-all-trades; you're the master of the trade they need.

- *Be specific about each resume.* The jack-of-all-trades problem is especially apparent when you're sending out fistfuls of resumes and hoping one will stick. Customization is admittedly more work, but it's the only way to give yourself the best shot possible. Each resume should be custom tailored to each specific opening.

The Shoebox Resume Revisited

Don't be too discouraged by the notion that you need a whole new resume for every application. One way to make customizing easier is to return to the shoebox approach. Start with that rough "resume" that includes everything you can think of. Put all that material together as if it were a real resume in the form of the roughest of rough drafts.

Don't worry about giving it a final polish, but make it coherent and make it inclusive. You may end up with the Great Scroll of Resumes, five pages that contain a lot of irrelevancies, but this is just for you. You're not about to submit this particular document to anyone.

Now, with everything even remotely useful on the page, you can pick and choose, editing as necessary, deleting what doesn't belong, and elaborating on the parts that seem especially relevant.

For many people, this approach to customization is much less daunting than starting fresh with a custom resume for each possibility. If you've already filled your shoebox, you have a head start.

- *Be specific about the way you say things.* "It's not what you say, but it's how you say it." Clearly, that sentiment is not entirely applicable to the resume, where what you say matters a great deal. You can, however, increase the impact of your content in several ways.

  - *Don't bury an achievement in a block of text that talks about responsibilities.* Call it out separately.

  - *Go easy on the adjectives.* Anyone can claim to be a customer-focused professional. Instead, provide an example. Were you recognized for your customer service skills? Recognition doesn't have to come in the form of an award. Perhaps you were given increased responsibility or work that was particularly challenging. If that's the case, say so.

  - *Avoid the nebulous and the passive.* Phrases like "was instrumental in" or "consulted with" tell us little. What's worse is that they tell us little while giving the impression that you were simply swept along with some workplace tide. If you were "instrumental in" something, what was the result? What did you actually do? Look over your phrasing with a critical eye, and if what you actually did is not readily apparent, find another way to make the point.

THERE'S A PLACE FOR CONVENTIONAL WISDOM

With each new season, the great minds at NFL headquarters determine certain "points of emphasis" for their officials. Which parts of the rules will get extra enforcement this year? One year, the emphasis may be on letting receivers run unhindered around the field. The next, the league decides that repeated blows to the head are to be discouraged. Often it's a case of actually enforcing seemingly forgotten rules that have long existed.

The points of emphasis in the rules of resumes don't change from year to year, but they're just as likely to be forgotten if they're not repeated. In that spirit, here's a rule worth harping on: Your job is to make it as easy as possible for the person—or machine, if it comes to that—reading your resume. That's why you want your resume to look good and to be easy to read, why you want your achievements to leap off the page, and why you want to answer all the questions that a job posting implicitly asks.

That rule should be enough reason to stick with certain tried-and-true resume formulas. A screener shouldn't turn to your resume and feel lost.

That's not to say that today's resume formats are the best formats possible, but the situation is a lot like the one that applies to your keyboard. There may well be better keyboard designs than the QWERTY approach passed down to us by our ancestors, but those "better" designs will take a lot of getting used to. Every peck of the keys will be a struggle.

So, even if you've developed a resume format that's clearly light years ahead of everything that's being done today, and even if it's the only format capable of capturing the "real you," think twice before unleashing it upon the world. There's actually a good deal of latitude in today's conventional formats, but those formats are what screeners expect to see. There's no point in submitting a resume that leaves screeners scratching their heads.

With that in mind, there are really only three formats to choose from: the reverse chronological resume, the functional resume, and the hybrid.

Reverse Chronological

The classic so-called "chronological resume" is actually a resume with work experience examples presented in reverse-chronological order.

Who it's for: people with steady experience in the same field

Who it's not always perfect for: people changing fields, people reentering the workforce, people with significant gaps in their employment history, people who've changed jobs often, or people who are just starting out.

Refer to pages 63 and 64 for an example of a before-and-after resume that has been converted to conventional reverse chronological format. And for a closer look, see the several sample resumes on www.shimmeringcareers.com.

Functional

What if your prior achievements are more important than your most recent experience? Or you have relevant experience in several different areas that you want to highlight? The reverse chronological approach may fail to deliver, so you may want the functional resume instead. Here, you highlight achievements and results first. This approach can also help obscure your older age, a multi-job history, a long hospitalization or unemployment, and any other drawbacks that the chronological form highlights. Hence, though the functional resume is perfectly acceptable and often clearly the best choice, it may raise suspicions. As always: Be aboveboard if asked, and don't apologize. You've done nothing wrong.

Who it's for: people with many gaps in their career history or who lack the requisite skills and achievements in their most recent job

Who it's not for: anyone with a solid chronological work history

See pages 66 and 67 for a sample functional resume.

An Image Problem

There's one problem with the functional resume that doesn't get much press: Rightly or wrongly, some hiring managers view them with suspicion. They like the idea of a chronological presentation; it's neat, organized, and traditional. A functional resume is a little odd. It may not be the last refuge of a scoundrel, but it's seen as a way to hide flaws that a chronological resume would make apparent, things like job-history gaps or a tendency to hop blissfully from job to job.

Since we're here to make hiring managers' jobs easier, it's fair to acknowledge that they have a point, and, after all, HR departments are hardly known for their out-of-the-box thinking or their comfort with things that seem unusual. Sadly, in the interest of getting hired, they have to be humored in the interest of getting hired. One way to humor them, especially if you come bearing an unusual history or don't quite fit the predetermined mold, is by combining chronology and function.

Funcological (aka Hybrid)

For many people, a combination of the two standard formats is the best option. It's good enough, in fact, not to need a ridiculous name, but who can resist the chance to bring some funk to the world of resumes?

A hybrid resume, one that makes it easy to see where you've been while bringing extra attention to the skills and abilities you've developed, allows screeners to find what they're looking for without jumping through hoops. Length can be an issue, so you may have to tighten up on the purely chronological sections, keeping job descriptions and responsibilities rather minimal, but you should be able to send the right message with a focus on achievements and results. Keep the work history in and make it easy to find, but lead off with, and keep the emphasis on, skills and accomplishments.

Who it's for: anyone and everyone, especially applicants hoping to join Earth, Wind & Fire

Who it's not for: no one

Other Resume Do's and Don'ts

In addition to conventions of form, there are other standards. Some are worth following, and some, if they're conventions at all, are best ignored.

Contact information always goes at the top of the first page. Your name should appear in a larger font than the rest of the resume. Your address, phone number, and email address should all be there, and you should—please!—check them twice for accuracy.

References available upon request? There is no need to make that promise. Employers will contact references when the time comes, and it's understood that you'll have them when asked.

Dates are mandatory in employment history, but they're not strictly necessary in education. Do not include your date of birth or any other personal data that's not strictly relevant. Your dress size makes a difference if you're a model. Your weight matters if you're a boxer. All others should keep personal data to themselves.

Only actors and models include photos. Everyone else should remain invisible until the interview.

There is a place for hobbies and interests, but they can be safely omitted if you're running long. If they're relevant to the job at hand, however, include them. If they're not relevant and they don't enhance your image—remember your brand—it's best to leave them out.

BEFORE RESUME

DAVID PERKINS
Edison Hill, CA 99989 • dperkins@isp.net

Objective: VP of Business Development

Astute technical executive with ability to interface in several industries and markets with financial expertise across sectors and in turn-around situations. Increase executive team productivity. Born leader! Strong marketing and budget development experience.

PROFESSIONAL EXPERIENCE

Senior Vice President, Vocalo, Inc., San Francisco, California, 2010 to Present

- Key executive in multi-million dollar business software services firm providing a comprehensive suite of services and applications. Led turnaround of firm including development of new strategy, vision and mission to target new, but related market to core engineering team's expertise.
- Revamped marketing department, established new business development goals utilizing lean principles.
- Sold graphics software business to industry leader, exceeding most analyst's expectations.
- Sold 25,000 square feet of commercial office space in Southern California.
- Applied capital from above-mentioned sales to jump-start VOIP product development, hiring top-notch software engineers to develop intellectual capital for sustained growth.
- Exceeded industry expectations for sales and market share growth (5%, 8% and 12%) for the past three years.
- Company earned *Standard Magazine* Award as one of top five U.S. software companies to work for.
- Able to consult to c-level executives.
- Software as a service innovator and entrepreneur.

Vice President of Product Development, Digital Mota Research Corporation, Palo Alto, California, 1998 to 2000

- Recruited to revive product lien of Silicon Valley internet security software firm. Managed team of design engineers, application developers and market strategists. Identified opportunity to apply company's patents in new applications to provide desktop and intranet protection against spyware, viruses and spam. Managed R&D projects that resulted in 12 new patents to reestablish market leadership.

- Led team that created first Web-based model for delivery of self-regenerative virus-destructing network server, from product scoping to implementation, testing and shipping. Product has since become award-winning application and challenging market leader for all similar web-based applications.

- Spearheaded the creation of marketing and communications strategy for spin-off companies, helping them gain exposure and new business opportunities.

- Recruited, hired, and managed teams of engineers, designers, artists, and writers to participate in an Internet advertising project for a cutting-edge technology tool that included a downloadable software kernel and separate content packages for display on client computers, which led to two patents. Product and service shipped in 2003.

Senior Software Engineer, Lodi Network Systems, Inc., San Jose, California, 2000 to 2005

Key technical implementation expert and programmer as well as contributing business development ideas for prominent networking company.

- Sold web streaming software portion of business to NWP Software Inc. in 1997. Continued as consultant to NWP for one year.

Additional Experience: Ariba, Inc. – Agile Product Development

EDUCATIONAL BACKGROUND

Stanford University – Palo Alto, California
Masters in Computer Science
Santa Clara University – Santa Clara, California
BS in Computer Science

AFTER RESUME
(Reverse Chronological)

David T. Perkins

Edison Hill, CA 406.444.2222 • dperkins@isp.net   https://www.linkedin.com/in/davidperkinscs

Chief Executive Officer
Solutions Engineer| SaaS Innovator

Spearheading Business Transformations by Integrating Data Analytics and Talent Management

More than 12 years of success propelling world class, high-technology product development initiatives. Empower teams to deliver innovative products to market, closing competitive gaps and exploiting a competitive edge in the market to achieve financial success.

Maintain multi-billion-dollar P&L administration and lead global technology operations. Optimize business operations and lead repositioning and restructuring efforts, driving revenue growth. Background includes launching industry-first programs that redefined customer experience in the mobile software environment.

EXECUTIVE STRENGTHS

· Operations Management	· Turnaround Management	· Project Management
· Team Building	· Executive-Level Decision Making	· Mergers & Consolidations
· Financial/Accounting Oversight	· Problem Resolution Management	· KPI Metrics
· Stakeholder Management	· Process & System Development	· Team Training

CAREER NARRATIVE & IMPACT

Vocalo, Inc.
San Francisco, CA | 2010–Present
Software services developer in mobile intelligence for the supply chain industry.

Senior Vice President, Software
Following a major reorganization, assumed management of mobile SaaS development for global team. Provide support for infrastructure to maintain and enhance industry standard software. Assure consistent quality and reliability of products. Oversee business development to maintain company's mobile technology leadership position. Negotiate licensing deals and purchases. Advise COO on multi-tiered business services progress. Manage $35M budget.

- ▸▸ **Led conceptualization and development of PI-E7** award-winning data integration platform, which provided key technology that led to sale of business line to IBM.
- ▸▸ **Managed company's first technology partnership** with a global hardware company.
- ▸▸ **Supported sales and business development** by serving as voice of customer.

(continued)

DAVID T. PERKINS, 2   406-444-2222 • dperkins@isp.net

Career Narrative (cont.)

Digital Mota Research Corp.
San Francisco, CA | 2005–2010
Global software research company with $10 billion in consolidated assets

Vice President, Software Development
Developed, assessed, and implemented process for implementing improvements in flagship database product line. Provided full support for infrastructure to maintain and enhance industry standard software. Assured consistent high quality and reliability of products. Oversaw business development for mobile project line. Identified opportunity for multi-protocol network and guided NTP implementation.

- **Launched mobile analytics imaging and fail-over solutions** for new mobile software line.
- **Identified technology and led team in early testing,** and installed technology in customer sites.
- **Managed development of internal chat and email** to ensure effective client satisfaction.
- **Defined programming environment** to provide client support.

> *"David ensured the success of every project he touched. He has an amazing work ethic and technical expertise that is brilliant."*
> —Harlan Atkins, CEO, Ariba, Inc.

Ariba, Inc.
Sunnyvale, CA | 2002–2005
Provider of Intranet and Internet-based business-to-business ecommerce solutions.

Assistant Manager, IT Services
Co-managed entire product development lifecycle (PDLC) for innovative agile development department. Provided program leadership and project management to develop a strategic technology roadmap, collaborating with cross-function and global-technology teams.

- **Created a company charter and managed a globally distributed team** that defined the company's product development process during rapid growth period.
- **Managed a team of Scrum Masters / Program Managers,** assuring two successful product development successes.

EDUCATION & CREDENTIALS

Master of Science in Computer Science, Stanford University, Palo Alto, CA

Bachelor of Science in Computer Science, Santa Clara University, Santa Clara, CA

Carnegie Mellon University: Technology Development Award presented by industry expert panel.

FUNCTIONAL RESUME

Morgan Chase

91712 Lombard Street, San Francisco, CA 94109 • 415-901-8000 • chasemorgan$cash.com

---

Qualifications for **Bank Manager**

Operational manager with 5+ years in sales leadership, applying financial skills, creating processes, and overseeing daily workflow. Record of managing teams and cultivating client-centric environment by leveraging customer service excellence and outstanding relationship management. Skilled at developing programs to achieve organizational and revenue goals.

Key Contributions

Operations Management

- **Earned promotion** from Sales Representative to Sales Manager, enabling honing development of skills in team leadership and workflow management.
- **Contained costs** and ensured budget requirements were met.
- **Generated steady increase in revenue** after building and implementing customer program, which attracted new clients while growing business with existing accounts.
- **Increased efficiency and productivity** by improving and creating processes and procedures that expedited cash register operations.

Team Leadership

- **Identified potential talent** and groomed new employees into top performers.
- **Demonstrated positive mindset and proficiency in employee motivation** to elevate employee performance potential.
- **Showcased skill in holding subordinates accountable** to goals.
- **Won branch contest as top salesperson** for 3 consecutive quarters.

Interpersonal Communication

- **Secured business with new clients** using competencies in active listening, persuasion, relationship building, and solution development.
- **Maintained solid relationships with existing customers**, adapting to new needs and continually seeking ways to upsell.
- **Attracted partners for employer** based on success while working together.
- **Defused tense customer scenarios** by using conflict resolution skills.

1/2

Morgan Chase

415-901-8000 • chasemorgan$cash.com

Experience Overview, continued...

Experience Overview

THE GAP – San Francisco, CA   *8-year tenure*

Store Manager (5+ years)

Promoted to leading 15 staff members in generating retail sales, opening and closing store, and in applying meticulous attention to overseeing cash register area. Managed inventory and stock levels. Hired and mentored staff members into top-performing sales representatives.

Sales Representative (3+ years)

Greeted customers and provided strong customer service. Identified opportunities to increase number of items that clients were interested in purchasing. Consistently ranked as top performer and offered creative and effective ideas to improve operations and grow sales.

TAB SUPERMARKET – Alameda, CA   5+ years

Cashier

Applied utmost attention to detail while scanning items for purchase and providing strong conflict resolution regarding any complaints. Leveraged mathematical aptitude to provide change to customers when there were issues with register.

Computer Skills

Microsoft Office Suite (Word, Excel, PowerPoint)

Education & Volunteer Work

Associate of Science (A.S.) in Business
Sunnau Community College

Other experience:

American Heart Association of Daly City
Community Treasurer

2 / 2

Resume Checklist

Before your resume is ready for prime time, give it one last once-over:

☐ *Does it make the right flash impression?* Employers scan the average resume for just 15 seconds.

☐ *Does it target the job?* All-purpose resumes are no-purpose resumes.

☐ *Does it showcase your successes?* It must indicate why you stood out, not just repeat your job description.

☐ *Is it specific?* For instance, does it quantify your achievements?

☐ *Does it include time-related successes,* such as "Finished project one month before deadline"?

☐ *Is it free of spelling or grammatical errors?* Sloppiness is the fast track to the wastebasket, and spellcheckers can't eliminate it.

☐ *Does it use strong action verbs?* Foggy terms like "facilitate" challenge the employer's understanding and memory.

☐ *Is it fat-free?* Has it stripped away clutter, such as age, health, and the pointless "References available upon request"?

☐ *Is it long enough?* Forget the one-page myth. If you've been an executive for 15 to 20 years, you may need two or three pages.

☐ *Does it highlight the heart of your career?* In most cases, it should cover just the last 10 to 15 years.

☐ *Does it look attractive?* Or does it resemble the legal notices in the newspaper? Insist on appealing use of white space, bullets, and boldface.

☐ *Finally, does it leave the employer wanting to know more about you?*

Key Lessons

✦ You are marketing yourself, and your resume is an ad meant to sell your candidacy to the employer.

✦ Keep employers interested by remembering to answer this question: What can you show employers that will make them want to find out more?

✦ Compile a list of all your courses, jobs, volunteering, and hobbies, along with your corresponding skills and accomplishments, as a starting point for your resume.

✦ Create customized resumes for each employer and job using the actual job posting to focus on the skills you know matter most to that employer.

✦ Make sure your resume adheres to each employer's formatting requirements, has an attractive and easily readable design, and is free of typos and other mistakes.

Chapter 4

Take Cover:
The ABCs of Cover Letters

*"My name is Sherlock Holmes. It is my business to
know what other people do not know."*
—Arthur Conan Doyle, *The Adventure of the Blue Carbuncle*

Do COVER LETTERS MATTER? A common refrain
in hiring circles is that they're mostly ignored.

Even if that's true, applicants should make their plans only after
a long, hard look at that unassuming "mostly." It's certainly a given
that the resume is what really counts, but there are enough people
out there who do read cover letters—along with a fair number
who read cover letters first—to make them an important piece of
job-search paper.

One small-business owner has this to say: "As the owner-
manager of a small professional firm, I always read cover letters
before reviewing the accompanying resume. I found that it gave
me a more personal sense of what the individual was like, and I
always noticed if they had taken the trouble to find out about us,
whether they'd addressed the letter to a specific individual, and
whether they expressed themselves well in writing. If I liked the

cover letter, I'd look to the resume to confirm the skills and experience we were looking for. If I didn't, I'd still review the resume, but good cover letters gave people an edge. This is probably not terribly practical for large organizations, but it seemed to make sense for a small shop."

The takeaway for applicants is that there's no reason not to write a cover letter and there's every reason to make it as good as it can be.

More Than an Afterthought

How do you make your first impression with an employer? With your cover letter.

Don't let the name fool you. "Cover letter" suggests afterthought, slap-on status. Yet it is critical, since:

- *It speaks for you before the resume.* It introduces you. A pleasant, clear, brief cover letter conveys one message; a remote, gnarled, wandering letter, another.

- *It highlights aspects of your career that might otherwise get lost in the resume.* It gives you a chance to aim spotlights at the right places.

- *It shows your care for detail.* Or, rather, it shows that you aren't careless, that you haven't dashed off a last-minute message.

- *It can reveal your judgment.* For instance, if you mention irrelevancies like hobbies in the cover letter, you can trip yourself up. No one wants an executive with poor judgment.

WHAT'S GOOD FOR RESUMES IS GOOD FOR COVER LETTERS

Almost every principle that applies to resumes is equally true for cover letters.

- *Be perfect.* Review your letter and eliminate mistakes. Grammar and spelling have to be flawless.

- *Be good-looking.* For physical letters, use good paper and a good printer. For all cover letters, format them so that they look crisp, clean, and professional. Play by the layout rules of business letters. The most common style is "block format." Everything is left justified, starting with your contact information, the date, the recipient's name, title and address; a salutation using the recipient's name; and the body of the letter. If you have your own letterhead, use it and omit the separate block of contact information, but follow the text with a closing ("Very truly yours," for example) and your signature, with your name printed below the signature.

- *Be personal.* Mass-produced cover letters are as bad as, if not worse than, mass-produced resumes. If you can find a name to write to, address your letter to that specific person.

- *Be informed.* Research is important—a sentiment that we will return to again and again. If you know something about the company, refer to whatever it is that's driven you to apply for this particular job at this particular company. With that in mind, provide a direct answer to this question: What do you bring to the table that will benefit the company and make you the right person for the job?

- *Be smart.* Make your life easier. You should personalize your cover letters, but that does not mean that you start with a blank screen and start from the beginning with each letter. Create a template that includes the bullet points you want to emphasize with every employer. They're likely to be fairly consistent. You can then customize your template with names, company specifics, and selling points that are especially relevant to each employer.

- *Be brief.* One page consisting of four or five paragraphs should be enough for almost any imaginable circumstance. Remember, you've got your resume attached, so there's no need to repeat everything you're saying there. A cover letter needs only the highest of your highlights.

- *Be direct.* Get to the point quickly, with no meandering along the way. Keep it simple. Use short sentences and action verbs. Avoid passive constructions; they feel weak, as if things were being done to you and not by you. Passive: "All testing procedures for the perpetual motion machine were developed by me." Active: "I developed all testing procedures for the perpetual motion machine." Try to be more Stephen King and less Henry James.

Know Your ABCs

In the movie David Mamet's "Glengarry Glen Ross," Alec Baldwin's character hammers his sales force with the mantra "Always be closing," seemingly the numero-uno rule of the ABC sales system famous, or infamous, among sales professionals in the real world. Cover letters have their own less maniacal ABC mantras: Always be contextualizing. Always remember the context in which you're working in every part of the job search. If you bear that in mind, you can avoid making one of the basic, if subtle, mistakes that plague many of these job-search documents.

Like your resume, your cover letter is not exactly meant to answer the question of why you are so wonderful in a general way. While a cover letter pays attention to your magnificently positive qualities, it does so in a very specific context and with a very limited agenda.

The real, in-context question a cover letter answers every step of the way is this: Given that you're so terrific, what can your wonderful qualities do for this organization? That's the question. You may be terrific in many ways, but the only qualities that matter are those that demonstrate to the reader that good things will happen if you're hired. In other words, if I give you a job, what's in it for me?

In a resume, you can provide a list of answers. By all means, give them a whole string of accomplishments that support your case. In a cover letter, though, focus only on the strongest of your strengths—the one or two things that will sell the reader on your prospects, the ones that will close the deal. (For a sample cover letter, see the following page.)

Handling Potential Trouble Spots

The cover letter is the one vehicle you have for dealing with issues that can trouble someone who has only your resume in front of him.

Cover letters can deal with all sorts of potential trouble. If there are gaps in your work history or frequent job changes, or if you're changing fields entirely, sometimes a few words of explanation are in order. If you're underqualified or overqualified, you can make a case for why it doesn't matter. If you're a new grad, you can emphasize experiences and personal qualities that your resume may not cover well enough.

This can be a delicate balancing act. You run the risk of calling attention to an issue that might have escaped notice, or of emphasizing an issue that, though noticed, was one a screener was quite prepared to ignore. Sadly, there's no hard-and-fast rule that will make the decision for you. It's barely even a case-by-case decision, because too many variables come into play. There's

Michael Masterson
Street Address, City, State Zip Code – Phone Number – Email Address

Date

Dr. Stuart Ehrlich
Chief Revenue Officer
Shelby Pharmaceuticals
15 Columbus Circle
Rochester, New York 47135

RE: Pharmaceutical Sales Representative

Dear Dr. Ehrlich:

My 10+ years of progressive experience in medical sales has led me to your available **Pharmaceutical Sales Representative** role. With a Bachelor of Science in Business, it's my conviction that your organization would count me as a valuable addition. Throughout my thriving career over the past decade, I've kept a close watch on Shelby Pharmaceuticals, and I have been impressed.

Over the course of my career with small businesses to major corporations, my efforts entailed building relationships with healthcare providers and educating them on the benefits of my employers' products. Additionally, my B2B sales, presentation, active listening, client needs assessment, solution sales, consultative sales, and negotiation skills enabled me to consistently help companies succeed. My co-workers and supervisors have recognized me as a driven and tenacious self-starter with exceptional interpersonal skills.

Proudly, in my professional history I...
- **Earned numerous sales awards,** including the prestigious Bartell Pharma Sales Award.
- **Consistently was recognized as a top performer.** At Bartell, I ranked #1 on a team of 60 reps.
- **Contributed to the development of highly successful sales programs.** I established a sales organization at Remington Biotech Pharmaceuticals for a new line of pediatric therapies.

Complementing these achievements is my credential as a CNPR, CRM competency, and bilingual (English / Spanish) communication strength.

This letter and the enclosed résumé are snapshots of my background. For a more in-depth understanding of how my skill set and experience would propel your organization to a higher level of growth, please contact me at your earliest convenience. I look forward to hearing from you.

Sincerely,

Michael Masterson

Enclosure

your specific history, the specific employer, and even the specific screener. The state of the job market itself also comes into play. When the job market favors applicants, many little imperfections will be overlooked. When employers are in the driver's seat, every imperfection becomes a reason for rejection. Still, there are some tips that will help:

- *First, as with any cover letter, keep it brief and to the point.* This is no time for rambling, long-winded explanations.

- *Second, keep it balanced.* Don't just try to explain away your weaknesses. Get some positives in there as well.

- *Third, focus on your strengths:* your skills, your accomplishments, and your experience.

- *Fourth, don't go negative.* If, for example, you've changed jobs frequently, this is not the place to say bad things about previous employers.

- *Fifth, use formatting to your advantage.* If your cover letter includes a short series of bullet points, for instance, don't devote all of them to your problem. Devote most of them to your strengths. Don't make your weakness the most important point you're making. Don't let it become the story. Instead, put the weakness you're worried about in the context of your many strengths.

Finally, if you're still unsure about the need to explain something in your resume, get someone to take a look. This time, you don't want a detailed review. You don't want to put it under the microscope. Have your reviewer give it something between a skim and a quick reading. See what jumps off the page. If what jumps is a problem, that may push you in the direction of using your cover letter to put that problem in its place. It may also lead you to take another look at your resume itself and to consider some changes. If so, take heart. We'll cover the options for people in special situations in the next chapter.

Key Lessons

+ Your cover letter is the employer's first impression, so strive to make it as good as it can be.

+ Use your cover letter to highlight aspects of your career that might otherwise get lost in your resume.

+ Format your cover letter so it looks crisp, clean, and professional, and use the "block format" style that is common for business letters.

+ Personalize each letter, and if you can find a name to write to, address your letter to that specific person.

+ Your cover letter should provide a direct answer to this question: What do you bring to the table that will benefit the company and make you the right person for the job?

+ Keep your letter to one page, get to your point quickly, and avoid passive language.

+ Each quality you mention should be framed in the context of what it will do for the organization.

+ Focus only on your top strengths and save the full list of your accomplishments for your resume.

+ Cover letters let you deal with potential trouble spots like gaps in your work history or appearing underqualified, but you should balance your weaknesses with your strengths to avoid overemphasizing the issue.

Chapter 5

Special Delivery: *Overcoming Difficult Situations in Your Resume and Cover Letter*

"My center is giving way, my right is in retreat; situation excellent. I shall attack."
—Ferdinand Foch

With a good start on resumes and cover letters, we can turn our attention to some special situations, the difficult predicaments many of us find ourselves in at some point during our working lives. They can all seem daunting, but not a single one is necessarily fatal.

For special situations, your paperwork has to work overtime. You have to handle your resume in the right way, and you have to make especially good use of your cover letter. If you do that, you'll keep your application in the running, and that's all we ask: Just get one step further down the road to an offer.

EMPLOYMENT HISTORY GAPS

There are gaps—and there are gaps. Not every period of unemployment needs to be explained. In fact, the best course for a short gap, one that lasts less than a year, is to let it be. You may feel that gap acutely, and, for that reason, it's tempting to give it a lot of attention. But that's counterproductive. Think of it as a minor disruption, treat it that way, and a hiring manager will be less inclined to make it a huge issue.

With too much emphasis, you risk calling undue attention to something that would not have much impact otherwise. Hiring managers are not living in blissful ignorance of the tough times that have troubled an entire national economy. They've had plenty of recent experience with this very situation. Don't encourage them to make it their focus by making it your focus.

Longer gaps are a different story. A chronological resume will make them stand out, so it may be better to use a functional or combination approach. The real key, however, is how you used your time. If you're unemployed, it is absolutely in your best interest to stay active, whether by volunteering or by learning something new. Did you volunteer somewhere? Did you coach? Did you take a course or learn something on your own? Was it work-related?

If you've been doing any of those things, they should be spelled out. Volunteer work often involves skills and responsibilities that translate nicely to the workplace, but people tend to neglect those activities because "it wasn't a real job."

In some cases, time away from work was not the result of layoffs or company closings. If that's the case, a cover letter can play a very valuable role. If, for example, you had to take time to care for a family member, explain that in your letter, and don't be too sure that you can't find room for it in your resume. You may have been embroiled in an endless series of complicated financial and medical decisions. Managing that turmoil is its own kind of work. Don't leave it at "Took time off because of family illness." Instead, make it clear that you negotiated a complex and emotionally taxing situation that took a great deal of strength, commitment, and organizational ability.

JOB-HOPPING

Frequent moves from job to job make hiring managers nervous. If you're hired, with all the training and recruitment expenses that entails, will you stick? Here's how to instill confidence:

- If you had a short-term position that does nothing to improve your resume, here's the good news: You don't have to include it. You may not be able to omit a long-term position because it can turn into a troublesome gap, but, while you shouldn't lie about it on your resume, this is not a sworn statement of every job you've ever held. Application forms are a different matter, since some require you to list every one of those jobs, but a resume is a marketing piece, not an affidavit. You're entitled to omit irrelevancies.

- If you've held the same position with numerous employers, organize your resume according to your continuing role: Chief Tiger-Groomer, Bronx Zoo, San Diego Zoo, and Columbus Zoo, 2008–2012.

- You can use that same approach if you've been freelancing and working on short-term projects in one field. Focus on the job description, not the "employers," and list multiple representative clients within a consolidated time period. Each client does not need individual dates, especially if, like many freelancers, you work for repeat customers in spurts, with time off between discrete projects for a given client.

- Use your cover letter to explain the (reasonable and very understandable) circumstances that led you to change jobs relatively quickly. Don't, however, base your explanation on a litany of your employers' faults. Bad-mouthing and negativity never go over well, regardless of how bad things were.

CHANGING CAREERS

A true career change calls for a combination resume. The idea is that you developed skills and reached results in your former career that are clearly transferable to your new one. If you're moving from sales to teaching, for example, you know how to make presentations, how to persuade, how to interest your audience, how to organize material, and how to relate to all sorts of people—all things that matter in both fields.

If the skills you need now are not the ones you used in your former career, what are those skills and where did they come from? Presumably, you didn't pick your new field at random. Did you go to school? Did you do any volunteering? Did you intern? Take a hard look at what you learned and what you achieved in those settings. Focus your resume accordingly.

A chronological resume won't deliver the right message. Use a combination resume that opens with a summary of your qualifications and a clear statement of your new goals. Add a brief chronological rundown of your employment in your former field. Finally, use your cover letter to underline a convincing explanation for the big change.

RE-ENTERING THE WORKFORCE

An extended absence from the workforce doesn't have to leave a yawning chasm in your resume. Consider your absence a long gap in your history, and focus on the same things that apply to people with employment gaps. In other words, highlight the things you did in the interim—even if you weren't being paid to do them.

- Did you go to school or participate in any form of continuing professional education?

- Did you do any volunteer work?

- Were you involved in any community activities?

- Did you take on any freelance work? Working from home is still working.

It is also worth highlighting ways in which you kept abreast of your field. If nothing else, make this a point of emphasis in your cover letter. It shows the kind of continuing commitment that employers want to see.

JUST STARTING OUT

Anyone can feel lost in the wilderness of the job market, but new graduates often feel more lost than most. This is true even for grads who have worked part-time throughout school and are looking at a first experience of a job that's not a self-limited stopgap. It's the first time they're crossing the line into a real career that could last for the rest of their working lives. By any definition, it's an important moment that can overwhelm.

What's needed is the kind of orientation that freshmen get when they first arrive on campus: Here's where you sleep, here's the library, here's who to talk to about your coursework, and here's how you make the most of this opportunity.

Of course, most new grads have heard of such things as resumes and cover letters. They know they'll need them, but they don't necessarily know where to start, what to include, what to leave out, and what, in the end, makes for a resume that gets results. New grads need a compass.

Break Out the Shoebox

As a new grad, you've taken courses, you've worked on projects, you may have participated in extracurricular activities, and you may have worked, full-time or part-time, on or off campus. All of that is going to end up in a shoebox full of everything you've done that has even the slightest chance of being relevant to what you want to do. Remember: The one-size-fits-all resume is not the goal.

When you're looking at job opportunities, you'll edit that mass of information so you're left with the things that actually apply.

- What courses did you take?

- Which of those were advanced courses?

- What was your major?

- Did you work on any special projects?

- Did you intern anywhere?

- Did you participate in extracurricular activities?

- Did you participate in work-study?

- Did you have any jobs of any kind during the school year or during the summer?

- Did you join any clubs or groups?

- Did you receive any honors or special recognition?

- Did you excel in particular classes?

Make the Most of Your Education

People who've been out of school for a while don't need to go into great detail about education. But new grads often do. List your major and your academic honors, and include your GPA if it's impressive.

If your major is relevant, list individual courses, especially if they're directly on point. If you're a business major applying for work with a property-assessment firm, for example, advertise the fact that you took courses in commercial assessment, industrial valuation, and principles of exemption and abatement. If your grades in those super-relevant courses were exceptional, include them.

If your major doesn't directly relate, make note of the courses you took outside that major and that do relate.

If you completed a large project, even if it was part of your coursework, consider including it as if it were a major work-related project. If the end product was impressive, put it online and provide a link.

In some fields, certifications are important, and some of those certifications have educational prerequisites. If you've completed educational requirements but can't quite get the credential yet—a common issue when there is also an experience requirement—let employers know that certification is almost within your grasp.

Make the Most of Your Experience

Think about the work you've done. You may have more to say about it than you think, so don't sell yourself short.

For the typical student, there are two types of work:

Type one: You went out on your own, cutting lawns and trimming shrubs in the neighborhood, for example. You had to drum up business, create a schedule, and follow through. You weren't just cutting the grass, though. You were running a business, and that's how you should frame that experience. You can think of babysitting or housecleaning the same way.

Type two: You were an employee, and you may well have been involved in some low-level drudgery that doesn't seem like much, but there may have been highlights. Perhaps you were the one charged with closing up at the end of the day or the one who trained new hires. When you're just starting out, all those little things can be good additions to a resume. Small they may be, but they're still achievements.

Don't forget that experience doesn't have to involve pay for it to be relevant. Internships should obviously be in the mix, but so should volunteer experiences and extracurricular activities, especially if they have some bearing on your career goals.

Beware the Millennial Curse

Many career advisors discourage applicants from including "irrelevant" jobs in their resumes, advice that makes sense if you have substantial relevant experience. While it's still true that relevant experience matters most, this can prove difficult for recent grads.

In reality, there has always been a case for not including all of a new grad's experience. For one thing, you don't want to devote so much space to your college career that your meager work experience is buried and barely noticeable at the bottom of the page.

In addition, today's graduates face a different problem. They're those awful millennials, the supposedly coddled generation of entitled, narcissistic "Trophy Kids," who lack a discernible work ethic—just what employers are *not* looking for.

Not all employers share that opinion. The smarter ones know that it never makes sense to paint a diverse group—any group—with the same broad brush. Whatever you make of the generational characterization, however, the millennial portrait expressed in overwrought editorials has gained enough traction to be worth countering.

The best way to do that is to make it quite plain that you've worked—and worked hard. Anyone who's been there knows that someone who's been waiting tables four nights a week—or doing any one of a thousand low-level jobs, relevant or not—has more than enough work ethic to go around.

The bottom line: If you don't have an abundance of relevant experience on display, don't exclude other experience as a matter of principle. It still has impact.

Key Lessons

- For special situations, your resume and cover letter have to work overtime to keep your application in the running for a job offer.

- Use a functional resume instead of a chronological one when you have employment gaps longer than a year.

- Frequent job-hopping makes hiring managers nervous, but you don't have to include every short-term position if it doesn't improve your resume.

- If you've held the same position with numerous employers or freelance clients, organize your resume under the continuing role or job description instead of the individual employers.

- Use your cover letter to explain the circumstances that led you to change jobs quickly, but don't base your explanation on your employer's faults.

- For a true career change, use a combination resume that focuses on the skills relevant to your new field and includes a brief chronology of your former employment, and then use the cover letter to provide an explanation for the change.

- New grads, make the most of your education by listing your major, academic honors, relevant courses and projects, and your GPA, if it's impressive.

- Experience doesn't have to involve pay for it to be relevant; internships, volunteer experiences, and extracurricular activities can all be included.

Chapter 6

Prepare to Launch: *Market Research for the Job Search Set*

"The good life is a process, not a state of being. It is a direction, not a destination."
—Carl Rogers

I<small>T'S TIME TO TAKE STOCK</small>. You've homed in on a career that fits. You've found it in a field that really speaks to you. That's no easy task, but you put in enough thought, time, research, and self-examination to reach a conclusion. Congratulations are in order.

On top of that, you've taken care of the two universal prerequisites: You've prepared the best possible resume and a compelling cover letter, both ready to be customized to meet any occasion. They're in place, prepared for launch! Lovely!

You've done it all, but where has it gotten you? Not very far, obviously, but you can certainly start right in on a massive marketing campaign, getting your paperwork out to anyone and everyone you can think of. At the same time, you may as well pick up the occasional lottery ticket. Your chances there are about as good, but at least they tell you the odds. The odds for your mass-marketing campaign aren't much better, whatever they may be. But at least you feel like you're doing something, and that may make it easier to stick to your strategy.

Don't follow that path. It's equivalent to putting all your money into lottery tickets. In both cases, there's an infinitesimal chance you'll get lucky—and, in both cases, there's a much better chance you'll be wondering how to pay this month's rent.

You need a plan. It should be practical and shouldn't stress you to the breaking point. It should be easy to follow and made up of things you'll actually do. It should make good use of your time. And above all, the plan should work.

INSIDE THE HR BRAIN

We've already seen a bit of how employers think because it's expressed in a rule we've mentioned, one that might be the Golden Rule of Hiring: Employers hire people who they think will benefit them, and applicants must make "benefit to employer" their overriding marketing concern.

That's a rule to live by, but it would be nice to know a whole lot more. Where do employers start? Where do they find the people they want? How do applicants get their attention? And, of course, how can you be one of the people in the running?

Armed with answers to those questions, we can focus on the areas with the most potential, and it should make it easier to adhere to another useful rule, the Pareto Principle, also known as the 80/20 Rule.

That rule holds that a small proportion of a large group is likely to be responsible for disproportionate results. For example, 20 percent of your customers may bring you 80 percent of your profits, or 20 percent of your customers—presumably a different 20 percent—are responsible for 80 percent of all complaints. In 2002, Microsoft CEO Steve Ballmer advised customers that 80 percent of all errors in Windows were caused by 20 percent of all the bugs in the system.

In the job search, the question is this: Where does it pay to invest your limited time and energy? Where do you get the most bang for your buck? What's the 20 percent that gets 80 percent of the results?

Employers seek candidates from all sorts of places: job boards, recruiters, career fairs, former employees, present employees, classified ads, online job postings, competitors' employees, and so on, all part of the hiring landscape for years.

In recent years, however, technology and social media have become more and more important to hiring strategy. According to *Job Outlook 2013*, the latest semiannual report published by the National Association of Colleges and Employers, 13.7 percent of employers planned to use more technology and 23.9 percent of employers planned to use more social media in 2010. In 2013, those percentages increased to 59.6 percent for technology and 57.3 percent for social media.

At the same time as they are moving with the social media tide, employers are, as always, looking at their hiring practices with an eye toward improving results.

Randall Birkwood has been around the block a few times, having directed recruiting at T-Mobile, Cisco, and Microsoft, and he has tried to quantify hiring sources according to quality of hire. Quality is a difficult subject to quantify, and Birkwood acknowledges that he "took the simple route" in his research. "Quality of hire is defined as the percent of new hires who pass their one-year anniversary and score at least 'meets expectations' on their first review," he wrote.

Of the six categories in Birkwood's analysis, the two sources that led to the highest quality were former employees and passive candidates. If you're an applicant looking for a job with one of your former employers, or if you're not looking for a job at all, you're in luck, but it's not likely you're in either of these categories.

Things start to get interesting with the category of employee referrals, which was next in line as a source that produced high-quality new hires. That's certainly enough to give employee referrals some added weight in hiring determinations, but there's also the question of quantity. It turns out that employee referrals made up "a much greater percent" of new hires than either of the top two categories.

What about job boards? They're easy for applicants and employers to use, so they tend to get a lot of traffic. While Birkwood acknowledges that they were the second-largest source of hires, they also yielded the lowest quality. Birkwood says he has no plans to avoid job boards in the future, but other options will get extra attention. "In our planning, we can focus on putting more resources and effort toward the good quality hire sources, such as employee referrals, passive candidates, and former employees."

You can't very well turn yourself into a former employee, but you can take a hint from a hiring manager willing to share his own thoughts about the best places to be in the job market. On one hand, then, we have an increasing reliance on social media. On the other, we have a situation in which hiring managers may tend to put great faith in employee referrals.

If it seems like we're heading into the worst possible case of "it's who you know, not what you know," that may not be far from the truth. What's needed, though, is a way to make good use of the situation as it really is.

Your Best Bet

Happily, there are steps you can take to get yourself in the best possible shape for today's redesigned job market and take advantage of the way it functions now. If social media is so important and employee referrals work so well, perhaps there's a way to tap into those resources and get things moving in the right direction. It is difficult to find many good things to say about the art of hiring in its current state.

Lou Adler, who is well known in recruiting circles for his advocacy of a performance-based approach, can't seem to find many good things to say about the art of hiring at present, and he has plenty of company.

Two problems stand out, and they're both of great relevance to anyone in the job market, although only one can be applied to this stage of the job search. First, the fact that today's job market is very much a buyer's market means that employers are inundated with resumes for almost any opening you can name, at almost any level. When 800 resumes arrive in response to one opening, no HR department has the ability, let alone the willingness, to do much careful screening. They resort to blunt instruments applied by machines, hence the ascendency of keywords. They're happy to accept applicants who are "good enough," if not great, and they're certainly not equipped to see behind the most superficial reading of a resume.

As a result, they don't afford much chance to the applicant who does not conform to the standard mold. Gone are the days when companies thought outside the box. When talent was in short supply, the world of finance took a shine to mathematicians, even if they didn't have occupation-specific credentials. Today, it's hard to imagine a similar reach by some other industry, regardless of how well the earlier experiment worked out. "Unusual" applicants get screened out early.

The second problem is one we'll deal with at length when the time is right: The interview process is broken. Not only is it broken, but there's a real chance that it never really worked in the first place. This is something applicants need to understand and come to grips with, and Adler, in particular, has a lot to say about improving that part of hiring. Applicants, however, don't need to conquer the interview until they've gotten past the screening process. Let's put the interview on hold for the moment while we work on getting a foot in the door.

Adler would like to see the entire hiring process put on a performance-based footing, maintaining that hiring managers are wasting their time if they're posting ads or looking for resumes on the web. He surveyed employees early in 2013, asking how they got their jobs. Adler reports that 81 percent of passive applicants were hired through internal moves or networking, a result he calls "astonishing," although it's hard not to see it as eminently predictable.

The combined results for active and passive hires, however, were more eye-opening: Some 58 percent of total hires occurred through internal moves or "some type of proactive networking activity," including referrals from hiring-company employees.

If we strip out internal moves, it turns out that networking, including those employee referrals, was far and away the leading means of getting a new job, accounting for 46 percent of all hires.

Meanwhile, only 14 percent of those surveyed got their jobs because someone searched for and found their resumes online, and 27 percent were hired through job postings. At 41 percent, those sources cannot and should not be ignored. In fact, applicants cannot afford to overlook any reasonable strategy, and resumes and online profiles at sites like LinkedIn should be as good as they possibly can be.

It's a mistake, however, to think that you can get those things in terrific shape and then just sit back, relax, and wait for employers to find you. Adler uses the survey results to reinforce his message to hiring managers: "If recruiters are spending more than 25 percent of their time posting ads or searching for resumes, they're missing the heart of the talent market."[1] Turn that message around, and it's a powerful message to applicants: Put yourself out there in every way you can think of, but put the bulk of your energy into networking and referrals. Otherwise, you're missing the heart of the job market.

---

[1]   www.eremedia.com/ere/why-source-of-hire-should-drive-a-companys-talent-acquisition-strategy/

With all his emphasis on performance, Adler is no believer in the screening power of skills-based resumes: "People who are hired externally, but are highly regarded and referred by a trusted source, are evaluated on a reasonable balance of past performance and skills and experience."

For the applicant, the lesson couldn't be simpler.

- You're one applicant among many.

- Even if you're the best applicant, the screening process can't be counted on to find you.

- Rather than relying on the small chance that your resume is among the chosen few, you need to find a way to get noticed, to differentiate yourself from the competition.

- Hiring managers, like recruiters, can't afford to ignore a referral; if anything, it's a sure way to make their jobs easier.

- If you already have a personal connection, you have an advantage.

- If you don't, making that kind of connection could be tremendously rewarding.

- You'd separate yourself from the crowd. You'd get a foot in the door.

- Getting that kind of payoff is worth your energy and time.

To be blunt, you'd have to be nuts to leave the possibility of a personal connection out of your job search strategy, especially with so much solid evidence pointing to its unequaled value.

But let's say you don't have that kind of connection at the moment. If that's the case, you're hardly alone, but most people won't make much of an attempt to change things. They don't know who to approach. They don't know how to start or what to say.

So our next order of business is to look behind the curtain, because finding personal connections in your field does not have to be a process shrouded in mystery. You'll still have to seek those connections out, but, with the right approach, you can find the kind of allies who will lift your job search to another level.

Internal or External: The World According to Wharton

If you're not already in place for promotion from within, your status as an external hire does have its advantages. For one thing, external hires make more money—up to 20 percent more—than their internal counterparts. The downside, however, is that they don't perform as well, at least at first, and are more likely to be let go in the first two years on the job. Once they pass the two-year mark, they have an advantage once more. They tend to be promoted faster than people hired from within.

According to a study by management professor Matthew Bidwell of the Wharton School, a lot of the pay differential can be attributed to the fact that outside candidates are hired on the basis of their impressive resumes. They often have more education than people already in the organization, and they look awfully good on paper. "Firms struggle to evaluate the true qualities of applications, and workers struggle to know which of the jobs available will best suit their preferences and abilities," Bidwell says. But hiring managers have, at best, incomplete information about external candidates, while an internal candidate is something of a known quantity.

If nothing else, the Wharton study supports Adler's notion that the most common hiring practices place undue weight on skills and experience when they would be better served by a performance-based approach.

Let's not get carried away, though. We wish employers the best, but we're here to get hired, not to solve the world's hiring problems. Even if every expert in the universe agrees that the traditional approach is flawed, it pays to have the brightest, shiniest resume possible. When those poor hiring managers have to grudgingly resort to external sources of candidates, give yourself the chance to be the unknown quantity that stands out.

COMPANY IDENTIFICATION

Looking at all the evidence about today's job market, two things stand out:

- The use of technology, including social media, has to be part of any serious job search.

- Nothing will do more for you than the personal connection that turns into a door-opening referral.

For anyone who is looking for the right contact in the right field, those two key points are, as we'll see, closely related. For those with contacts in hand, there's still the question of how you can enlist a friendly contact in your search, a question that applies to everyone. First, though, those of us without personal connections need help. How do you find the right people? Once you've found them, how do you approach those people—strangers, after all—so that they end up on your side?

The answer is that you need a plan, one that starts with a practical step, continues with a practical step, and ends—you guessed it—with a practical step. This part of the search is really about three things:

1. Finding where the jobs are in the field you want to pursue.

2. Finding the employers you'd want to work for.

3. Finding the people who are involved in those jobs, are working for those employers, and who, if all goes well, might just be willing to give you a few minutes of their time.

Making a List, Checking It No More Than Twice

Like many plans, this one starts with a list. The list in question is made up of companies, those in your field of choice. There's a very good chance that you can list a dozen qualifying companies off the top of your head. Some may be household names. Throw those big organizations in, but don't stop there. Of the tens of millions of companies in the United States, very few of them are the ones we've all heard of, and the ones we've heard of tend to be the most competitive, and that, in turn, is because everyone knows them. When everybody knows your name, you get a lot of job applications.

Your list should not be limited to the biggest of the big. Smaller companies, the ones with fewer than 100 employees, outnumber the big guns by a factor of ten. And even though the largest employers, those with over 500 employees, account for a large share of the nation's jobs, that share is still under 15 percent.

The bulk of companies and the bulk of jobs are found among smaller organizations, many of which you may never have heard of. But here's where technology comes to the rescue. You can search databases, like www.indeed.com, www.simplyhired.com, www.glassdoor.com, or www.monster.com, which aggregate job listings from companies that are hiring in any given field.

This is most emphatically *not* supposed to be an exhaustive list. Instead, in keeping with our overarching theme, this is a chunk of activity that's eminently doable on a small scale. You're not trying to create a definitive pointer to the place you want to work. You're not trying to include every company in existence. Those sorts of big, ill-defined projects can paralyze those of us with even the slightest tendency to procrastinate or the smallest hint of ADD.

So take this task for what it is—a simple list of companies in your field, perhaps 50 of them as an upper limit. Don't forget: It's not that 50 is the goal. If you come up with 20, that will do perfectly well. The point is to avoid turning this step into the kind of research project that consumes days at a time.

Next, perform some equally simple triage. Some companies might be too large, some too small. Sometimes geography makes the decision. You'd never live in certain places. You'd never want to live so far away from family or, perhaps, so close.

The specific reasons don't matter. Keep it simple, and cross off the companies that have disqualified themselves. You're the one making the decisions.

Once you've reduced the list to 15 to 30 candidates—the precise number is not set in stone as long as it's at least a dozen or so—we can start to apply other criteria, the ones that speak more directly to the business of getting hired.

 ### Or Try Harvard

It will take some effort to establish the kind of contacts we're describing here, but you do have an alternative. For a mere $63,675 per year—tuition only, of course—you could attend Harvard Business School, where it's all about the networking. You'll rub shoulders with the ultra-rich from many lands in a school where, *The New York Times* says, "the only middle-class students here are the Americans." The *Times,* while explaining what business school is all about, also makes it quite clear that you'll have to mind your manners. "Because many students attend business school in the specific hope of building a network of influential contacts, they tend to fear offending anyone, especially wealthy classmates who might one day provide connections and financing."

> If dear old Harvard looks like a reasonable option,
> feel free to skip ahead to the next chapter. If not, read on,
> and be glad you're saving $100,000 or so in the process.

Defining Companies—and People—of Real Interest

You now have a list. As it stands, that list is not terribly useful, but it will increase in value exponentially with a little organization, and that little bit of step-by-step organization will reward you with a list that will make your search a whole lot easier.

Step 1: Who Are They?

At this point, you're faced with a gaggle, or perhaps a slew or a pride, of companies. They have to endure without a distinctive collective noun, but you've heard of some of them already. Some leapt to mind even before you started your research. There are also going to be some unknowns. Clearly, you can't organize your list when you know nothing about some of its members, so it's time for some further searching. Visit the unknown companies' websites. Google them. Follow a couple of links to information that isn't company-generated. Look for mentions of them in the business page of any newspaper and in blogs that have solid reputations in your field. You don't need to know everything, and you may be surprised by how quickly you get a sense of whether this place is right for you.

Use a method of ranking these companies. Any method will do, as long as it gives you a way to identify the companies on a scale of "closeness to your dream job." Rank them in order, if you like, and don't be concerned if some companies cluster together at the same level of relative dreaminess. On a similar note, don't be surprised if a little bit of information about some of the formerly unknown companies is enough to make you lose interest entirely. Banish them forthwith.

Let's not get carried away with the research, though. The only reason we're looking at companies through this lens is to eliminate the losers while establishing a preliminary determination of where it may pay to put the most energy.

Step 2: Who's Hiring?

Since we're not doing any of this for the sheer fun of it, we want to know who, in our ordered list of employers, might actually be hiring these days.

So far, we've figured out where we'd love to work, where we'd really like to work, and where we'd like to work. Now we need to know which companies actually give us the sense that they have jobs to fill.

Job-specific search engines, sites like Indeed, Monster, SimplyHired, Glassdoor, and many more, will do most of the heavy lifting here. They should give you a quick sense of whether the company is hiring at all and, if you narrow your search terms to include your own field, whether they're hiring people like you. Both points are important, with one caveat: Since you're screening via keyword in the same way that employers screen resumes, there's no guarantee that your chosen keyword is a match for the employer's keyword. Therefore, it's important to know whether a given company is hiring at all, even if results don't appear for a specific job description.

Speed trumps almost everything, according to Steve Dalton, author of *The 2-Hour Job Search*. He has a point. You don't want to find yourself falling down the rabbit hole of every job posting you come across, following every link until you somehow find that two hours have passed and, while you have newfound respect for the honey badger, you are none the wiser about jobs.

The fact that searches are imperfect by nature and that no one aggregator finds every job out there argues for a more flexible approach that reflects your priorities.

In this case, flexibility means spending a little more time on the companies at the top of your list, those dream employers. Visit the sites of those employers. See what jobs they've posted. Conduct a search of the web in general, using specific search terms that combine the job and the company you want. You can do this without turning a small detour into a major project, and it's worth spending an extra few minutes of your time on your top-rated employers.

If, in any of this, you find the posting of a lifetime, the perfect job at the perfect company, resist the temptation to dive right in. Applying at this point is a sure way to consign your resume to a black hole from which it will never escape. You may be unique and very special, but the perfect-job-perfect-company combination is guaranteed to attract hundreds, if not thousands, of resumes from unique and special people everywhere, and you get no edge for being among the first to respond.

The plain truth is that the winning applicant will not get the job by responding to the posting unless he has something more going for him.

The Black Hole in the Hiring Galaxy

One part of the job search that almost all applicants find brutally frustrating is the failure of employers to offer any response at all. As it turns out, that failure doesn't just happen at the beginning of the process.

According to a 2012 survey by Harris Interactive for CareerBuilder, 29 percent of applicants get no acknowledgement of their applications at all, and 75 percent of applicants are never graced with word of a decision. What's more amazing is that 60 percent of applicants hear nothing further even after they've interviewed for a position.

Companies have all sorts of reasons for behaving this way, some of them even legitimate. For example, legal trouble can follow a corporate communication that runs afoul of existing regulations, although that excuse assumes that employers will not only respond, but respond in illegal detail.

The bottom-line reason for this employer behavior is depressingly simple: Employers do it because they can. They have plenty of applicants. Their lack of response won't change that, at least in the immediate future. They'll still have plenty of applicants.

In any event, applicants should know that they're hardly alone if they're hearing nothing. They won't know why they didn't make the cut or how they could have improved their chances. They'll have to roll with the punches or—the real message here—find a way around the broken system.

Step 3: Making Connections

It should come as no surprise that our quest takes us into the world of personal connections once more.

To begin with, we don't have to look for people who are already found. If you have a contact at one of the companies on the list, put that aside for the moment. You'll still need to decide how best to approach that person, but that exercise can wait until we've filled out the list with contacts for the rest of the desirable companies.

If you're starting from scratch, you could, of course, try the "cold call," but if you've ever done any cold calling, you know what a hard road that is. Even if, like most of us, you've only been on the receiving end of a cold call, you know just how receptive you were to that unsolicited, out-of-the-blue contact.

On the other hand, you can argue that the potential payoff of a cold call is big enough to make the venture worthwhile. That's what cold callers and telemarketers tell themselves. If the prize is big enough, one sale makes all the other rejections worthwhile. As a job search strategy, however, approaching someone out of the blue should be a last resort, used only after you've exhausted all your other options.

And those options are many. Fellow alumni are a great place to start. You have a built-in connection and a wonderful way to introduce yourself. There's no need to look for something in common. You should be able to find an alumni database online through your school's alumni association, for both undergraduate and graduate schools. Work in reverse chronological order, starting with alumni from your most recent institution. If that was a graduate program, you already have a database that is self-selected for its interest in the field you've chosen. If it was an undergraduate program, there's bound to be significantly more variation, but you're only looking for people who are already working at the places on your list. You may also find information about people's majors, another potential area of commonality. The more you find in common, the greater your chance of striking the right chord.

If your alumni search doesn't pay off, all is not lost. Social networks can serve a similar purpose, even without the built-in help of a shared academic background. Not all social networks are created equal, however.

Among career-oriented networks, LinkedIn is the undisputed champion. In January 2013, the company announced that worldwide membership had passed the 200 million mark, with the United States leading the world with 74 million members. You don't have to go further than Wikipedia to get a sense of LinkedIn's value in the job search. In a bulleted list of eight LinkedIn uses, we find this: "Job seekers can review the profile of hiring managers and discover which of their existing contacts can introduce them."

Wikipedia's onto something, but it misses the real power of LinkedIn. It would be nice, of course, to go right to the top of the hiring hierarchy, but it would be unrealistic to think that hiring managers are not already inundated with referrals from even their most tenuous connections. We want to go a little broader and a little deeper into LinkedIn's potential, going beyond the possibility of connecting with hiring managers themselves. The beauty of LinkedIn is that you can use it as a way around the standard hiring process. Connecting with hiring managers only scratches the surface.

We'll consider LinkedIn in depth, but what about other social networks? With a membership of over a billion monthly active users and 665 million daily active users, Facebook dwarfs the competition.

It's no secret that Facebook is not a professional network. It often seems more like the anti-professional network, with people showing themselves at something less than their best, but it still has its uses. Perhaps its best use is as an almost-last resort, just ahead of the cold call, when other options are not paying off. A simple Facebook post, letting everyone know that you'd like to connect with someone at Company X opens that request to your network and, by extension, to the different networks of the people in your network.

 ### Handle with Care

Is it really necessary to remind anyone to be careful with what they post on Facebook? You're not about to update your status with evidence that you've committed a crime, although that's hardly unheard of on Facebook, but you should review your profile and your timeline, cleaning up as necessary.

Facebook allows you to control what people see, so you can always adjust your privacy settings, but beware: This can be a minefield. Facebook's privacy policies are an ever-changing adventure, and you can't assume that what was private last week will be private today. Err on the side of caution. Don't just "set and forget."

Let's say, though, that you've thoroughly scraped your profile of information that doesn't flatter your image—your brand. That, too, can pose a danger. Strangely enough, there is risk in doing too good a job. You can end up with something so bland and lacking in personality that it's no brand at all. It's barely human, and employers—even hiring managers!—are human. No one wants or expects a potential employee to forgo every part of life that's not directly related to their careers. Outside interests, hobbies, a sense of humor, and a life outside of work don't damage your prospects. In the worst case, in fact, a presentation that's especially sterile invites skepticism: Just how bad was the material that's been deleted? Was there nothing worth saving?

Key Lessons

+ Remember the Golden Rule of Hiring: Employers hire people they think will benefit them, so applicants must make "benefit to employer" their overriding marketing concern.

+ Networking, including employee referrals, is the leading means of getting a new job, so put the bulk of your energy into cultivating connections.

+ The use of technology, including social media, has to be part of any serious job search, so online resumes and profiles should be as good as possible.

+ Make a list of companies in your chosen field, rank them in order of closeness to your dream job, and then do online research to identify which are hiring.

+ If you find the perfect job posting, resist the temptation to respond immediately; the winning applicant will not get the job this way.

+ Use your existing resources, such as online alumni databases and social networks, to make personal connections with people who can provide a door-opening referral.

Chapter 7

Undercover: *Searching for a Job While Employed*

"We must leave this terrifying place tomorrow and go searching for sunshine."
—F. Scott Fitzgerald

ADVICE ABOUT THE JOB SEARCH always seems to focus on the searchers who are unemployed—generally, those who are new graduates, have been laid off, or are re-entering the workforce after a prolonged absence.

Times have changed, however. There is another group of searchers, people who have jobs but need help just as much as the unemployed. They're the underemployed. These are the people who trained in a given field and had career expectations that, in today's job market, are unrealized. They're working in low-level jobs, often in fields that have nothing to do with their ambitions. They're working because they have to, at whatever job will take them. They're working part time because that's all they can find.

At one time, people who were both employed and looking for jobs were a different breed. They might be working in the right field but for the wrong company. They might be working at the right company in every way except that there was no room for advancement.

Unemployment has been falling, but if you look at the broader picture, one that includes people who have settled for part-time work out of necessity and people so discouraged that they've simply stopped looking for work, the rate doubles. Add in the people who are working full time at jobs that don't begin to reflect their education and ability, and the number of people who, in one way or another, make up the "unhappy employed," and it is a very large number indeed.

The exact number is hard to pin down. On the one hand, it's easy to poll workers and ask part-timers if they want full-time employment, the kind of yes-or-no question that lends itself to a simple survey. On the other, there's a lot more nuance when you're asked if you're holding a job that aligns with your qualifications or abilities, let alone one that aligns with your aspirations.

It's impossible to derive meaningful information from questions whose answers are so dependent on personal idiosyncrasy. Where does the full-time retail clerk with a philosophy degree fit in? How do we account for the customer service representative who's a few credits short of her degree in psychology? Are these job-holding people underemployed? Did they get what they should have expected when they failed to make the job market part of their academic choices? Is there a line we can draw between a "foolish" decision and underemployment? If they're making marginally decent livings in relatively stable situations, should that remove them from the ranks of the underemployed? Or does it matter that the work has nothing to do with their educations and ambitions?

There are no clear answers to these questions, but one thing that is clear is that a bad situation appears to be even worse for college graduates. A recent report by the Economic Policy Institute (EPI) underscores the fact that new college graduates are alarmingly unemployed or underemployed, despite the official end of the Great

Recession in 2009. The report found that college graduates have an unemployment rate of 7.2 percent (compared with 5.5 percent in 2007), and an underemployment rate of 14.9 percent (compared with 9.6 percent in 2007).[1]

If you think the situation is only temporary, a hangover from the Great Recession that robust growth will solve, that same EPI report may make you think again. It also shows that since 2007 the share of new college grads working in jobs that do not require a college degree has increased from 38 percent to 46 percent.

We're talking about widespread problems for many people, employed or not. The essentials of the job hunt don't really change according to your employment status, but employed searchers do have to consider a number of special issues that don't affect their unemployed counterparts.

10 RULES OF THE ROAD
Rule 1: Mum's the Word
The first rule of the searching-while-employed club is: You do not talk about searching while employed.

The one exception applies when, and only when, your boss tells you it's time to look for a new job. For example, layoffs have been announced, with your imminent unemployment the result. You've been told when the end will come, and your employer may even have offered assistance with finding other work. In that case, everyone knows what's going on and there's no need for secrets. In that case and that case only, you can go to colleagues and supervisors for advice.

In every other case, the risks of disclosure outweigh any possible benefits. At the very least, you'll be seen, quite rightly, as less

---

[1] Alyssa Davis, Will Kimball, and Elise Gould, "The Class of 2015," Economic Policy Institute, May 27, 2015, http://www.epi.org/publication/the-class-of-2015/#young-workers-are-not-"riding-out"-the-recession-by-"sheltering-in-school (accessed March 1, 2016).

committed and less loyal. As a result, your assignments may suffer. You won't get the more interesting or important projects, and you certainly won't be given increased responsibility. Your chance of advancement will be reduced to zero.

These are all perfectly sensible responses to the news that you're looking for the door. What's worse, though, is the possibility that your job search doesn't bear fruit. Think of it: Not only are you the guy who wanted out, you're the guy who couldn't find something better. You don't have to see your career as an exercise in brand management to know that you've done a lot of damage to your prospects.

Many of the other rules for searching while employed are related to this first principle. Even when they seem to lack that relevance, it's always best to remember the first rule and to make decisions on that basis.

Rule 2: Use Your Own Tools

If you want your search to stay private, and you do, don't be tempted to use company equipment in the process, whether it's your computer, the office copier, or a company-issued phone. To one degree or another, your employer has access to all those things. Similarly, don't use your work email address for search-related communications.

Be careful with social media, especially your use of LinkedIn. Don't use your work email address, and don't log in at work if you can help it. LinkedIn remembers you and your visit, and anyone who accesses your computer after you've logged in can see your profile.

Even if privacy was no concern, there's an ethical issue. Your employer has a reasonable expectation that the tools you've been given will be used to benefit that employer. Yes, there's some flexibility, and people use equipment for all sorts of purposes that don't meet that expectation, but this is different. If you're a valuable employee and your departure would be a loss to your employer, you're using that equipment to your employer's detriment.

If neither privacy nor ethics are enough, consider the view through the eyes of a prospective employer. They're trying to predict what you'll do if offered a job. They'll base that prediction, at least in part, on how you've behaved at other jobs. They're likely to wonder if this is what you'll do if hired. It's not necessarily a fatal doubt, but it's not the kind of thinking you want to encourage. Instead of taking a chance, keep things separate.

Rule 3: Use Your Own Time

Just as employers have expectations of how you'll use the things they provide, they have expectations of your use of time. Again, there's leeway. No sane employer expects that every second of every day should be spent in unwavering attention to your work, although you might not want to test the limits if you're assembling circuit boards in China. What flexibility there is, even among more relaxed employers, does not extend to using time on the clock to find greener pastures.

Time should not be much of an issue when you're updating your resume, investigating openings, and researching companies. It can be more problematic when you're scheduling interviews, but it's a problem that's easily solved. Schedule meetings during your lunch hour or outside of working hours. Explain the situation to prospective employers, who already know that you're currently employed, and they'll understand. If they can't accommodate you, it may be a sign that this is not the new job you want.

Rule 4: Stay Positive

If you're actively looking for a new job while working at your current job, it's logical to assume that there's something you don't like about your current situation. That's fair enough, and perhaps it's true. You're working at a horrible job for a horrible company in a horrible place. Keep it to yourself. Negativity is almost never a desirable quality. A prospective employer, as an outsider, is in no position to judge your workplace, and he's likely to see your negativity as something fundamental, a quality you're all too likely to bring to a new workplace.

Instead, stick firmly to the positive. If you're looking for a job, it's because of the exciting opportunity it represents. It's because of the wonderful things you know about this new company and because you hope to contribute amazing things in a new environment.

Perhaps your office is a notorious nightmare. Its miseries are legendary, and you assume that everyone in the industry knows how bad it is. Even then, be positive. For one thing, you may be wrong. Perhaps it's not as infamous as you think. Even if you're right and it is notorious, your positivity will be all the more impressive when you leave a lasting impression as the candidate who was able to rise above it all.

Perhaps, however, you're cornered. An interviewer, hearing all your attempts to be positive, asks something specific about your workplace. It's obvious from the question that he knows the negative facts. "How did you handle it when the company adopted the lash as a motivational tool?" You can't very well deny it or give it a positive spin. You can, however, avoid the ad hominem. Don't attack Captain Bligh for his monstrous doings. Instead, offer an impersonal response that deals with structural issues of the organization: Resorting to the lash was counterproductive. Productivity actually fell. The organization hadn't even considered more enlightened—and possibly more effective—strategies. If it had, things might have been very different, and, by the way, you were really impressed by what you learned of this company's approach.

Rule 5: Take Care with References

If you've kept your job search private, be careful with references. Prospective employers will want your references to be as current as possible, and that obviously includes current supervisors. If you don't want those supervisors to know about the search, ask if any contact with them can be postponed, at least until it's clear that an offer will be forthcoming. If possible, get the offer first, and see if it can be made contingent on satisfactory current references.

In any case, take the matter into your own hands. Break the news yourself. An unexpected call from a prospective employer to a supervisor you've kept in the dark puts you in a very awkward position.

Rule 6: Dress as Usual

If your workplace dress code is casual, don't expect your sudden appearance in suit and tie to escape your colleagues' notice. They always notice, and they almost always comment, whether you're aware of those comments or not. Before you know it, your strange new formality will be the subject of speculation and rumor. Remember that the workplace environment is second only to the high school cafeteria as a place where gossip thrives. If you have to, scope out a restroom on the way to the interview where you can change, and build in time to do so.

Rule 7: Use Discretion on the Web and Social Media

Your Facebook posts are of abiding interest to more than your friends and the National Security Agency. Anything you publish, even if you think you're restricting your readership to a few select friends, is liable to be noticed by people you'd rather keep in the dark. Prospective employers are very interested in your presence on the web. They'd be crazy not to be.

There's really only one safe approach to your online communiqués—keep quiet about your job search until you're willing to make it public. The corollary to that principle will serve you well here and throughout your professional life: Assume that anything you post will eventually become public, and that the likelihood of it becoming public is inversely proportional to your desire to keep it private.

Rule 8: Update LinkedIn

Not everything on the web is dangerous and evil, as you probably know, so make your online identity as good as it can possibly be. This especially applies to LinkedIn. Update your profile and give it whatever polish you can before starting your search. Even if they look nowhere else, employers will look here.

Updating and improving your LinkedIn profile does present one potential pitfall, however, since LinkedIn is perfectly happy to notify every one of your connections whenever you make the slightest little change. You can easily put a stop to this, though, by adjusting your privacy settings so that your changes are not automatically included in connections' news feeds. The danger, of course, is that you may not even be aware of what's being broadcast, so visit the privacy settings in your account at the earliest opportunity.

If you're intensely worried—some might say "paranoid"—about being found out, consider disconnecting from your boss. Even if he notices the change, there's a very good chance it will be written off as a connection that fell between the cracks, or somehow discontinued, and there's no real harm done.

Rule 9: If the News Gets Out, Be Honest

It happens. Despite your best efforts, someone in your office finds out what you're up to. There's nothing to stop you from underplaying it—you're just testing the waters, for example—but there's nothing to be gained by denial. Depending on your specific situation, the fact that you're testing the waters won't endear you to your supervisors, but honesty will always do a lot less damage than dishonesty.

LinkedIn, again, needs some special attention. Even if you've kept your profile updates private, some inquisitive soul may notice that you've made changes. If that happens and you're not prepared to reveal your plans, remember that LinkedIn has many legitimate uses well beyond the job search. For example, it's a good way to stay in touch with contacts in your field and to keep up with industry developments. These are arguments you can make with a straight face.

Rule 10: Be Prepared to Stay Put

The search doesn't always end with the offer of a dream job. Either the offer doesn't come or the change is not quite as dreamy as it seemed when you set out on the quest. In either case, be glad that you haven't burned any bridges, and use the experience for what it's taught you. Perhaps it gave you a new perspective on your current job or on the alternatives available in your field. You may have learned something about the application process, and you'll be a better interviewee in the future. Perhaps you've realized that you should expand your skills or that it would be a good idea to gain some experience in facets of the business you'd previously ignored. All this hard-won knowledge can be incredibly worthwhile, whether you've decided to stay put for the duration or if you simply opt to put your search on hold for the moment.

BONUS ROUND: ALWAYS BE SEARCHING

What is the best time to be looking for a job? The answer that's come down to us through the ages, one that rings true to everyone who has ever ventured into the job market, is that the best time to be looking is when you don't need a job at all. There are two big reasons for this:

First, you look better to employers. If you're out of work, things get more difficult, and the longer you've been out, the harder things get. Once a few months have passed, your odds of getting hired decline precipitously. Hiring managers will assume that you've been out of work for a reason, that you've been passed over by employers who had every chance to hire you and that they're better off following in their colleagues' footsteps. Why bring you in for an interview when you've probably been interviewed several times already? Why not spend valuable time on more promising candidates, especially when there's no shortage of applicants? Why not take advantage of the fact that you've been given an easy way to dismiss a whole pile of resumes?

Second, it affects more than the employer's thought process. It affects you—and your own mindset matters a great deal. If employers want candidates who are confident and positive, no one is in a better position to demonstrate those attributes than the candidate who doesn't need the job right this minute. The one who can afford to stay put while looking around for the best possible option is the one who is relaxed and secure. Meanwhile, the one who really needs this job, who's tightly wound and trying too hard, is the one who comes across as desperate. That's not what hiring managers want to see.

There's another side to the notion that the best time to be looking is when you don't need to find something, and that is where you find the real lesson for employed searchers: You don't have to be conducting a full-blown job search every day of your working life, but you should always be doing some of the things that are part of that search.

The best thing about these activities is that they'll all be beneficial even if you don't plan to dip a single toe into the job market.

Cultivate Your Network
Keep up with old contacts and make new ones. You can touch base with the occasional phone call, send an informal email or, if the physical world is more your style, attend meetings, seminars, and other industry events. And if you are looking for a job, these are the contacts who can make all the difference. They'll know about openings before they're posted. They may be willing to put in a good word for you with their own hiring managers. If the tables are turned and it's your company that's looking to hire, they're a great source of candidates. If the job market doesn't enter into it at all, personal connections are still supremely useful as a way to

stay on top of developments in the industry and changes at your contacts' companies.

Keep Up with Industry Developments

Contacts can help with this, but it's worth staying abreast of trends by more formal means. Keep up with industry publications. Pay attention to the news. Visit competitors' websites, where they're more than happy to showcase any big news they've made. Every field has events that offer some form of continuing professional education. Take advantage of those resources so that you're the one with a finger on the industry's pulse. You're knowledgeable. You're committed to the field, and you want to understand the trends that are shaping its future. It's hard to imagine a workplace in which these wouldn't be very desirable qualities.

Extend Yourself

The simplest fact of office life is that the best employees are the ones who can do the most for their employers. You might, of course, object to that statement. It doesn't explain why the boss's nephew has the corner office. It doesn't account for the promotions given to that manipulative weasel in marketing. In real life, nepotism, office politics, and a variety of extraneous factors make a big difference. Marry the founder's daughter, by all means, but if that kind of end-run is not on your horizon, one of the best things you can do for yourself is to expand your competence.

Find a skill that's relevant to where you are and where you want to be—a "complementary" skill. If you're a programmer fluent in one language, learn another. If you sell residential real estate, learn the commercial side of the business. No matter what field you're in, there's bound to be a set of skills that will expand your horizons. If you're looking for a new job, those kinds of skills add value to your candidacy, but they also add value to your employment if you stay right where you are.

Key Lessons

+ When searching-while-employed, do not talk about your job search with your colleagues or on social media.

+ Do not use your company's computers or other resources for your job search, and schedule interviews on your lunch hour or outside of work hours.

+ Keep any negative feelings toward your current employer to yourself in interviews, and focus on the positives the new opportunity will bring instead.

+ Ask if references from your current supervisors can be postponed until after an offer is made.

+ Your colleagues will notice if you show up in a suit when your usual dress is casual, so make a plan to change clothes before your interview.

+ Update your LinkedIn profile before starting your search, but adjust your privacy settings to keep notices from appearing in your connections' news feeds.

+ If someone in your office finds out what you're up to, you can downplay it as testing the waters, but be honest.

+ Be prepared to stay put if your search doesn't end with the offer of a dream job.

+ The best time to look for a job is when you don't need one, and you should always be doing some of the things that are part of that search.

+ Keep up with old contacts and make new ones, stay on top of industry developments, and expand your horizons by learning a complementary skill that will add value to both your candidacy and your current job.

Part 3

HIT THE LINKS

Chapter 8

Come Together, Part 1: *LinkedIn Packs a Punch*

*"Pay attention. It's all about paying attention.
Attention is vitality. It connects you with others.
It makes you eager. Stay eager."*
—Susan Sontag

For better or worse, social media has made a place for itself in the job market. For better, because you can put yourself in the best possible light when you take the time to polish your online presence. For worse, because that same presence can do you harm, either because there's nothing there that distinguishes you from other candidates or because you've managed to do things that are overtly damaging.

According to a survey by ExecuNet, a network that claims "over 250,000 senior-level executive members," almost every recruiter will at least search the web for a candidate's name, and half of those surveyed reported that they had eliminated a candidate because of what the search revealed.

At the same time, 82 percent of those surveyed said that some candidates' chances had improved because of what the Internet revealed. They were particularly taken with candidates who displayed presentations and articles that proved subject-matter expertise, who were connected with top names in their fields, and who were mentioned in press releases.

Obviously, those criteria don't apply across the board. If you're slaving away in a company's lower echelons, no one is expecting you to star in company press releases, for example, but it's an indication of the kind of positive appearances that make a difference. The biggest negatives are also fairly obvious. If your online presence revolves around partying as hard as you can, employers will run away as fast and as far as they can. Sex, drugs, and rock and roll do not an employable profile make.

Suffice it to say, then, that social media, whether it's Facebook, Twitter, or Google Plus, cannot be ignored and should not be misused. You'd think that, by now, everyone in search of a job would have gotten that point. You would, of course, be wrong, and people still insist on sabotaging their career chances by posting inappropriate material as if only their closest friends were paying attention.

The Good and the Bad

Recruiters are definitely paying attention to what candidates are up to on the web, and 42 percent of recruiters have been influenced by what they've found in social media, according to Jobvite, a social recruiting and talent acquisition technology firm. Sometimes, the influence is positive, but the list of positive factors is alarmingly short. Recruiters look with favor on only one kind of content: 65 percent of them say they look kindly on evidence of volunteering or charitable donations.

The list of negatives is considerably longer:

- 83 percent have been turned off by evidence of the use of illegal drugs.

- 71 percent have had problems with sexual material.

- 65 percent objected to profanity.

- 61 percent were unhappy with errors in spelling or grammar.

- 51 percent disliked references to guns.

- 47 percent were troubled by pictures involving alcohol consumption.

Although this seems like a common-sense list of turnoffs for recruiters and employers, it bears repeating for as long as people keep sabotaging their prospects by making the same old mistakes.

It may be time to say that applicants who are still committing the most egregious online sins are beyond all help, but that doesn't mean that everyone else is using the web's potential to the fullest. It's not just a matter of avoiding the worst mistakes. It's also a matter of getting the most out of the sites that make up the social web.

Out of all those sites, one stands out. It's the one we all know, the first site that comes to mind when anyone says "professional network." It's the one with an enormous user base and a global reach, the one with something for every industry and every stage in your career. You've likely already figured out that we must be talking about LinkedIn. Nothing else compares.

JUST THE FACTS

LinkedIn has been up and running for a little over a decade. In that time, it has amassed over 347 million users, about a third of whom are in the United States. It's available in 20 languages and 200 countries. It gets 184 million unique visitors every month, and

40 percent of them check LinkedIn daily. The company now gets 38 percent of its visits via its mobile website.

LinkedIn doesn't dominate the entire social web. When independent sites require logging in via social network identification, Facebook logins account for almost half the traffic, Google almost a third, and LinkedIn lags far behind at a mere 2.4 percent. Lest that number look terribly anemic, business-to-business sites tell a different story. There, LinkedIn's share of logins via social network jumps to 26 percent, second only to Facebook's 33 percent.

And LinkedIn's business is, after all, business. It hosts 3 million business pages and showcases 1.2 million products and services. When it added options for educational institutions late in 2013, it took LinkedIn only six weeks to host 1,500 school and university profiles. Meanwhile, its membership includes 30 million students and recent graduates.

It seems, then, that LinkedIn has conquered the world, and that notion is consistent with LinkedIn's own goal of reaching a membership of 3 billion. According to VentureBeat CEO Jeff Weiner, speaking at the 2013 TechCrunch Disrupt conference, LinkedIn "hopes to have a profile for every one of the world's 3 billion working people and its entire store of companies and higher education institutions."

All this popularity might make you think that everyone is on LinkedIn or, at the very least, that everyone with even the slightest concern about their career has whipped up a compelling profile. Strangely enough, the reality appears to be a little different. Millennials, the famously connected and tech-savvy generation, the people who can't stop looking at their smartphones, may actually be underrepresented on LinkedIn. Despite the fact that 80 percent of them use social media, only 13 percent use LinkedIn.

For job seekers of that generation, that's an opportunity. The vast majority of your peers are missing out on one of the most important tools available. Anyone who's in the job market should invest the modest amount of time and energy it takes to create a profile.

You can argue that having a presence on LinkedIn doesn't necessarily mean that you're a serious and dedicated job applicant. Obviously, you're not the most qualified candidate simply because you're on LinkedIn. You cannot argue, however, that your absence from LinkedIn won't make a recruiter or hiring manager wonder, at least a little, about your priorities. If your career is important to you, why wouldn't you be interested in the world's biggest professional network?

There's much more to LinkedIn than profiles, and we'll look at the many ways it can be used to power a job search. But, whatever you do, don't ignore it. Recruiters certainly pay attention, with 94 percent of them using LinkedIn to screen candidates. In other words, everyone is using LinkedIn.

Once you understand that LinkedIn should be part of your career, the next step is to learn how to use it for the best possible results. That's where LinkedIn's power can really make a difference.

LinkedIn, Beyond the Job Search

"But wait," you say. "I have a job, and I've had the same half-baked LinkedIn profile since I joined the site. I may be testing the job-market waters, but I sure don't want to advertise the fact. If people here at work think I'm on my way out the door, I see nothing but heartache and misery ahead. Won't my spiffy new profile and my whole LinkedIn revival give them the exact message I'm desperately trying to squelch?"

We're glad you asked, because there are things you can do and say to keep the situation under control. First, LinkedIn isn't just for the job seekers among us. Admittedly, the site can feel like it's primarily there for members who want to find new jobs. Perhaps that's the result of LinkedIn's understandable emphasis on a function it can monetize, but there's actually a lot more going on. LinkedIn can help you get a better job, but it can also help you do a better job, regardless of your current ambitions.

LinkedIn is best known, and rightly so, as a worthwhile place to network, and it fulfills that function whether you're looking for something new or not. LinkedIn makes it easy to keep in touch with people in your field for any reason, and it's hardly a stretch to say that it can bring value to people who have no interest in the job market.

We all know that it can be hard to maintain connections in the real, non-virtual world. Packed schedules and long distances often make face-to-face contact difficult. LinkedIn solves some of those real-world networking problems, extending your potential connections to people you wouldn't ordinarily meet, whether it's a former colleague who's half a world away or a prominent individual whose door would otherwise be awfully hard to open. You don't need an appointment. You don't have to set aside time. You don't have to pick up the phone. You're not limited to people you already know. As you'll see, in that context, LinkedIn groups are one particularly good way to make some seemingly unattainable connections.

Second, LinkedIn is people-centric, but that's not all it is. It's also a place that can help you keep in touch with news and trends in your industry, again providing an excellent medium for that kind of keeping up. If there's a hot industry topic, it's bound to come up for group discussion. If there's a trend that everyone's talking about, there's bound to be that same talk on LinkedIn.

In sum, your suspicious co-workers should understand that LinkedIn is good for things besides job hunting. Why is your profile looking so much better these days? Well, you've become fairly active in a group, and you've had some very engaging interactions with some prominent members. You know that people will often take a quick look at your profile, after an initial contact, to find out more about you. You don't have to be looking for a job to want to whip that profile into shape.

We can take it as a general principle that LinkedIn has uses beyond the job search. Those uses are legitimate, and anyone who's interested should be able to see that LinkedIn is more than a job board.

What if you are in the job market, however, and you want to keep that news to yourself? If that's the case, you can take steps to add a bit of privacy to your LinkedIn life by limiting what's broadcast throughout your network.

If activity broadcasts are turned on, it may seem that LinkedIn is anxious to let everyone know about every step you take. The list of things that trigger updates is long: adding a new job or a new school; adding a link to a site; recommending someone or beginning to follow a company; adding a connection, if you allow your connections to see the rest of your connections; changing your current title or adding skills; and sharing content. It's a long list, and you may want to spare your network the endless barrage of updates even if you're not in the job market. Given that LinkedIn will send alerts about almost anything if you let it, here's a good rule to follow: Broadcast judiciously or not at all.

Remember that you can help secure your privacy from bosses and co-workers by disconnecting from them, and, as we stated earlier, there's a very good chance that they'll attribute your lack of connection to a simple oversight. There's an equally good chance that it will escape their notice entirely. Most people are not spending lots of time on LinkedIn unless they're in the job market with you, in which case they may not be terribly interested in adding employment status to the general conversation.

Job applications themselves are a bit of a special case, and LinkedIn does try to keep some applications—especially the ones that use the site's own tools—out of the public eye. In other words, if you apply through LinkedIn, you won't find any public indication that you did so. Note, though, that if you make changes to your profile itself, those changes are not automatically exempt. They'll follow the standard rules of broadcasting and sharing.

If you've opted for the site's premium account for job seekers, be careful there as well, because LinkedIn will add a "Job Seeker" badge to your profile. That badge can be turned off, but remember to check. Its sudden appearance is not something you want to explain after you've publicly reaffirmed your lifetime commitment to your current job.

Groups, though useful, also make for treacherous waters. If you decide, for example, to investigate groups for job seekers, a group's logo can end up in your profile. If the group is called something like "Desperate Job Seekers," you've created another opportunity for awkward conversation. Thankfully, you can choose not to show that logo—again, as long as you remember to check. You can also use your profile settings to disable updates about groups you join. Remember to check that setting before it does any damage.

In the end, it shouldn't take superhuman powers of persuasion to convince anyone with a career that it's worth investing some time in LinkedIn. To make this point, you have truth on your side, and the truth is that LinkedIn, used well, helps you do a better job of the job you have right now. If, on the other hand, you're using the site to help you get a better job, LinkedIn can help there too, and it will *certainly* let you keep your job search under wraps. Be careful out there, though, and pay attention. You'll only have problems if you don't know about and use the site's options—all just a click or two away—that let you keep your secrets to yourself.

Key Lessons

+ Social media has made a place for itself in the job market, and you can put yourself in the best possible light when you take the time to polish your online presence.

+ LinkedIn is the world's largest professional network and one of the most important tools available.

+ Most recruiters use LinkedIn to screen candidates, and anyone in the job market should invest the modest amount of time and energy it takes to create a profile.

Chapter 9

Come Together, Part 2: *LinkedIn Profile Basics*

"Little things make big things happen."
—John Wooden

T HE ONE THING YOU'LL have on LinkedIn, like it or not, is a profile. Sign up for LinkedIn and it's there. You don't have to lift a finger. If you're absolutely anti-finger-lifting, your profile will be empty of everything but your name.

Let's take two things for granted, though: You want to create a professional profile, and you want that profile to do as much for you as it can. If that sounds like the kind of job you'd like your resume to do, you're right. Your profile substitutes for a resume. Until the Internet-distant past of 2012, you could simply upload your resume for all the world to see, and LinkedIn gave you tools that made the process easy. As profiles became more feature-filled and more detailed, resumes became redundant, at least in the sense that they were worth maintaining as a feature unto themselves.

As you'll see, the difference between profiles and resumes, especially for job seekers, is really one of terminology, and many of the rules that apply to resumes apply with equal force to profiles.

Who Are They?

We'll focus on the many ways that LinkedIn can establish and enhance your professional identity, and on creating and nurturing connections through the site, but LinkedIn also provides learning opportunities in different spheres. Two of those opportunities stand out:

First, there's LinkedIn as a research source for company information. Earlier, we discussed interview preparation at length, and, as part of that, we touched on company LinkedIn pages as a source of information. In general, employees' LinkedIn pages can give you a picture of an employer that's more complete and more revealing than the picture revealed by the company's own website or its own LinkedIn page. Employee pages are always worth checking. They're most valuable when they're the pages of people in the position or group you're interested in, places where you're likely to find something of an inside view of the company's current focus. (Refer to the image below and the following page, for samples of company pages.)

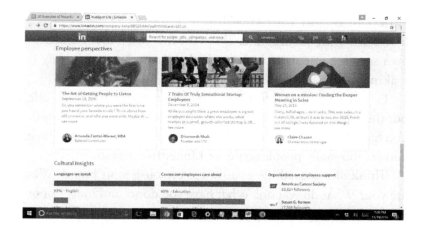

The best value comes, however, if you've scheduled an interview and you know your interviewers' names. Check them out on LinkedIn without fail. You may find clues to the kinds of keywords that will resonate in an interview, along with information about projects they're involved in. With that bit of LinkedIn stalking, you can emphasize your own experience with similar work.

Second, there's LinkedIn as a measuring stick for career changers. If you're looking at a new field, you may not know exactly what you need to do or what your next step should be. You can find out, though, by seeing what those who have gone before you have done. If you look at the profiles of 20 project managers, and 18 of them hold PMP certifications, you'll have a compelling indication of what matters in the field. Tying qualifications to actual people who are working in the real world is a lot more compelling than reading about theoretical qualifications in the abstract. Take a look at people's backgrounds. How did they get where they are today? Again, that's the real world telling you what the career path is like.

Where to Begin: Your Headline

It all starts with the headline. That's the first thing that LinkedIn's own search engine will index, which means that it's the key to making sure that you can be found.

Left to its own devices, LinkedIn will use your current job title, but the only limit to what you can do with your profile is length. You have 120 characters in which to deliver a compelling message, and far too many people settle for LinkedIn's default.

Think of the headline as a way to establish your brand. Who are you? What do you do? What have you done, and most important, what will you do for an employer who wants to hire you? Keep it clear, simple, and direct. It's a hook that's meant to grab the reader's interest.

What not to do:

- List your current tasks.

- List your various duties.

- List all your previous jobs.

- List all your past employers.

- List each and every one of your credentials.

Not one of those inclusions gives you the kind of hook we're looking for. They're marginally better than simply using your job title, but they don't draw people in. Let's say that LinkedIn would very much like to populate the headline field with "Sales Manager." Instead of leaving it at that, elaborate: "Sales Manager, High-Volume Auto Sales/10+ years/Implemented award-winning social media strategy yielding 20% growth." You might also consider including variations on the job title if it applies to one of those many jobs that are called different things in different places. "Business Analyst" and "Project Manager" are often interchangeable, as are "Account Manager" and "Sales Representative."

Should you include the name of your current employer in the headline? It all depends on the employer's identity. If we're talking about Google, Apple, or Microsoft, or any of the big brands in your industry, name away. If you're working at Murray's Computer Repair and Auto Detailing, that distinction can be safely omitted.

You can treat qualifications in the same way. If your qualification, a Ph.D. or some specific certification, is important in your field, it certainly has a place. If it's minor or if it's not directly relevant, save room for something with more impact.

No single headline style works for everyone. Different fields, for example, call for different levels of formality. One thing they all have in common, however, is a phenomenon that also affects resumes: Keywords matter. You're on LinkedIn because you want to be found, and keyword searches are the way that happens. Be sure to include the name of the industry you're in, as that's a common starting point for searches. Check job postings and look at the profiles of other people in your industry. What did they emphasize? Are there keywords that appear in headline after headline? There's no reason that you shouldn't avail yourself of the wisdom of those who have gone before you.

That advice holds throughout LinkedIn. You don't have to start from scratch. Find someone who's already doing the job you want now or the one you'd like to have in the future. What do their profiles look like? What keywords are they using? What qualifications are on display? What core competencies are they emphasizing? Treat those profiles as templates for your own.

One more useful approach is to put yourself in the shoes of the searcher. If you were looking for you, how would you start? What words would you type into the search box?

In any event, take a tip from sales and tell a story. For our sales manager above, it's a story about someone with a bunch of experience who's put a successful new program in place. If I own a string of dealerships and have my eye on new ways to boost sales, this may be someone I'd like to talk to. He's told me who he is, where he's been and, crucially, what benefit he may be able to provide.

This is all very well, you say, for people with jobs. They have an easy jumping-off point for that little story, but what do I do if I'm unemployed? You can still make good use of your headline. This time, you'll indicate the position you've held in the past, but in a more general way. If you've managed marketing in the past, your profession is still "Marketing Professional." If you've worked in the auto industry, say so, and if you're an expert in marketing via social media, print, or broadcast, make that known. If you have an accomplishment that really stands out, include it. Just don't go overboard; keep it short and sweet like this: "Technology Marketing and Internal Communications Executive Seeking Product Marketing Leadership Opportunity." You don't have to use every one of your allotted 120 characters, and there's always the danger that you'll dilute your primary message if you do.

If you're just starting out, especially if you're fresh out of school with a relevant degree, you can ignore some of the "don'ts" that apply to people with experience. For instance, you'll want to include degrees or certifications that matter. You'll also want to include important skills. If you're fluent in Java or have mad CSS skills, let the world know.

The other headline-related question that job seekers have to answer is whether to make the job search explicit. Should you add "Open to New Opportunities" or something of that ilk? There's no answer that's absolutely correct, but here's one place where LinkedIn can do some work for you. Take a look at your statistics. How many people are finding you with or without mention of the job search? What's generating more activity? Remember that you can tinker with every aspect of your profile to see what works. You can do it as often as you like. You can tear everything up and start from scratch. There's nothing to keep you locked in to a given headline or a profile that's not working for you. If you're doing a lot of revision, however, keep an eye on your activity settings, as explained below, so that you don't inundate people with constant stylistic changes that make no material difference.

When Not to Spread the Word

A word for those who are already using LinkedIn and want to revise their profiles: Do your update "silently" by turning off updates in your activity feed. If there's nothing really new—except, of course, for the vast improvements you've made to the existing content—there's no reason to alert everyone to changes in your profile. Save the broadcast updates for things that matter. This goes double for employed people who are trying to keep a job search out of a current employer's line of sight.

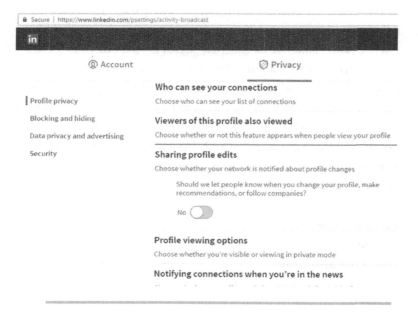

Ready for Your Close-Up: Your Profile Photo

Add a photo to your profile. LinkedIn reports that the addition will make it 11 times more likely that a recruiter will view your profile. That's not a small difference.

But don't just use any old photo you happen to have available; or a photo of you and your cat, unless you're in the cat-sitting business; or a photo of bikini-clad you and your pals at the beach, even if it's the best you've ever looked on camera. You also don't need to get a professional involved; what's important is that your photo is professional-looking. Pay attention to the background, to what you're wearing, and to the expression on your face.

Use a resolution that's high enough to be crisp and clear. Don't use the kind of blurry images that look like they emerged from a 10-year-old flip phone.

It doesn't have to be a formal portrait, the kind of thing that would grace the boardroom upon the chairman's retirement, but it has to be consistent with the message you're trying to deliver. In essence, and reductive as this may seem, it's part of your brand.

If you're not sure about what works, take a look at what other people in your field, especially people at similar points in their careers, are doing. Which ones seem to have the right effect? Which ones send the right message? Which people would *you* consider if you were looking to fill a job? Take your cue from your own responses. They're just as accurate as anyone else's when it comes to making these very impressionistic judgments. Trust your instincts.

Fleshing Out the Profile

The headline and photo may be the least "resume-like" parts of your LinkedIn profile, but that changes as you continue. Much of the remaining profile is self-explanatory. You add job titles and employers, educational history, and credentials to a point at which it's almost a resume alternative. In fact, you can certainly cut and paste portions of your resume where they fit.

Be sure to include your industry in the summary, since it's one criterion hiring managers use when they search for appropriate candidates. It's also a good idea to include more than one professional position you've held. According to LinkedIn, the addition results in a 12-fold increase in profile views.

A LinkedIn profile and a resume may be similar, but they are far from identical. LinkedIn offers some features that, while they would amount to excess baggage in a resume, work very well on the web.

One such feature is the LinkedIn "summary," a blank space that allows for a bit of exposition. You can use it for a personalized narrative that expands upon the bare bones of titles and companies. Play up the things that are most important to you, and give the reader a coherent sense of where you've been, where you are, and where you want to be in the future. Make it inviting and easy-to-read. Bullet points and short paragraphs work better than large blocks of text. Highlight special accomplishments.

We considered some of the potential drawbacks of the strictly functional style when we analyzed resumes, but the summary is one place where a functional approach makes perfect sense. Faced with an actual functional resume, some readers are skeptical. They want to see the cut-and-dried progression from one job to the next. They want each change to involve a little more responsibility. They don't want to parse your resume to find out exactly where you were and what you were doing. In other words, they want their jobs made easier. At its worst, the skepticism is a manifestation of the suspicion that a functional resume has something to hide. That may be misguided, but it does happen. An online summary, however, is not subject to that same skepticism, so the functional approach works.

As a result, the summary can be a boon to new graduates and the unemployed alike. You're not trapped by the limitations you run into when you're forced to fill in the "Job Title" blank. You don't need to have held a long series of jobs to provide some meaningful content.

List your specialties in the summary, and think, once again, in terms of keywords. This is a chance to include keywords that you may have missed in other sections. Some keywords simply don't fit well into the more typical layout. You know, though, that they need to be somewhere, because you also know that hiring managers will be looking for them.

Sample LinkedIn Summary

Here is Shimmering Careers' LinkedIn summary. Although it is for a business, it uses the same principles as you would for an individual:

I work with you on job search and career change. My talent lies in creating a powerful professional resume, the finest LinkedIn profile, cover letters, and a clear strategy. I will get your job search moving so you succeed.

I work with C-level execs, senior managers, sales and marketing professionals, and technologists. Whatever the field, I help you reach your career goals by crafting excellent documents and providing job interview coaching, job search, and salary negotiating. My salary tips alone will pay for my services.

I have helped my clients get hired and promoted at many organizations you know: Tesla, GoPro, McKinsey & Company, Apple, Google, Facebook, LinkedIn, Genentech, Microsoft, Salesforce.com, Amazon, Intel, Chevron, Wells Fargo, Charles Schwab, Stryker, Gap, Adobe, Intuit, Stanford University, Oracle, Facebook, and more.

- ▶ Professional Resumes
- ▶ Executive Resumes
- ▶ Software, Engineering, and IT Resumes
- ▶ Science Resumes

- LinkedIn profiles for job seekers
- Attention to keywords and branding
- Expertise in hiring, job interviews, job search strategy, salary negotiation & promotions
- Support all career levels and industries
- Social media programs
- Communications Initiatives to reach external audiences
- Job interview preparation

My books include *When Can You Start? Ace the Job Interview and Get Hired,* and *Fire in the Valley: The Birth and Death of the Personal Computer.*

My technology background helps me aid software developers, semiconductor engineers, scientists, product managers, and executives.

My clients are talented executives, IT professionals, administrative assistants, sales professionals, project managers, marketing directors, analysts, and more. I create documents to prove that you make a difference.

If you have experience as a volunteer, you can add a section to your profile that reflects that experience, and it's something that's not done often enough. LinkedIn reports that 41 percent of the professionals it surveyed viewed that experience as a meaningful part of the profile, and 20 percent of those surveyed claimed to have based hiring decisions on a candidate's volunteer activity.

One great advantage of LinkedIn is that it allows you to link to material that can't be easily incorporated into the traditional resume and cover letter. In the "additional information" section, you can include links to your website, a company site, your Twitter account, and anything that is relevant and persuasive. If you have a professional blog, include a link. If you belong to industry associations, include those links as well. There's even a spot for outside interests, and, while a section dedicated to hobbies and the like is rarely a good choice for a paper resume, it somehow fits well in the virtual world.

Your LinkedIn profile is not set in stone. If you get a new job, have been involved in a major project, or recently accomplished something of note, update your profile. If nothing else, a profile that's current says you're engaged and interested in your career and not just coasting along on automatic pilot. When your profile hasn't been touched in years, those qualities are not so evident. There's a lot more to LinkedIn than your profile, of course, but, without question, this is the place that starts putting LinkedIn to work.

A Friendlier Profile Link

Once you've made your profile as good as it can be, make it work for you. One of the best ways to do that is to include the link in your email signature. Give people an easy way to learn more about you.

The link to your profile is generated automatically by LinkedIn, but the default style is the typical alphanumeric soup of meaningless characters. You can change that and create a link that's friendlier and more professional at the same time, something closer to your name, in LinkedIn's profile settings. When you sign up for LinkedIn and receive your profile, it will be something like linkedin.com/ins/ mindyschwab14689. Customize it to your first name and last name, such as linkedin.com/ins/schwabmindy.

Watch the Clichés

After putting all this energy into creating a profile that tells your story, you want it to stand out. LinkedIn thoughtfully provides a list of the top 10 buzzwords that have been beaten to death by U.S. professionals:

- Extensive experience

- Innovative

- Motivated

- Results-oriented

- Dynamic

- Proven track record

- Team player

- Fast-paced

- Problem solver

- Entrepreneurial

They're not only overused, but they're abstractions— qualities that anyone can claim—because they aren't supported by anything concrete. If they're qualities that apply to you, try to find ways to translate them into specific accomplishments that reflect those qualities. That's a much more convincing approach.

THE VARIETIES OF LINKEDIN EXPERIENCE

Outside of the standard profile, LinkedIn is not a one-size-fits-all experience. It offers a free basic account and, for the general audience, several tiers of premium service. In addition, there are specialized options meant to fit particular needs, including premium plans for job seekers and recruiters.

Is it worth paying for a premium LinkedIn membership?

After all, LinkedIn doesn't have to cost a thing. There's the expenditure of time and energy it takes to maintain an account, but a basic membership is free. It's a useful option that works well enough for most of us, but it's hardly the only option. LinkedIn offers a range of premium plans for users with different needs. There are special plans for businesses, recruiters, sales professionals, and job seekers.

Every LinkedIn user should know something about these offerings, but that's especially true for job seekers. Rightly or not, they're the ones most likely to feel they need all the help they can get. LinkedIn's Job Seeker plan just might provide some of that help, and you can test drive it for free.

First, however, a caveat: LinkedIn's premium plans are everchanging. When it comes to pricing and features, nothing is written in stone, but there's a certain degree of continuity between iterations. Plans for job seekers tend to revolve around the same general themes—increased visibility, better search, and messaging—even if the details change.

As is typical in the LinkedIn world, it all starts with your profile. With the premium plans, you get a larger photo, an expanded header, and additional background images. You can also open your profile to LinkedIn's entire membership. You'll display more profile information, and when you appear in search results, LinkedIn claims you'll be twice as prominent as the nonpremium competition.

You'll also get "top keyword suggestions" when you're editing your profile's summary. According to LinkedIn, adding those top keywords will increase the likelihood of appearing in relevant search results. In addition, a premium account gives you "Featured Applicant" status that moves you to the top of the list when you do appear in those results.

Perhaps that's analogous to other kinds of search. Google claims, for example, that only a minority of users get past the first page of results when searching the web. If the same principle applies to hiring managers searching for candidates, being at the top of the list can make a difference.

In search, the premium plan provides additional filters that free accounts lack, letting you filter results by seniority, company size, or even the interests of the people you're trying to find.

You also get to see everyone who's viewed your profile within the preceding 90 days, a big improvement over a free account's five-person limit. Beyond that, a premium account adds useful information about the people who have used those searches to find you, letting you know their industries, locations and, perhaps most important, the keywords that led them to your door. If you know how people found you, you'll know what parts of your profile are drawing the most interest, and you can tailor your presence accordingly.

A premium plan also comes with "Applicant Insights," a tool that shows the number of other applicants for a job you've found and tells you something about them, breaking the competition down by education, seniority, and top skills. Again, these are good things to know.

Finally, there's InMail, a feature reserved for premium accounts. As you probably know, LinkedIn puts limits on who you can contact with a free account. You have your connections and your connections' connections, but you hit a wall once you try to extend your reach beyond that.

InMail allows you to contact anyone on LinkedIn directly through LinkedIn's own messaging system. You don't need a connection or that person's email address—something that can be hard to find in any event—and InMails are delivered via email as well as through the on-site system. Using InMail, you've added at least a touch of credibility to your image. It shows you're serious enough to use a premium account as part of your job search. It takes your message a step beyond "easily ignorable message from a total stranger," and it lifts you above the netherworld of cold calling. As a result, recipients are more likely to hear what you have to say and to respond.

When all is said and done, investing in a premium plan certainly won't hurt, but the real message here is that it pays to be active on LinkedIn regardless of your status. Activity is what makes the difference. Use LinkedIn for all it's worth, take full advantage of groups, and your free basic account will serve you quite well. Sit back and wait for results to come to you, and even your premium plan won't do much for your prospects.

Key Lessons

+ On LinkedIn, your profile substitutes for a resume.

+ Use LinkedIn to research companies, including checking employees' pages to get a more complete and revealing picture than what you see on company websites.

+ Your headline is the key to making sure you can be found and should be customized to deliver a compelling hook.

+ Find people who are already doing the job you want and treat those profiles as templates for your own instead of starting from scratch.

+ Add a professional-looking photo, include more than one position, and be sure to include your industry to make it more likely a recruiter will view your profile.

+ Use the summary section to provide a personalized narrative that highlights your strengths and to include the keywords that don't fit in other sections.

+ Volunteer experience can be a meaningful part of your profile and may help increase your hiring chances.

+ You can include links to your website, Twitter account, and other relevant material that can't be easily incorporated into a traditional resume.

+ LinkedIn offers a free basic account, plus premium plans that provide additional benefits for job seekers, like top placement in search results.

Chapter 10

Come Together, Part 3: *Making the Most of LinkedIn*

"We all have ability. The difference is how we use it."

—Charlotte Whitton, first female mayor of a major city in Canada

W<small>E'VE COVERED THE BASICS</small>, but there's a lot more you can do to maximize your profile's potential. Before we move on to the other side of LinkedIn—the one that is all about the connections you can make—there are ways to bring your profile to the next level. Since this is how you greet the professional world, there's a lot at stake.

It's too easy to say, however, that your profile has to be clear, complete, and compelling, that it has to let people know how you can benefit them, that it's all about your brand, that it has to deliver your message, or that it has to sell you as a professional. We've said all that, and they're all worthy goals. By themselves, however, they don't get you very far.

If you're pitching for the Yankees, you know that your goal is to get outs, to avoid giving up runs, to win the game, and to do all that without destroying your shoulder. You'll certainly keep those goals in mind, but it's hardly information you can apply when you take the mound. You need something useful, and what you learn is that reaching your no-run, no-hit goals, preferably with your arm intact, depends on doing a lot of things, both little and big, right. LinkedIn works the same way; there is a long list of big and little things you have to do along the way. They're not abstract. They're not general. They're not platitudes. They're concrete steps to take, and they work for everyone. If we roll up our sleeves and get practical, the rest will follow.

KEYWORD SOUP

Keywords matter. They're the way the Internet looks for things, and LinkedIn is no different. If you're a graphic designer, you'd better have "graphic design" prominently displayed in your profile, but some profiles take the concept way too far. You'll run across profiles, especially in the summary section, that have gone keyword-crazy. The summary makes no sense—it doesn't seem to have been written in any known language—but it's stuffed to overflowing with keyword after keyword. People will indeed find you, but they'll be sorry they did. Instead of keyword-stuffing, write in clean, simple English. If keywords fit naturally, use them. If they don't, don't worry about including every keyword you can think of. Always err on the side of telling the reader something like a story, and don't sacrifice your profile to the keyword gods.

FLESHING OUT THE SUMMARY

Yes, our robot friends are ever advancing and will likely achieve sentience soon, but, for now and the foreseeable future, employers are looking for humans. You probably qualify! As a human, you may even have interests that aren't strictly work-related. When creating your profile, consider including some outside interests or activities, perhaps by adding a few words to the summary. You're a whole person, and people are more attracted to someone they can relate to, someone who's not necessarily all career all the time. Give them a more rounded look at who you are. If you're an avid runner, for example, and you're proud of the personal best you set in a recent 10K, throw in a few words about that activity. Make it simple and place it under "Other Interests": "I have been an avid runner since 2004, and I'm out there whenever time and weather permit. I run competitively occasionally, and recently set a personal best in the 10K."

Not all outside interests need to be showcased, however. A recent personal best in shots of tequila per hour is an achievement best kept to yourself, but you can add interests and activities to a LinkedIn profile that you wouldn't include in your resume. Give those additions the "resume test" first, though: If it's something that wouldn't be remotely appropriate in your resume, it's not likely to work for you on LinkedIn.

THE ORDER OF THINGS

Optimizing your LinkedIn profile is really a matter of customizing it, and you're given a lot of options. For instance, you can move sections around to find the optimal presentation. One of the most basic options is the power to change the order in which your educational history and professional positions appear. If you're a new graduate with little or no work experience, you may want to focus on your education, and LinkedIn allows you to put that front and center. The options are not unlimited, however. Past positions, for example, will always be shown in reverse chronological order, and whatever appears as the first entry in education will appear at the top of your profile.

WORK EXPERIENCE

If your work history is lacking, don't forget that you can include positions for which you weren't necessarily paid, and those inclusions can give your profile a much more complete look. If you've worked as a volunteer or an intern, add those positions, especially if they're relevant to your field. You can even include work done as part of your education, whether that work involved participation in a relevant project or enrollment in the kind of activity that falls under the rubric of a "clinical" program or a practicum. In other words, don't be afraid to stretch the definition when it helps your brand.

YOU COME HIGHLY RECOMMENDED

You can extol your own virtues until you run out of space, but a recommendation is in a category of its own. LinkedIn also allows for "endorsements," but that's a more limited, skill-focused option that we'll cover as a feature in its own right. You can ask any of your connections to recommend you. LinkedIn will associate the recommendation with something from your past, either a past position or an educational institution, but you can customize that association and use the recommendation even if your connection is not associated with some discrete moment in your past.

LinkedIn lets you automate recommendation requests. Find connections in your address book, check them off, send requests in bulk, and wait for the plaudits to roll in. Each connection receives an individual message, but it's the same message, not a personalized request. For best results, don't automate. Always ask for recommendations individually. Make your request personal by including something unique to each relationship, and always make it clear that you're happy to do something in return. Don't forget to include a word of thanks. Recipients will appreciate the personal touch, and they'll not only be more likely to respond, but they'll be more likely to respond with something worth adding to your profile. Once you have a recommendation, you can decide whether to accept it, you can ask the recommender to revise it, and, once you've accepted it, you can choose whether to show it or not.

Whenever LinkedIn allows you to choose between one of its default forms and something of your own—and that's a frequent occurrence—choose the latter. Recommendations are a good example. You have so much to gain by getting the right recommendation from the right person. It is totally, absolutely, completely, unequivocally, and inarguably worth the five-minute investment. Period.

What makes for a good recommendation? It should be short and to the point. It should indicate how the recommender knows you. It should summarize what makes you wonderful as specifically as possible, ideally with some reference to a meaningful achievement. You turned a dysfunctional team into a well-oiled machine? You solved a daunting programming challenge and brought the company's website into the 21st century? Specifics are what matter, not the kind of adjective-heavy blurbs that leave the reader wondering what you actually did. The ideal recommendation will deliver two messages: The reader will understand that your work was of benefit to your organization and will also understand how it will be of benefit to someone who hires you in the future.

Recommendations are displayed under each of your jobs. And apparently, the site makes a random choice of two recommendations to display. The obvious conclusion here is that it's worth making your recommendations as good as they can be. (To see a sample of LinkedIn recommendations, refer to the following page.)

I ENDORSE THIS SKILL

Recommendations have substance, if only because they carry with them the implication that the recommender had to take a little time to put their thoughts into writing. (Yes, there are occasions when the recommender tells you to write the recommendation for them, but it's not as if those self-recommendations are labeled, and the effect isn't really diminished by the mechanism involved.) Endorsements, by comparison, are a lightweight alternative to

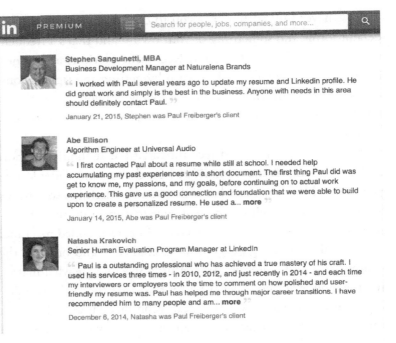

Stephen Sanguinetti, MBA
Business Development Manager at Naturalena Brands

" I worked with Paul several years ago to update my resume and Linkedin profile. He did great work and simply is the best in the business. Anyone with needs in this area should definitely contact Paul. "

January 21, 2015, Stephen was Paul Freiberger's client

Abe Ellison
Algorithm Engineer at Universal Audio

" I first contacted Paul about a resume while still at school. I needed help accumulating my past experiences into a short document. The first thing Paul did was get to know me, my passions, and my goals, before continuing on to actual work experience. This gave us a good connection and foundation that we were able to build upon to create a personalized resume. He used a... **more** "

January 14, 2015, Abe was Paul Freiberger's client

Natasha Krakovich
Senior Human Evaluation Program Manager at LinkedIn

" Paul is a outstanding professional who has achieved a true mastery of his craft. I used his services three times - in 2010, 2012, and just recently in 2014 - and each time my interviewers or employers took the time to comment on how polished and user-friendly my resume was. Paul has helped me through major career transitions. I have recommended him to many people and am... **more** "

December 6, 2014, Natasha was Paul Freiberger's client

recommendations, but they're still necessary to round out your LinkedIn profile. Like recommendations, endorsements come from someone else, and they are each attached to a specific skill that, presumably, relates to your career.

You can add as many as 50 skills for endorsement. As you type them into your profile, LinkedIn will try to match them in a drop-down list, but you're not limited to LinkedIn's choices. You can add a whole new skill, something that's not among the suggestions, at any point. What you can't do, however, is tell LinkedIn exactly how you'd like those skills ordered. The site will insist on listing skills with the most endorsements first. It will then list unendorsed skills in the order in which they were added, but you can change that order in any way that suits you.

What if you have a skill that's no longer relevant? You can simply delete it, and its endorsements will disappear along with the skill.

Changed your mind? You can make it all reappear by adding the skill again, but take note: Your endorsements will only reappear if you add the skill exactly as it first appeared.

You can—and should—ask for recommendations, but you can't ask for endorsements, at least as a matter of built-in LinkedIn functionality. Despite that internal limitation, there's nothing to stop you from asking for an endorsement from someone you think would be willing. As always, that kind of request is more likely to succeed when you're offering something to the person you're asking.

What if you're having second thoughts about a particular endorsement? That endorsement from Bernie Madoff was nice, but it's taken on something of a negative connotation now. You can hide it. You're worried, though, that Bernie, a man with a lot of time on his hands, will just endorse you all over again. Here, stern measures are called for. The only way to get Bernie under control is to remove him as a connection. He won't be notified of your action, although he may figure it out on his own, and, frankly, he's probably used to it by now. You'll both be better off.

Two Bits of Branding

Here are two small things you can do to add a bit of polish to your branding efforts:

1. *LinkedIn will add the logos of employers and volunteer organizations when you add them to your profile, and it makes for a more complete, professional look.* They'll only appear, however, if the name of the organization matches the name by which it's known to LinkedIn, so visit the company page to be certain of a match.

2. *LinkedIn, bless its automated heart, is following what you're following, and it displays the news and companies you follow in your profile.* To take a cynical view,

it doesn't matter if you're really paying attention. It does matter, though, that you appear to be someone interested in the latest industry news and the activities of the industry's big players. Even if your interest is an illusion, that kind of following helps your brand and gives a more complete picture of your interests.

Of course, you really should be following these things, especially if you're a job seeker. It's exactly the kind of information you need to have at hand before walking into any job interview.

FROM CONNECTIONS TO CONTENT

Networking is still the heart of LinkedIn, but the simple act of making connections has decreased in importance as LinkedIn has added features over the years. Bit by bit, the focus has shifted to content hosting, and LinkedIn's recent decision to open its publishing platform to all members is another step in that direction.

Job seekers should take note: This platform is a nice addition to the existing options. It can do good things for your job search if you use it—and *great* things if you use it well.

The simple ability to add content is not new. Members have long been able to add a variety of content types to their profiles, including simple text, pictures, slide shows, video, and more elaborate writing like white papers. In those cases, content was associated with the member's profile, and it wasn't necessarily hosted by LinkedIn. It was always useful, and it continues to have an important place in job-search strategy, but it was aimed at a more limited audience. In the end, people had to find you first to find your content.

Now, the sequence can be reversed. Your content can lead people to your profile. It can even lead them away from LinkedIn to your blog or website. A stop at your profile is no longer strictly necessary, although it's still an option for anyone who's interested.

Your profile is still in the loop, however, because your posts on the new platform automatically appear alongside that profile. In other words, you can now complete and enhance your profile in two ways, either by posting to the profile itself or by posting to the new platform. If you haven't taken the time to complete your profile, the platform gives you a new option. It's worth a closer look.

Post-Worthy Content

LinkedIn places few limits on what you can post on the new platform. It warns against posting "anything obscene, shocking, hateful, intimidating, or otherwise unprofessional," and it expects you to actually own what you publish. Clearly, though, content should be "professional" in three senses of the word:

1. It should be content you'd happily share with customers, clients, and current and future employers.

2. It should relate to the working world and the LinkedIn world, but not a less formal world, like Facebook.

3. It should be free of typos, grammatical errors, and misspellings. If you're a great salesman who confuses "its" and "it's" on occasion, get a grammatical friend to take a look before posting.

There are two other subject matter limitations. Your posts can't be purely promotional or about job openings or opportunities.

How Much Content?

There's no limit on length. If your magnum opus, *Marketing Snowshoes in the Amazon,* makes *War and Peace* look like a quick read, no holds barred. Apparently, LinkedIn will publish it, but you may want to think twice. LinkedIn itself thinks a three-paragraph post is ideal, but that limit may go too far in the other direction, especially given the emphasis on the "long-form" potential of the platform. It's best to find a happy medium. Say what you have to say. Be brief if you can, but write more if you need to. Try to keep it interesting.

Beyond Text

The platform extends beyond the written word. You can add links to external sources, and those can be your own sites or independent ones containing relevant information. If you're in the snowshoe industry, for example, you might link to the Snowshoe Manufacturers Association's chart of sales trends, the government's announcement of the latest safety recalls, or an opinion piece about the industry's future in light of Apple's rumored introduction of the iShoe.

On that note, there's nothing to stop you from publishing a blog post of your own on the LinkedIn platform. You can add a note explaining the source of the post and a link back to your blog. If people are interested, they may well be tempted to follow that link and read more.

It also works in the other direction. If you've written something on LinkedIn, you're free to use it as a post on your blog. And if you're not sure you need your own blog, give the idea a chance. If you have a passionate interest or some ideas about your industry, a blog can enhance—or establish—your reputation as a thought leader.

You own what you post, so you're free to do whatever you please with it, but LinkedIn reserves the right to distribute your work as discussed below, to annotate it, and to sell ads alongside it.

You can also add images and videos to your posts, and you can do more than add a link to an external video host. The new platform allows embedding, and it supports YouTube, SlideShare, and several other sites. To embed, simply find the video where it's hosted, find the "embed" link among the host's sharing options, copy the embed code, and paste it in the box that appears after you click LinkedIn's embed icon. Click "Add Media" and you're done.

Why go beyond text? The simple answer is that other media can be more powerful and more persuasive. Those are good things to add to any presentation, but they should resonate with job seekers who are looking for an edge in the search.

In a recent experimental study from the University of Chicago, researchers had candidates present job pitches in two forms. In one group, the pitches were written. Hiring managers recruiting for one phase of the experiment simply read the pitch and judged the candidate's merit accordingly. In the other group, the hiring managers had the same pitches read to them by MBA students, the very people they'd be evaluating in real life. The content of the pitches was identical, but hiring managers rated the audio candidates significantly higher in measures of intellect and likeability. Most telling of all, they rated them higher in the ultimate criterion of *hiring likelihood*.

The medium is a big part of the message, but it's a variable job seekers overlook. When the study's candidates were asked to predict results, they guessed that text would work as well as audio; the results came as a surprise. If job seekers make the same mistake, they may not know what they're missing, but they're denying themselves a powerful tool.

Platform vs. Profile

LinkedIn's new platform hasn't reinvented the wheel. The content you can publish is not fundamentally different from the content you can—and should—add to your profile. Both options allow for text, slides, and video. Both let you link to content that's hosted elsewhere.

There are differences, however. The first and simplest is a matter of search. Posts on the new platform are searchable on and off

LinkedIn. In theory, at least, your audience can consist of the entire Internet-using population, LinkedIn membership not required. As a practical matter, this may turn out to be tremendously important in the context of the job search.

Let's say a hiring manager uses a quick Google search to start evaluating a candidate. Her results include a series of links to smart, professional content the candidate has posted on LinkedIn. That has the makings of a very positive first impression.

To make your post easier to find, add appropriate subject-matter tags, and include an autobiographical snippet at the end to add a touch of personal information. That can make a stronger connection with your readers, and it's a great way to emphasize your professional identity in a very natural way.

The second difference lies in distribution. By using the new platform, you open your work to a wider audience. Posts and updates will still be distributed to your connections, but now people outside your network can choose to follow you, and they'll also be notified of new posts.

The new platform also offers options for sharing. Posts can be shared using Facebook, Google+, and Twitter. They can be shared via email and can also be distributed through LinkedIn groups you've joined, but there's a caveat for people who belong to multiple groups: Anything shared with more than a group or two is liable to be seen as spam.

There's also a wider world beyond your connections or followers who have essentially volunteered to join your LinkedIn audience. As part of the new platform, LinkedIn will distribute your content for you.

Like Google's algorithm for search, LinkedIn's criteria for wider distribution are not transparent, but they revolve around three features inherent in the new platform. People can comment on a post, give it a Facebook-style "like," and share it with their own networks.

According to LinkedIn, distribution depends on some combination of those three factors. The details, however, are a mystery.

If a post gains enough traction, it can graduate to LinkedIn Pulse. When that happens, the post is featured by LinkedIn on its site and in email updates that reach inboxes all over the world. With Pulse, all of LinkedIn's 347 million members are in the audience.

New Platform or Old?

The new platform certainly offers some new things. Posts can be longer. They're more accessible to people who aren't connections. They're more searchable, and they can be more widely distributed. Those are meaningful additions to the LinkedIn ecosystem and worth exploring. And the fact that posts attach directly to your profile might be the deciding factor if you're thinking of giving the platform a try.

At the same time, you don't *need* those new capabilities to make LinkedIn work, just as you don't need the widest possible distribution to create an effective LinkedIn presence. The core functionalities are already there. The key is to add content that shows you at your professional best. If you want wide distribution, use the new platform by all means. Whatever you do, though, use *something*. Don't let your profile languish when it can do so much.

KEEP CURRENT

Keep it current. That's the most obvious bit of LinkedIn advice imaginable, but you can do much more. Share updates through your profile, and share often. You have 600 characters of text you can use to talk about anything of interest. You can choose to make an update public, to share it with first-degree connections (more on this to come), or to make its first 140 characters visible on Twitter. You can add links to anything, with special abilities for LinkedIn's partners like *The New York Times*. You can send updates via email, a function adjustable in your email settings.

If you share quality content and you do it regularly, it confirms the fact that you're engaged in your field and on top of the latest developments. If you stick to it, people can start to see you as a valuable resource. Does it even need to be said that "valuable resource" is exactly what you want a prospective employer to see when there is a position to be filled?

IT TAKES WORK!

It's probably all too clear by now that a good profile, like a good resume, is not something you can throw together in a few minutes, but it's work that has to be done. LinkedIn shows no signs of slowing down. If anything, its influence keeps growing, and, at this point, it's completely accepted as a natural part of the hiring process, something that gets a lot of attention from hiring managers. Some recruiters and managers use LinkedIn as a de facto candidate database, turning to it instead of or in addition to their internal databases. After all, it makes their jobs easier, so don't expect LinkedIn's importance to fade in the foreseeable future.

We're now at the point at which a good LinkedIn profile is more "basic requirement" than "optional extra." Whether you're looking for a job now or think you could be in the market at a later date, a condition that realistically applies to all of us, put in the work and get your profile up to speed. A great profile can pay big dividends. A hastily assembled, bare-bones list of a degree and a few job titles can do mortal damage. If you're in doubt, take a tour through LinkedIn and look at what the competition is doing. That should be motivation enough.

If this makes you fearful, don't let it. Once you dive in, you'll find that LinkedIn tries hard to be a user-friendly experience, especially for a site that offers so much. It's well organized, it always tries to point you in the right direction, and it offers extensive on-site help. But you do have to dive in.

Don't Get Carried Away

Despite its great value, there's a danger hidden in all this LinkedIn work, and it's similar to a problem that afflicts people who obsess over their calendars and to-do lists and agendas to such an extent that nothing actually gets done. LinkedIn is just a part of the job search. Don't fuss over your profile, rewriting your summary and rearranging your bullet points, at the expense of the other important parts of the search like networking or, of all things, actually applying for jobs. Set a limit and stick to it.

CALL IN THE CRITICS

When you think your profile is complete, call in a critic. It can be a friend, a colleague, a fellow student, or a family member. It doesn't matter if your critic knows everything there is to know about you, your career, or your industry. In fact, it's sometimes better if they're not experts. Hiring managers don't always have detailed knowledge of the technical aspects of jobs they're trying to fill, a failing that may be more common in more technical fields.

Ask your critic to look over your profile. Is everything clear? Are there things that are hard to understand? Does anything raise a question? Don't worry if there's some qualification they've never heard of. But remember, the best profiles are simple and direct enough to be understood by just about everyone. If your critic is confused, consider whether that confusion results from some weakness in your profile. If it does, revise.

If said critic says your profile is good to go, there's still one more step before you unleash your profile on the world: Proofread, and proofread again. Little mistakes loom large when your profile is the means by which you greet the world, and it's a law of nature that we tend to miss typos and grammatical errors in our own work, even the ones we'd catch if they were made by someone else. Get some help, perhaps from the same critic you've already enlisted. Another set of eyes can find mistakes that are effectively invisible to you. Don't let a missing apostrophe become a professional catastrophe.

Key Lessons

+ Keywords matter in your LinkedIn profile, but avoid keyword-stuffing and only use the ones that fit naturally to create a clear, well-written story.

+ People are more attracted to someone they can relate to, so include outside interests or activities to provide a more rounded look at who you are.

+ If your work history is lacking, include unpaid positions, like volunteering or internships, especially if they're relevant to your field.

+ You can ask any of your connections to provide a recommendation to display on your profile, and for the best results, you should make each request.

+ Although endorsements aren't as impressive to recruiters as thoughtful recommendations, they are still necessary and reveal much about your skills.

+ Consider using LinkedIn's publishing platform to post content that demonstrates your industry expertise and lets your personality shine through.

+ Be sure to keep your profile current, and call on trusted friends or colleagues to review its content for grammatical and spelling errors and any red flags.

Chapter 11

Come Together, Part 4: *Linking into the LinkedIn Network*

"Social networks do best when they tap into one of the seven deadly sins."

—Reid Hoffman, LinkedIn founder

Your LinkedIn profile is only part of the picture. We've touched on another side of LinkedIn, the networking side, that's at least as important. Just as your profile has become a mandatory career tool, whether you're employed right now or not, your LinkedIn network can change the career game in a very big way. Everyone can benefit from having a complete profile, but job seekers get special benefits from LinkedIn networking. If you're looking for a job, those benefits align perfectly with the idea that, when you're looking for a job, nothing is more effective than getting the right person on your side.

As you'll see, there are two sides to effective LinkedIn networking. First, you have to understand how things work in order to make them work for you. Second, you have to put in the effort it takes to get the right results. The LinkedIn universe is not impenetrably complicated, but it does function according to its own set of rules.

If you learn those rules and put in the time, you can end up with connections you never would have made without LinkedIn's help.

At the same time, LinkedIn won't do it for you. It doesn't make everything easy, and some obstacles exist by design, so don't expect a LinkedIn account to magically make you and Bill Gates BFFs. You have to make a conscious effort to expand your network, but here's where things get interesting: It may be unlikely, but it's not impossible for you to connect with good old Bill when all is said and done.

IT ALL STARTS WITH CONNECTIONS

Just as atoms are the building blocks of matter, connections are the building blocks of LinkedIn networking. If you're a physicist, though, it's not enough to know how the universe is structured. You need to know how the elements of that structure, the atoms, interact with one another. Once you know that, you can make reliable predictions about the results of actions you take.

Again, LinkedIn connections call for a similar approach. You need to know about the different connection types, their mutual interactions, and the ways they can be used. You need to look behind the curtain. Physicists do that, hoping to read the mind of Mother Nature and discern the laws that govern the universe. Our job calls for a similar approach: In effect, we'll try to read LinkedIn's mind. What are the rules? What can you do within those rules? Why does LinkedIn operate the way it does? What does that tell us about the best and most effective ways to work? What are the obvious steps? And, even better, what are some of the least obvious steps that lead to a powerful LinkedIn network?

We start with the basics. In the LinkedIn universe, connections are organized by "degrees," and everything starts with the first-degree connection. Those are the people who explicitly agree to join your network, so they tend to be people with whom you already have some sort of direct connection.

Those connections won't magically appear. Each one needs to be invited, and each can accept or decline your invitation. That looks like a straightforward system, but complications arise quickly. You have four options for first-degree connections, but, even at this early stage, small differences appear:

1. *Find someone's profile.* Click "Connect." You can add a personal note.

2. *Search LinkedIn for someone.* When you see the result you want, click "Connect." You can add a personal note.

3. *Go to "People You May Know."* Click "Connect." Again, you can add a personal note.

4. *Head to the "Add Connections" page.* Here, you need more than a simple click. You can invite connections using their email addresses, but you don't get the simple one-click function that lets you add a personal note.

Little Differences Can Mean a Lot

The options for inviting someone to connect are simple enough, but even small differences matter, and some choices can actually undermine your efforts to create a useful network.

Consider, for example, the fourth method of making a first-degree connection, the one that starts at "Add Connections." You may be thinking that the email requirement and the lack of a note function can't possibly matter that much, but, in the right circumstances, they matter a great deal. The email requirement is absolute: Without your contact's email address, you can't send an invitation to connect.

The personal note matters. When your contact can't remember exactly who you are, your note can serve as a reminder. If your contact draws a blank upon receiving your invitation, however, LinkedIn allows him to respond with an indication that he simply doesn't know who you are. That's fair enough, and it's usually not the end of the world, but his blank look can have an additional ramification in this situation. If you send too many invitations to people who say they don't know you, LinkedIn recognizes this and will start to limit your ability to send invitations. It will insist that you provide a prospective contact's email address, and it will apply that requirement regardless of the connection method you're using.

That scenario is just one way in which little differences can mean a lot, and it's important to understand LinkedIn pitfalls in greater depth as they arise. For now, suffice it to say that you can't make the best use of LinkedIn without knowing which choices are encouraged and which are discouraged by the site itself. LinkedIn has definite ideas about how its users should behave.

Once you've established direct connections, you have the start of a first-degree network, but you may be wondering where that gets you. After all, you already know those first-degree folks, and it hasn't opened the hiring door to you so far. Connecting with them on LinkedIn is, in and of itself, unlikely to generate the magical key you need.

How, then, do you get that key into your pocket? One thing that would help is to grow your connections and have the biggest network you can. With more and more connections, you're more likely to find the one person who knows of an opportunity that's perfect for you. Does that seem like a tall order? What are the chances of getting great results when you only have a handful of direct connections? Have faith, and consider an old, old story that demonstrates the remarkable potential of even the smallest beginning:

Long ago, the inventor of the game of chess, a fellow sometimes known as "Sessa," brought his creation to the king. The king loved it and offered to pay Sessa for his work. Sessa didn't want much. Instead of asking for gold or silver, he wanted only rice, with the proviso that the king place a grain of rice on the first square of the board and, each day thereafter, place twice the preceding amount on the next square. We all know where this is heading. Simply by doubling the amount each time, Sessa ended up with more rice than the king had in his entire realm. Indeed, before he even made it through the first half of the board, the king is on the hook for more than a billion grains of rice, and it only gets worse from there.

So it is with LinkedIn connections. Perhaps you have only five direct connections. Let's say, though, that each of your connections has five connections of their own. We now have 25 additional possibilities, and if each of those 25 has five connections of their own, suddenly there are 125 people out there whose help may be available.

In LinkedIn's own view, quantity is not the goal, and there's no prize for having the biggest network. In fact, LinkedIn limits members to 30,000 first-degree connections, and caps invitations at 3,000 per member. Those limits, generous though they are, are understandable, and they haven't stopped some members from amassing connections of different degrees that number in the tens of millions. Without some restrictions, the site risks becoming less useful, and less attractive to the people it wants to enroll, especially if communication between members starts to feel at all like spam. As a result, LinkedIn expressly emphasizes connection quality.

We get it. Some connections are more valuable, or simply more meaningful, than others. To use LinkedIn as a job-search tool, however, we want the best of both worlds, even if we don't envision connecting to millions of users, delightful though they may be. We want high-quality connections *and* exponential growth, and those goals are not mutually exclusive. With the right approach, LinkedIn can accommodate both objectives, but first we need to extend the network and increase our odds of finding the right people in the right places.

Stretching Your Network

The potential is obvious, and you're ready to add connections by the truckload. You have your handful of first-degree connections. Now what?

As is often the case, it helps to know what's happening on the other side of the fence. When you prepare a resume, for instance, you prepare it according to how you think a hiring manager will react. On LinkedIn, the people you'd like to connect with have several options for handling requests, and you have several options for how best to approach them.

How do you find these wonderful people who are going to do you so much good? The place to start is with your first-degree connections. The people we want are those who have connected to those connections. Once you've found them, they take on the status of—no surprise here—second-degree connections.

Per the LinkedIn default setting, you can see the connections of your first-degree connections when you visit their profiles, but users can customize the display. They have the option to hide all of their connections except for the ones you share. Those shared connections are always visible by default and they never disappear. Obviously, a layout that hides every connection that might be new to you is not much help. You're already well aware of the connections you share. It's those other connections you want to uncover.

Don't Be Shy

Even if one of your first-degree connections insists on hiding her connections, you always have the option of asking a direct question. After all, these are your closest connections, at least for LinkedIn purposes, and there's nothing wrong with asking one of them if she is connected to someone at Company X or if she knows someone involved in your industry in any capacity. Any contact has the potential to be a useful contact. The key, however, is the ability to approach those people through someone you already know—a much better option, as we'll see, than approaching them out of the blue as your unknown and unvouched-for self.

LinkedIn doesn't give us much to go on in determining relative numbers of members hiding or displaying their connections, but an extremely unscientific perusal of the site supports the idea that most members are happy to reveal their connections.

As long as connections are visible, you'll be able to browse through every one of your connections' own connections. You can also limit your browsing to connections that your contact has recently added, a useful option if you've visited the same profile recently.

What are you looking for? As a job seeker, it should be obvious. You're looking for people who are in the right field, first of all. You're looking for people who are working at companies that interest you, the kind of companies you identified early in your search, the ones that seem to value the skills and experience you have and, most of all, the ones that seem to be hiring. You're also looking for other areas of commonality. Perhaps you're fellow alumni or you have similar interests, whether work-related or not, or some shared experience in your respective histories.

In other words, you're looking for a reason to connect, something mutual to support that connection. Whatever that "something" is, it must be well beyond the fact that you happen to be looking for a position in a field in which that person happens to work. Remember that one goal here is to open doors. Sometimes that means arranging for an informational interview. Sometimes it means being first to be told of an opening that just might be a good fit. You don't expect this person to hire you or to get you a job. You just want some help moving a little closer toward your goal.

Beware, though: There are an awful lot of people out there with enormous numbers of connections, and browsing through pages of possibilities is not the best use of your time and energy. To get around this problem, use LinkedIn's "search" function, accessible when you click on the connection number displayed on your connection's profile page, represented by a magnifying glass. You can enter a search term and, if you're still overwhelmed with results, opt for "advanced search" and narrow the results to the ones that matter. As in any search, there are no hard and fast rules for what constitutes the best possible terms to use. Trial and error is generally the order of the day. Search by job title, company, or location, but don't forget to search by educational institution. Alumni connections are particularly valuable in a job search.

 Desperate Measures
Remember that while LinkedIn users are not always available to you for connection requests, you can invite anyone to connect if you know their email address. If you don't already know that address, you may be able to find it or figure it out with a bit of sleuthing.

Company websites often provide the information. When they don't, you may still be able to decipher the company's email naming convention from publicly available information. Let's say, for example, that you're hoping to be hired as quarterback by the New York Jets, a job that may be closer to your grasp than you might think. If you once knew one address, j.namath@jets.com, for example, you have reason to believe that the team's coach might be reached at w.ewbank@jets.com, and that you might want to start getting back into playing shape.

Still no luck? Even if you don't have those clues, head to Emails4Corporations. The site supplies email formats for over 1,000 businesses, and that will give you an excellent starting point for your efforts.

This is hardly the best method for making contact, and failures will probably outnumber successes. Up your connection chances with a clear, polite note that shows you are a serious professional seeking to connect for professional reasons, and include a bit of background and biographical information about yourself and your work. At the same time, you may have found someone perfect, except for the fact that you have not uncovered another way to connect. This is a last resort, to be used when all else fails, but there are times when the job search makes last resorts necessary.

Connecting at the Second Degree

Picture yourself in the role of a second-degree connection. There you are, signed into your LinkedIn account, and up pops a request from someone who'd like to connect. You search your memory for any hint of this person's identity. Is she the person you met at last year's Christmas party? Maybe she attended that seminar you went to back in June? No, she's none of those people. You've come up empty. You're not terribly inclined to connect to someone you've never heard of.

But wait! There's a note included in the request. It seems she knows old Fred at Amalgamated Widgets. He's one of her first-degree contacts. Good old Fred, you think—maybe I should touch base with him and see what he has to say. He'll tell me what he thinks, so I'll just put this on hold until I talk to him.

This little bit of existential theater, deeply insightful though it is, will not win any awards, but it is an accurate portrayal of what goes through the mind of a second-degree connection upon getting an invitation to connect from someone he doesn't know. Generally, the direct route is not the best way to win second-degree hearts and minds. That's not to say that it's completely off the table. It can work, especially if that personal note gives a compelling reason for connecting, but LinkedIn provides another, better option: the introduction.

Note that a second-degree connection is always going to ask himself what the person you both know thinks, and he's very likely to want to find out for himself before granting your connection request. LinkedIn understands this, and it allows one member to pave the way for another by making an introduction where a direct connection is lacking. Introductions are so important in the LinkedIn universe that you get a limited supply of introduction requests—the number varying according to the type of account you have. (See "The Varieties of LinkedIn Experience" on page 146 for further details.) Even with these restrictions, the introduction is simply more polite and, most important, more professional than a random invitation to connect. If you have the choice, always ask to be introduced.

It's certainly an advantage to have someone put you in touch with a potential connection, even if he leaves it at that, but you can ask the person making the introduction for a little more. When you request the introduction, be clear about why you're asking, and see if the recipient might be willing to say a word or two on your behalf to the person you want to contact. The person on the other end of this process, the one you're introduced to, may get to see the content of your introduction request, so bear that in mind when composing your message.

Once the introduction request has been made, the recipient doesn't have to respond, and six months without a response will cause the request to expire. If the recipient accepts, you've established a new connection and, as LinkedIn puts it, you can "do business." The relationship between the two of you does not automatically enter the exalted first-degree realm, however. Introductions don't circumvent the standard LinkedIn restrictions, and a first-degree connection can only be established when one of you expressly invites the other to connect.

Even without the automatic creation of a first-degree connection, you've accomplished something. You now have a new contact, at whatever level, who may be helpful in the future. Perhaps he'll even be the source of another introduction. Whatever happens, each new connection is a step along the road to a LinkedIn network that can power a job search.

As we've said earlier in the book, regardless of the outcome, always thank the person who was kind enough to put you in touch with someone in his network. An introduction is something of an endorsement in and of itself. If the introduction was successful, tell your original connection something about the experience. Make him feel good about the introduction by letting him know how it helped.

Does all this introduction business feel like imposition? If so, it's worth revisiting the Ben Franklin Effect, the psychological phenomenon whereby a person who has done you a favor is likely to do you another—more likely, in fact, than someone who has *received* a favor from you. Favors apparently beget favors. We don't need to elaborate again on the mechanism behind this counterintuitive phenomenon, but the existence of the Franklin Effect should keep you from feeling that you've somehow used up your quota of favors with a given contact and that you don't dare ask that person for another. The reality is quite different.

A Degree Too Far?

In old-school detective fiction, the third degree is not something to wish for. What about on LinkedIn, where third-degree connections are the most distant contacts deemed worthy of a name? There's no fourth or fifth LinkedIn degree.

Consider what a third-degree connection really means. You know Ann, and you and Ann are first-degree connections. Ann knows Beth, who you've never met, but if you were to run into Beth at a party and the talk turned to mutual friends, you'd have a point of meaningful connection. "You worked with Ann? We were college roommates for a year! Did you know she just started a new job at Universal Tectonics?"

Now move one degree more. You know Ann. Ann knows Beth. Beth knows Carol. When you run into Carol at another party, the fact that Carol knows Beth, someone you don't know, means little or nothing to you. The fact that you know Ann means little or nothing to Carol. After all, Ann is a stranger to Carol.

At the third degree, we're talking about a connection's connection's connection. If one criticism of seeking introductions from a first-degree connection is that it can take time, how much more time is involved in enlisting the aid of two people, one of whom you don't even know? When a relationship is this attenuated, it starts to feel like one of those ancient curses that will visit ruin upon your children's children's children, unto the seventh generation.

As usual, we're not dealing in absolutes. Third-degree connections are not completely useless all the time.

They have their place, but they tend to be slow, they're awkward, and you can reasonably argue that they're not really connections in any meaningful sense of the word. Simply put, they're not the connections into which you should invest most of your energy.

The Benefits of Open Networking on LinkedIn

The point of LinkedIn is networking. It's why the site started, and it continues to be its fundamental reason for existence. What does that mean, though, when you're growing your LinkedIn network? Should you be selective about connections? Should you reach out to anyone and everyone? Should you accept requests indiscriminately? There are good reasons to consider opening your network to one and all—with just a pinch of selectivity, perhaps—because a large network can yield correspondingly large benefits.

Those benefits stem from the way LinkedIn connections work in the first place.

Consider two people, Bill and Hillary, who are at different points in their networking efforts. Bill has more than a thousand LinkedIn connections; Hillary has only a handful.

Once they connect, they become Level 1 connections on the site, and all of Bill's many connections become Level 2 connections for Hillary.

As it happens, Hillary is very much in the job market at the moment, and she's particularly interested in a job with Amalgamated Government, a company located just south of Maryland. She does the sensible thing and runs a LinkedIn search for people affiliated with the company, hoping to find someone who can help her get a foot in the door. While the search turns up no personal connections, it shows a list of names, and a link attached to each name reveals its source.

That source turns out to be ultra-connected Bill. These are the Level 2 connections she made through him, and it's given Hillary an indirect link to people tied to her chosen employer. That's already a benefit. At least she has a starting point.

So far, though, that's all she has. If Hillary contacts people on the list, they aren't likely to drop what they're doing to take up her cause. Luckily, Hillary has a better option. Instead of contacting them directly, she can go back to Bill and ask him to help. He can introduce Hillary to the people with whom he's connected at Amalgamated Government. With a kind word from Bill, Hillary's chance of receiving a warm reception is greatly increased. It's a priceless advantage. The right introduction is worth more than tossing a thousand resume hats into the job-market ring.

Once you open up your connections, they expand exponentially. Each new addition can add links to hundreds of people who may someday help you get a foot in the door.

A larger network also leads to increased exposure. More people will see what you post on the site, and you can use brief updates to showcase your thought leadership in your field. There's always the chance that the right person will see the post and be favorably impressed, leading that person to think of you as a worthy job candidate at the right moment.

Even if you're opening your LinkedIn network, you don't have to be utterly indiscriminate about making connections, hence the "pinch of selectivity" mentioned above. That approach opens the door to endless LinkedIn spam. And you certainly don't have to follow the lead of the LinkedIn Open Networkers, the so-called "LIONS," who advertise their willingness to connect with anyone and everyone. For them, the point is to amass as many connections as possible, but sheer volume shouldn't be an end unto itself. A bit of quality control—declining invitations that don't seem to come from real people and focusing on contacts who work in the same industry, for example—makes for a network that's both large and meaningful. It's those two qualities together that give any network its real value.

Key Lessons

+ For job seekers, the benefits of LinkedIn networking align perfectly with the idea that nothing is more effective than getting the right person on your side.

+ First-degree connections are the people you already know, but each connection needs to be invited to join your network.

+ You can increase your odds of finding the right people in the right places by extending your network with second-degree connections.

+ Search the profiles of your first-degree connections to identify their connections who are working in the right field or at companies that interest you, or who you share common interests with, like fellow alumni.

+ Asking your first-degree connection to make an introduction for you is more professional and effective than sending a random invitation to connect, and provides an opportunity for your connection to say something positive on your behalf.

+ If the recipient responds to your introduction, you've gained a new contact who may be helpful in your job search, but you do not attain first-degree status until one of you invites the other to connect.

+ Consider opening your network—with a bit of selectivity to avoid spam—because each new connection can add links to hundreds more who could help you get a foot in the door.

+ A larger network leads to increased exposure and a greater chance that the right person will see your posts, be favorably impressed, and think of you as a worthy job candidate at the right moment.

Chapter 12

Come Together, Part 5:
Becoming a Groupie with LinkedIn Groups

"Nothing truly valuable can be achieved except by the unselfish cooperation of many individuals."
—Albert Einstein

PROFILES AND CONNECTIONS are what most of us know best about LinkedIn, and it's probably fair to say they're the features that made LinkedIn famous. There's a third feature that deserves more credit than it gets, especially because it's one that can do wonders for the job search: LinkedIn Groups.

It's not that groups live in an obscure corner of the site that's rarely visited by users. There are over 2.1 million LinkedIn groups out there, and 8,000 new ones are added to that total each and every week. People communicate with one another in groups at the breakneck pace of 200 conversations per minute.

There's no doubt, then, that groups are the focus of a great deal of LinkedIn activity, but, rather than saving the best for last, let's look at one very good reason for anyone in the job market to make groups a priority. Strangely enough, it's still about connections. As we've seen, your ability to connect with fellow LinkedIn members is sometimes restricted, either by the rules of the site or by the preferences of the person with whom you'd like to connect.

Groups, however, live by their own rules.

Once you're a member of a group, you can communicate with a member who is otherwise unavailable, so long as he is a member of that same group. Once you select the group you want, reached by way of "interests" on your profile page, you can click on the number of members in the group to get a list. Once you have that list and find your target's name, you can generally send a message to that individual group member. You can do something similar from the "discussions" area, this time by clicking on a group member's photo.

You don't always have this messaging option. LinkedIn allows members, even group members, to opt out of receiving messages from fellow group members via a simple check box in the "settings" menu, a choice you can make on a group-by-group basis.

When you do have access, though, this is a way to connect with people who you wouldn't be able to reach through other LinkedIn channels, and it has some advantages of its own. For one thing, you've established a mutual interest through membership in the same group, something that can serve as a natural icebreaker. You can get to know people, and get yourself known, through group activities, just the sort of thing to ease your path to connecting on an individual level.

Groups are almost a parallel universe within LinkedIn. They can open doors completely outside the structure of first- and second-degree connections. That fact alone makes them worthy of further investigation, but groups can be a useful part of your LinkedIn presence, even if it's not a matter of making new individual connections. First, though, you need to know more about how the group ecosystem functions.

GETTING STARTED WITH GROUPS

When a network numbers its members in the hundreds of millions, those members are bound to demonstrate an enormous range of interests, and that is assuredly the case with LinkedIn, where the only discernable common denominator among members is the hope that LinkedIn will be a positive influence on their working lives. Beyond that, the sky is the limit, and the enormous diversity of interests becomes obvious when you look at the groups that are already out there.

There are industry groups, company groups, networking groups, alumni groups, recruiting groups, job-hunting groups, software groups, real estate groups, marketing groups, and sales groups. There are specialty groups that focus on the smallest slivers of specific industries. Are you a Java programmer? There are, of course, general groups for you, but you might have a special interest in Java on the mainframe, job openings in Mumbai, or user groups in Ohio. Whatever your field and specialty within that field, there's likely to be a group for you.

It's not all business, however. Are you crazy about poetry? There's a group for that. Do you have concerns about parenting? There's a group for that. Are you a football fan? There's not only a group for that, but there's probably a group for your favorite team, regardless of whether you're talking about the game that's played in helmets and pads or the one with goalies, extra time, and yellow cards.

You're likely to find a group for anything that isn't outright illegal, and the range of subjects is a wonder to behold. By the same token, the sheer number of groups can be overwhelming and, in some fields, the number of members is staggering. For example, *Forbes* magazine reports that group participants include 661,000 social media marketers and 180,000 Java developers.

With crowds that large, finding a place for yourself can be a challenge. What groups are worth joining, and how many should you join? When you find an interesting group, how do you actually become a member? What if you change your mind? What about starting your own group? And what should you do once you've become a member? Don't forget that we're considering these questions from a particular perspective, that of a LinkedIn member who wants to advance a job search. It's the job seeker who should pay the closest attention to what's happening in the world of groups.

LinkedIn, of course, puts some limits on participation, for both group managers and group members. You can be a member of 50 groups and 50 subgroups at a time, and you're limited to following no more than 5,000 people.

We're most interested in limits that apply to members, but for a little more insight, note that group management has its own restrictions. Each group can have only one owner, but it can have 10 managers and 50 moderators. You can only moderate 50 groups and 50 subgroups at a time, and no groups can have more than 20,000 members. Those are some rather generous limits, and there are plenty of groups with less than 10 managers, less than 50 moderators, and far less than 20,000 members. Furthermore, if you're bumping up against the 50-group limit as a member, you're almost certainly overextended, especially if you'd like to accomplish something in the group environment.

An important point to remember: Just as LinkedIn emphasizes the quality of connections and not their quantity, groups work best when you focus on the ones that genuinely interest you and on the quality of your contribution to the group. Despite the fact that you do want to benefit from the experience, the first rule of effective membership is this: Ask not what the group can do for you; ask what you can do for the group. Don't make personal benefit the first order of business. Instead, focus on making a contribution, helping others, and sharing your knowledge.

Finding the Right Group

You can search for groups from any page by using the drop-down menu next to the general search box and typing in whatever seems likely to get you to the right place. If you're on your home page, select groups from "interests" at the top of the page. LinkedIn will give you suggestions of "groups you may be interested in."

Once there, get the lay of the land by visiting a group's home page. Poke around a bit and you'll learn a lot. You'll find out how long the group has been around, how many members it has, and how fast it's growing, if at all. You'll also see how active it has been and the volume of comments and discussions, in the past and present, with specific numbers for the past week. Some groups, you'll find, are humming with activity. Others are fading away, and still others never really got off the ground. You'll see whether members have been added over the past week, and LinkedIn will give you the group's week-over-week rate of growth.

A group that has flatlined is not a great candidate for your attention. There, no one is listening. At the same time, a group that's overwhelmingly busy is not the answer. There, your voice may be lost in the din. Look for groups that are active but not overcrowded, places where your contribution will be noticed and appreciated.

Not all groups are equally transparent. Some groups are "open," and posts are visible to one and all. Other groups make things more difficult, hiding posts until you've joined, and joining, as we'll see, is not always automatic.

If you continue your investigation, you'll also find useful demographic information. How senior do the members tend to be? What are their functions? Where are they located? What industries are they associated with?

Some of that information is more valuable than others. If you want to work in software development, you might find categories like engineering, project management, information technology, consulting, and entrepreneurship. Those are functions of a sort, and it certainly starts to narrow things down, but it's a little too general to be of much use. In addition, there's so much overlap between categories that it's hard to know how well the group matches your needs.

Things change when you actually join a group. Doors open, and one particularly important door grants access to advanced search tools. As a member, you can refine your searches and specify functions that matter to you. Say, for example, that you are interested in the sales side of software development. With advanced search tools, you can use keywords to specify sales as the function that interests you, and you stand a much better chance of finding members whose own interests are relevant to your goals.

You don't get those tools until you join, though, and that sometimes takes more than a simple click of the "join" button.

When in doubt, ask. If you're having trouble navigating the group landscape, look to your connections, especially those in your industry, for advice. What groups have they found useful? Which ones put out the welcome mat for new members? Which ones would they avoid? An old LinkedIn hand can be an excellent source of inside information.

Joining a Group

If you don't get automatic admission with a click of the button, there are two routes to acceptance. The easiest, although it comes with the obvious prerequisite that you already know someone, is by invitation from someone who is a member or manager of that group.

Without an invitation, there's no way around the approval requirement, and it's not necessarily one of those automated processes that happen in the blink of an eye. Unless the group has made special provisions, a group manager has to actually review your bona fides.

 The Manager's View

Even if you're not a group manager now, it's always useful to know what's happening on the other side of the fence, and—who knows?—you may take on the management role someday or, if the situation calls for it, start a group of your very own.

When you manage a group, LinkedIn gives you several options for handling membership requests.

- The first, and broadest, option is "auto-join," a group setting that lets anyone become a member at any time.

- A group manager with a properly formatted list of contacts can upload the list to LinkedIn. If you're on the list, you're in. The list need only include first names, last names, and email addresses.

- A group manager can preapprove entire email domains, although LinkedIn won't let you approve certain domains, like gmail.com or yahoo.com, because they're "too generic."

- Finally, a manager can specify email addresses for membership by adding them to the preapproved list individually.

All other requests require individual review. If you're deemed unworthy, the manager can click "decline." If you're deemed especially unworthy, there's a "decline and block" option that prevents you from reapplying in the future.

If your application is declined, try not to take it personally. There could be a range of reasons: The group owner may think you don't have the necessary technical expertise or may simply believe the group has grown too large. With over a million LinkedIn groups, the easiest thing to do is find a similar group. There's no shortage of alternatives and, in the unlikely event that you don't find a group that fits, take up the challenge and make a group of your own. That shouldn't be the first option you pursue, but it's not as far-fetched as it may sound.

You may end up in the limbo of the "pending" status, when your application hasn't been acted upon. In that case, you can send a message to the group manager and remind them of your request. This is not a message you should send after a day of waiting. Give it some time; understand that the group manager may well have more pressing concerns; and keep your request professional, positive, and polite. Don't be demanding, don't complain, and don't push too hard. If you're left hanging for too long—a couple of weeks, say—move on. LinkedIn doesn't require managers to respond at all.

It can be difficult to gauge the quality of a group from a brief visit, even if you're able to see what people are contributing. As you wend your way through the many groups crying out for your attention, however, there are some categories that make sense for just about everyone.

A group that relates to your industry, even in a fairly general way, can help you keep in touch with developments and trends. They may not relate to the absolute specifics of your career, but it's likely that you'll interact with several subspecialties in your working life as a matter of course. Think of a general industry group as a way to keep an eye on the big picture.

It can be a group unto itself or a subgroup of some larger group, but look for a group that drills down to your specific field within a given industry. This will give you another perspective on things, and it's a place that you can pick up information, including hiring information, that's relevant to your niche.

Don't neglect alumni groups. They can be one of the most fruitful sources of connections on LinkedIn, just as they are in the world outside LinkedIn. If you went to a big school, you may find an alumni group that's overpopulated, but you may also find subgroups, based on majors, areas of interest, or shared experiences, that help to make things more manageable.

While LinkedIn is certainly about work, it's not only about work, and there are lots of groups that veer from the strict career orientation of the site. Living a life of all work and no play does have the proverbial dulling effect, and there's no reason you can't or shouldn't indulge in non-work activities, even on LinkedIn. If you have a genuine interest in something that's not part of your career, look for a group that relates to that interest. Your genuineness will come across, and there's no telling where connections you make in an "extracurricular" group might lead. Remember that we're looking for people who may know people in the right places, even if they're not in the right places themselves. It doesn't necessarily take a first-degree connection to help your career. The important thing is to keep yourself open to possibilities, wherever you find them.

TEN TIPS FOR MAKING CONTRIBUTIONS

Despite the site's professional slant, a LinkedIn group is a lot like any other online community. There are regulars and occasional visitors, valued contributors and people who are largely ignored, people whose posts are relevant and those whose posts verge on spam.

At the same time, the best approach on LinkedIn, while it resembles approaches that work almost anywhere, is a little more businesslike than the virtual chaos that can characterize other parts of the Internet.

1. *Keep it positive.* Treat other members with respect. Don't attack anyone. If you disagree with someone, disagree politely, and keep an open mind. And if someone disagrees with *you* in a less-than-polite manner, just ignore them— you have better things to do. You can always resign from a group if you find it has many ill-mannered members.

2. *Keep it professional.* No one expects your posts to resemble the exquisite sophistication of a paragraph by Henry James, the lapidary prose of Nabokov, or even the technical

complexity of a corporate white paper, but that doesn't give you license to cut loose entirely. An occasional LOL can pass, but don't litter your posts with slang and, especially, "text-speak." It's "you are," not "u r." Write as if you were addressing a professional audience and want to make a good, if friendly and informal, impression.

3. *Keep a lid on self-promotion.* In groups, leave aside the ABCs of "always be closing." Relentless self-promotion gets very old very quickly, and people are very quick to spot it. Ultimately, you'll be ignored if all that's on your mind is a new and better way to advance your own agenda. A little subtlety is called for.

4. *Do unto others.* Look for ways that you can help fellow group members. Answer a question. Offer a link to relevant information. Although you're there because there might be something in it for you, you'll be appreciated if you pay attention to the needs of others.

5. *Think before you post.* Many of the mistakes, some of them career-ending, that people have made in their online lives can be traced to their eagerness to hit the "send" button. Give yourself a minute to reread what you may be all too ready to say. A little restraint can go a long way, and, if it needs to be said, posting when you're not entirely sober can be its own special invitation to disaster.

6. *Keep the job search under wraps, at least a little, and especially at first.* If you attend a networking event in the offline world and make your need for a job your first and only topic of conversation, you won't be surprised if people start to avoid you. It's no different in an online group. Don't make your need for a job the first words out of your mouth.

7. *First impressions matter.* In any group, online or not, it can take a while for a new member to be accepted, and it takes time to get a handle on group dynamics. Which members are leaders? Who is respected? Whose contributions tend to be ignored? Sometimes, your place in a group is established very quickly, for better or worse, and a bad first impression is particularly hard to overcome. Tread lightly at first, not only with respect to the job search but with respect to the ways that you interact with other members. A LinkedIn group may have explicit rules, dealing with the kinds of links that are allowed, for example, but groups may also have unwritten rules that are just as powerful, and it can take some time to make sense of these.

8. *Don't hesitate to ask.* You'd like this whole experience to help you in your job search, and that means you'd like people to see you as a knowledgeable person with lots to contribute. That doesn't mean you can't ask questions of other group members. People like to be asked. They like to be seen as the experts who someone would approach with a question. Asking intelligent questions won't hurt your cause in the least.

9. *Use your newfound messaging powers judiciously.* Just because you can send messages to group members doesn't mean you always should. Save your ammunition for a time when you've established yourself as something other than a desperate job seeker in the group. Desperation is generally not a quality that will endear you to recipients of your messages. When it comes time to contact someone whose help you want, you'll already have established a basis for connection.

10. *Keep up your profile.* People will check your profile for a variety of reasons. Fellow group members may check

out of curiosity, but it's virtually guaranteed that anyone whose help you request will take a good, long look. In the midst of establishing your group presence, don't forget to keep your profile up to date and in the best shape possible. Follow the profile guidelines we've laid out and you'll be fine, but do follow them.

It should be clear from all this that there are restrictions that apply to your LinkedIn persona. As part of your mission, for example, you want to get to know people and you want people to know you. You don't, however, want people to know you "warts and all." Instead, you want to show yourself at your best. People should see you as a positive, intelligent, energetic, and productive force. In particular, people should see you as someone they can imagine sharing a workplace with. If they can make that leap, they're much more likely to give you the kind of lead that gets you closer to a job opening.

If it sounds like we're talking once more about your brand, you're quite right. If that brand seems to embody the desirable qualities you'd want to project in a job interview, that's very much the point. In fact, interview behavior is a good analogy for an effective style of group participation on LinkedIn. You may not have the most fun, but you'll stand the best chance of getting results.

A GROUP TO CALL YOUR OWN

What if you don't find a group that works for you, or you've found something appealing but can't become a member?

Perhaps it's time to strike out on your own and create the very group that doesn't seem to be there waiting for you. It takes some care in the inception and some work once your group is up and running, but it's a viable option when nothing else fits your needs. Remember, though, that you really do need to plan things out. Sit down and think things through beforehand, bearing in mind that you have absolutely nothing to lose if you decide to take the leap.

What does it take to make your group a success? First of all, it takes members. You can be a one-man band, but you can't be a one-man group.

Since you need members, you have to get other people interested. Your group's subject is important, and some subjects naturally attract more members than others, but the subject is a secondary consideration. The first order of business is to be sure that the group does not remain a secret.

Invitations

LinkedIn will help you get the word out. For starters, it will give you the option of announcing the group's creation to your connections. That's a good place to begin, and it requires nothing more than a single click of a check box.

The Group Directory

LinkedIn will also add your group to its group directory, and now you need to think about ways to make it easy for people to find your group when they search that directory. The rules are simple. We're talking about web-based search, so, as usual, we're talking about searching a database, which means we find ourselves back in the wonderful world of keywords. Without the right keywords, people simply won't find you.

Choosing Keywords

How do you select those keywords? It's the same method used to choose keywords for a resume when you need to account for the automated scanning that's part of today's hiring process. What words and phrases would you use if you were looking for this very subject? What words have others used for groups with subjects that are similar to yours?

If you're James Bond starting a group for international secret agents, you'll certainly want to mention spies, espionage, and licenses to kill. If you want to be found by your fellow countrymen, you might mention MI6. If your group will focus on high-tech weaponry, make "high-tech weaponry" a keyword. If you want cryptographers to find you, mention codes and cyphers. It's not complicated.

Putting Keywords to Work

Now you need to attach those keywords to your group. Again, LinkedIn makes it easy. When you set up the group, LinkedIn asks for some information, and there are three areas where keywords appear: group name, summary, and description. Both the name and summary will appear in the group directory. The description, which LinkedIn defines as an expanded version of the summary, will appear on the group's own page.

Categories

LinkedIn also asks you to assign your group to a category. You can choose alumni, corporate, conference, networking, professional, or the always popular "other." Chances are that you'll be able to fit your group into one of the existing categories, and they do have the advantage of providing a quick, one-word notion of what you're all about. If nothing fits, though, feel free to create a category of your own.

Specialize

With so many groups already out there, it's hard to attract members, and it's especially hard if your group tries to establish itself in a relatively broad area. You won't gain much traction if you start a group about marketing through social media. You stand a better chance if you narrow your focus and find your special niche. Perhaps you'll have better luck with a focus on marketing through Twitter or, if that's too broad, Twitter marketing to millennials, or Twitter marketing to millennials in San Francisco. Think of the people you'd like to attract, and consider what would get them interested.

Be Different

The idea is to see what's out there and find something different, but you can't let that be your only criterion. Don't pick a subject simply because it's scarce. Pick something in which you have a real interest. If the choice is between a group that's different and a group that reflects a genuine passion, always go with the passion. You'll have work to do once the group gets going, and you don't want to devote your energy to some topic that you've forced yourself to choose.

Open or Closed?

You'll have several other important decisions to make. The first is whether to have an open group or a members-only group. Members-only groups have their place, but you're trying to attract members, not discourage them, and that calls for openness. In members-only groups, outsiders can't even see discussions, let alone participate in them, so the group is a mystery. In addition, discussions in members-only groups are not indexed by search engines. Finally, there's no feature that allows members to share content to social media sites like Facebook and Twitter.

In an open group, on the other hand, all those options are available. On top of that, you still don't have to allow unfettered contributions from anyone who happens to stumble upon the group. You can restrict commenting to people who are group members. That's the sensible choice. If you open the door any wider, you'll find yourself buried under an avalanche of spam and promotions before you know it, and you'll spend all your time digging yourself out of that morass.

Make It Useful

There are far better uses for that time. Once you've started the group, you need to give members a reason to stick around and contribute. The group has to be useful to those members, and you can help it along by making your own postings relevant, interesting, and meaningful. That doesn't mean that every post has to be deeply profound. Start a discussion about an issue that's important to your field. You don't need all the answers. It's enough to throw things open to discussion. Ask people's opinions. Ask for feedback. Encourage debate. When you do that, show your appreciation to members who contribute. Comment on their contributions and, for particularly worthwhile posts, share them on social networks.

Nurture Your Group

In the end, starting a group and attracting members is only half the battle. You have to nurture that group over time. If you get things rolling only to sit back and hope for the best, it's not enough.

Stay active. Be a consistent presence. Members can receive weekly group digests via email, and you want to make sure that your name is there, reminding people of the leadership role you've assumed. That kind of presence can certainly help your career at any stage. Group participation can also be motivation enough to keep you on top of the latest news and trends affecting your industry. To manage your group well, you have to stay in touch with your field.

LINKEDIN IN A NUTSHELL

Your presence in online social media has become increasingly important to the hiring process in recent years. You can safely assume that hiring managers—anyone, in fact, who's considering you for a job—will make stops at all the big sites, especially the "Big Three" of Facebook, Twitter, and LinkedIn. They all have different uses, and some people believe that they fill different roles. It's said that recruiters look to Facebook and Twitter for a sense of cultural fit with an organization, while they look to LinkedIn to assess skills and experience. That's one theory, at least.

Whether the theory holds true or not, there's no doubt that, of all the social media sites, LinkedIn has the greatest potential to help your job search, and its help is perfectly in line with the principle we've harped on from the beginning: Connections matter a great deal in the job market. That may not be the fairest market, or the most noble, or the ideal, but it's the reality. LinkedIn is about connections, and that's why we've given it such a close look.

When you dive into the site, LinkedIn's options seem endless, but there are really only 10 laws of LinkedIn that you have to remember:

1. Make your profile as good as it can be. Make it complete, pay attention to details, and keep things up to date.

2. Grow your network of connections, regardless of degree, but don't expect too much of connections who are relatively distant.

3. Don't aim for record-setting numbers. Focus on quality, not quantity.

4. There's no denying that you, like many millions of other members, want to get something out of LinkedIn, but focus on giving, not getting. Be helpful and contribute when and where you can.

5. Join groups and use them for all they're worth, both as a way to polish your brand and as an indirect way to connect to people who might be inaccessible through normal channels.

6. Like connections, group memberships are not something to seek in quantity.

7. Look for groups that speak to real interests, even if they're not directly related to your work. You never know what connections you may find.

8. Don't forget that alumni groups can be particularly useful.

9. If the right group isn't there, start your own, and let people know about it.

10. If you start your own group, stay active and involved. Don't expect to "set it and forget it."

Consider those the Ten Commandments of LinkedIn. LinkedIn itself will undoubtedly continue to evolve, and specifics will change as the site adapts, but these principles are likely to serve you well no matter how things change. They also may be easier to follow than those other, better known commandments revealed by Moses, and here there's no mountain climbing required.

A Vote for Quality, Civility, and Some Caution

Any site with a couple of hundred million members and a focus on business is bound to attract the kind of promotional activity that qualifies as spam, and LinkedIn has always attracted spammers in droves. It may be a given that LinkedIn members are all trying to use the site to their own advantage, but groups are an easy target for excessive self-promotion.

By the end of 2012, the problem had grown to the point that LinkedIn felt compelled to take steps. Clearly, the site becomes less useful and less attractive to members as spam proliferates. The powers that be had to do something, but by choosing to act with a heavy hand, they created some new problems.

Early in 2013, LinkedIn gave moderators the power to consign group members to a status that made all their group postings subject to moderator approval. Posts could sit for days, or forever, without appearing, and members would have no idea what was happening. Moderators didn't have to justify their actions, nor did they have to notify the hapless members of what was going on, or even respond to members who had been affected.

Worst of all, once you fall into the category of "members whose posts need moderation," that status affects you in all groups, not just the one that started the whole mess. To add insult to injury, LinkedIn offers no appeal process. Instead, you have to try to fix things on your own, one group at a time.

If you've been using the Internet for more than a day or two, you won't be surprised to learn that when people have the power to "ban" members, or at least their posts, that power is sometimes abused. The LinkedIn forums are filled with members complaining of bans for all sorts of petty personal reasons. They disagreed with the wrong person. They mentioned some competitor who was not to be named. They spoke harshly of something dear to someone else's heart.

It's impossible to evaluate the claims of the injured here. There's every chance that they really did break the rules. There's an equal chance that they were completely innocent. Since the consequences of a ban are relatively far-reaching, though, it's, at the very least, one more reason to think before you post, to remain civil, and, especially, to keep self-promotion to a minimum. Groups can be so useful that it's not worth testing the limits of what's acceptable and what puts you in forever-moderated limbo.

Key Lessons

✦ Join LinkedIn groups as a way to polish your brand and to connect to people who might be inaccessible through normal channels.

✦ Groups exist for almost every field, specialty, and interest, including subjects that aren't business related.

✦ Look for groups that are active but not overcrowded, where your contribution will be noticed and appreciated.

✦ Some groups allow automatic admission, but others require an invitation from a group member or approval of the group manager.

✦ Alumni groups can be particularly useful and are one of the most fruitful sources of LinkedIn connections.

✦ Join groups focused on your genuine interests, even if they're not related to your work, because you never know where a connection might lead you.

✦ Keep your contributions to the group positive and professional, and think before you post.

✦ Limit self-promotion, don't talk too much about your job search, and look for ways you can help fellow group members.

✦ If the right group doesn't exist, start your own. Let people know about it through invitations and choosing the right keywords, and nurture it by staying active and involved.

Part 4
SHOWTIME!

Chapter 13

If the Suit Fits . . . *How and Why to Dress for Interview Success*

"Clothes make the man. Naked people have little or no influence on society."
—Mark Twain

"Clothes make the man." "You don't get a second chance to make a great first impression." "Dress for success."

The number of sayings that play up the importance of how we look and dress seems to trump the number of sayings that advise us to look beyond appearances. We know, of course, that we shouldn't judge a book by its cover, but it's more of a wish than a reality. We'd like to see ourselves as people who don't make superficial judgments, whose decisions aren't driven by things that don't really matter. We want other people to be like that, too.

The problem, however, is that human beings aren't built that way. We have visceral reactions far beyond our conscious control. Appearance matters, whether we like it or not. It matters whether we're aware of it or not.

We can't judge a book by its cover? Try telling that to any publisher whose marketing department knows full well that we do just that. We make cover-based judgments all the time, we do it everywhere, and we do it quickly, taking no more than a few minutes, for example, to draw conclusions about the person inside any given suit of clothes.

It's no surprise, then, that we do it in job interviews, a place we use for the explicit purpose of judging the other person in the room.

If you're being interviewed by a machine, this particular problem is solved, and you can stop reading here. Machines don't care how we look or dress. If your interviewer is a human being, however, you can assume that your appearance will have a significant effect on the way you're seen and judged. You could, of course, argue that interviewers should be above all that, but that's an argument for a more perfect world. In our world, interviewers jump to appearance-based conclusions as quickly as any of us.

It's a given, then, that people will judge you by how you look, but that's only one side of the story. The other side is just as important, and it's one that may seem immediately familiar. The fact is that the clothes you wear don't just affect others. They influence your feelings about yourself, and, by doing so, they affect the way you conduct yourself in the world. If you're looking good, wearing your favorite jeans and that oh-so-flattering jacket, you feel good. You're more confident, more self-assured. You're more at ease in your surroundings. You feel better able to take on the world.

In fact, when you dress for a particular part, you're better able to play that part. T.E. Lawrence, otherwise known as Lawrence of Arabia, knew this. As a British officer charged with assisting Arab forces rising against the Ottoman Empire during the First World War, he famously ditched his uniform in favor of Bedouin garb. The change had a two-fold purpose. It meant something to the Arabs fighting alongside him, helping them to see him as one of them, and it meant something to Lawrence himself. It helped him to see himself as someone who belonged, and it served as a concrete expression of his admiration for the culture around him.

Psychologists, undoubtedly aware of all of this from personal experience, could not help but turn a scientific eye on the phenomenon.

Studies had already established that many physical variables influence how we feel and act. Two Northwestern University researchers, Hajo Adam and Adam D. Galinsky, summarized those findings in a paper published in the *Journal of Experimental Social Psychology*:

> It has been shown that physical cleansing influences judgments of morality. In a similar vein, experiencing physical warmth increases feelings of interpersonal warmth, walking slowly activates the stereotype of the elderly, nodding one's head while listening to a persuasive message increases one's susceptibility to persuasion, holding a pen in the mouth in a way that activates the muscles associated with smiling leads to more intense humor responses, carrying a heavy clipboard increases judgments of importance, clean scents increase the tendency to reciprocate trust and to offer charitable help, and adopting an expansive body posture affects one's sense of power and associated action tendencies—more so than being in a powerful role.

These all fall under the heading of what's called "embodied cognition," the idea that physical conditions have powerful consequences, and that we humans are awfully susceptible to influences from the world outside. The physical conditions don't have to have obvious connections to the behavior they influence. Clean scents and charity? We certainly don't have to know what's happening, or to like what it says about us, to be easily manipulated by our environment. Our minds go about their peculiar business, and they don't even need our help.

If the physical environment has its own subconscious influence, that doesn't get us very far when we're faced with an environment we can't control. Our primary subject here, the job interview, does not take place in an environment we can shape to our liking. It is what it is, so we'd better focus on things we can control. Our body language might be one of those things, but we're not always conscious of the messages we're sending, at least not without some conscious effort and practice (see the "It's Not Just What You Say" section on page 213 for some pointers).

HANDLE WITH CARE

The one aspect of the physical world that's different, the one that is utterly within our control, in the interview and elsewhere, is the way we dress.

Our clothing exerts its influence in two different spheres. On the one hand, we all know that our clothing sends a message to other people. That's clear enough, but Adam and Galinsky looked beyond the effect of attire on others. They asked a different question: How does clothing affect the person wearing it?

Their work did more than confirm the intuition that what we wear affects us. In a series of experiments, they administered attention-related psychological tests to different groups of subjects. Some subjects would be shown a white coat during the test, with one group told that it was a doctor's coat and another told the identical coat was a painter's coat. Other subjects actually wore the coats, again with two different descriptions, again using the identical coat.

The effects of hearing about the coat or seeing it were negligible. Regardless of what it was called, the coat's mere presence was not enough to make a difference. Wearing the coat after being told it was a painter's coat did nothing. Subjects' performance showed no measureable difference, either up or down. One small change in the experimental variable, however, led to a surprisingly marked change: Those subjects who wore the so-called "doctor's" coat showed significantly better test results.

"We posit that wearing clothes causes people to 'embody' the clothing and its symbolic meaning," the researchers wrote. The coat-wearing experience, they said, is less direct than other physical experiences. It needs not just the coat but an interpretation of the coat. As the authors put it, "The symbolic meaning is not automatically embodied because it stems from the clothes—so it is not realized until one physically wears and thus embodies the clothes."

The point, though, and the basic principle of "enclothed cognition," as the authors call it, is that your choice of attire actually affects your own performance. It happens largely because your attire means something to you. It's not a case of simply feeling better in the right outfit or of subjective improvement. Judged by objective standards, the right outfit actually enhances your performance.

This little bit of cognitive magic is an important point for job seekers. When interview day rolls around, your choice of outfit matters, but it's not just the choice alone. It's the selection of attire that brings with it its own meaning. Whatever you wear, it's the meaning you attach to your clothing that makes the difference.

That's certainly a lot of weight for a coat and tie to carry, and, if it doesn't quite get to the level of "you are what you wear, no more, no less," it certainly provides a very good reason to make your sartorial choices with care.

FOLLOW SUIT

If your choices were unlimited, you might be tempted to throw in the towel in the face of such a fraught decision. For once, though, you can be glad that there are built-in limits. "Business attire" follows some simple rules. Here, ordinarily soul-crushing corporate uniformity is your friend. You can sit back, relax, and let the office environment be your guide.

For Everyone

The keyword is "appropriate." Unless you're interviewing with a fashion house, your clothing shouldn't make a statement or call attention to itself. It should blend in and be conservative.

- *Even in an informal workplace, an office where every day is casual Friday, an interview is generally a formal situation.* When in doubt, err on the side of increased formality.

- *Dress for the interview, not the job.* If you're interviewing for a construction engineer position whose workday attire will be a hard hat and work boots, leave those items at home.

- *Take a tip from all that psychological research and give your outfit a test run.* Does everything fit? Is it all clean and pressed? Are you comfortable in it? And, perhaps most important, how does it make you feel? Awkward and uneasy? Try something else. Empowered and put together? Go for it.

- *Be sure to see how things go both standing and sitting.* Some choices work well until you sit down and find things going wrong.

- *Keep scent to a minimum.* There's no need to announce your arrival long before you're within eyesight.

- *Gather intelligence if you can.* If you have a friend working for the company, for example, ask about what people are wearing.

- *Give yourself a last-minute inspection when you arrive at the site.* Fix whatever needs fixing.

For Men

Men have it easy. They'll never go wrong with the utterly traditional office uniform.

- *Wear a suit that fits, preferably in dark blue or gray.* Here, fit really matters. You'll look lost in something that's too big. You'll be uncomfortable in something too small. The point here is to look put together so that you feel put together.

- *Choose a solid-color shirt in white or blue.* If you must have a pattern, keep it subtle and understated, and don't pick something that's declared war on your tie. A button-down collar is always a safe bet, and it provides built-in collar-controlling power.

- *Don't even think about straying from black, polished shoes and black socks.* Your belt, by the way, should match your shoes.

- *Wear a tie that's simple and subtle, nothing that's too loud, too cute, or too odd.*

All of this is fashion advice without much actual fashion, but the point here is to use corporate uniformity to your benefit. You don't want to stand out. You want to blend in. You want to look at home in the environment and, by extension, to feel at home there. You have enough on your mind without adding worries about how you look. Stick to the tried and true, however dull that choice may be, and pay attention to your associations with the outfit you select.

For Women

Women have to make more difficult choices. If you're female, this comes as no surprise. Whether you're dealing with the "male gaze," with broad issues of differential workplace treatment, or with tensions between family and work that don't hit men nearly half as hard, you're coping with some thorny issues. Meanwhile, all you're doing is trying to be hired.

- *Taking the most pragmatic approach possible, you should be guided by the same principle that guides men:* Go with the corporate uniform as much as possible.

- *This means downplaying the stereotypically "feminine."* When faced with a choice, go with the outfit that seems more masculine. Like it or not, there's workplace research in support of better interview outcomes for more masculine outfits.

- *There are limits, of course—we're not talking about full-on Marlene Dietrich in white tie and tails.* If you can pull that look off, more power to you. You'll make a memorable impression, but an offer may not be immediately forthcoming.

- *In light of what's been shown to get results, you're looking at the same dark suits that work for men,* this time with a simple sweater or a classic blouse that doesn't stray too far from the cut of a man's shirt.

- *If you're wearing a skirt, don't choose anything too short or too long, and don't forget the hose.*

- *For shoes, choose flats or moderate heels, preferably with closed toes.* Just as it is for men, polished leather is your best bet.

- *Don't overdo the jewelry.* A couple of tasteful items are enough.

- *Don't overdo the nails.* A moderate length is best, and polish shouldn't call much attention to itself.

In the end, both men and women should be aiming for a look that's eminently forgettable and utterly inoffensive. The right clothing will help people to see and remember you as a competent professional who seemed to fit in. It will do this, in part, by making you feel like that competent professional who fits right in. If the psychologists are correct, it's more than a feeling. Clothes actually make the man—or woman—better.

IT'S NOT JUST WHAT YOU SAY

Let's return to a subject we touched on earlier in the chapter: body language. If you've thought through your answers to any possible question and feel completely capable of handling anything an interviewer can throw at you, you're still not ready to walk into an interview without a care in the world.

Regardless of the circumstances, people don't communicate by spoken language alone when they meet. There's an entire subconscious medium, whether it's called nonverbal communication or body language, that has a profound influence on the messages we give and receive when we interact. Since this nonverbal medium is subconscious, there's no guarantee that the message you think you're sending is the message your audience receives. At the very least, we want to ensure that your message is not being sabotaged by nonverbal behavior that operates outside your conscious control.

In short, it pays to know what signals you're sending out.

While no one doubts that nonverbal behaviors are influential, the extent of that influence is open to debate. At one extreme, James Borg, author of the book *Body Language*, a popular treatment of the subject, claims that 93 percent of what's communicated between people comes from everything except the words. We're always looking for the "hidden secrets," like body language, that reveal the truth behind appearances, so the 93 percent claim resonated with people.

On further review, however, Borg seems to have exaggerated the true power of the nonverbal. He based his calculation on the work of Albert Mehrabian, a research psychologist at UCLA who specialized in studies of the way people communicate. He broke communication down into three components:

1. **Verbal:** the words themselves, which carry 7 percent of the message

2. **Tone of voice:** vocal characteristics, responsible for 38 percent of the message

3. **Facial expressions:** the visual component, which carries 55 percent of the message

Since publishing those results and seeing them take root in the popular imagination, Mehrabian has been careful to distance himself from the notion that 93 percent of all interpersonal communication is nonverbal. He doesn't disclaim it entirely, but he warns readers that it applies only in limited situations: "Unless a communicator is talking about their feelings or attitudes, these equations are not applicable."

In the end, there is no universally accepted ratio of nonverbal to verbal communication in our everyday interactions. For interviewees, it's enough to say that a substantial, if unquantifiable, part of the impression you make is produced by body language and other nonverbal cues.

And it's not only a question of the impression you make. There's another reason to take a serious look at body language. Your body language can influence your state of mind.

To take a simple example, consider the advice that's often given to people who are about to be interviewed by phone, a practice that is especially common in initial screening interviews. Phone interviewees are advised to dress up, remember to smile, and to stand for the interview. None of this is visible to the interviewer, but it still helps the interviewee to give a better presentation—more positive, alert, engaged, and professional.

In a similar vein, the way in which you hold yourself, since it reinforces your attitude, is a natural target for someone who wants to change that attitude. For example, a "closed" posture, with arms folded across the chest and fists clenched, may actually buttress a person's unreceptive state of mind. If you're selling to that person, you might want to change that posture as a first step toward changing his unreceptive attitude. In that situation, an old sales technique calls for handing something to your prospect. Give him something to hold, and he's compelled to open the closed posture, a first step toward making him more open to your pitch.

An old boxing adage is surprisingly apt: Kill the body and the head will follow. In interviews, the head that follows is not just the one attached to someone else's neck. It's your own head, too, and it's that phenomenon that makes a basic familiarity with body language doubly important.

Keeping Your Head—Eyes, Legs, Hands, and Face—in the Game

It would be awfully nice if we could take all the research into body language and turn it into a few clear rules that always work. "Sit like this, and your body language will get you the job!" Alas, it's not that simple. There's no magic bullet, no posture you can assume that guarantees instant rapport with your interviewer.

Still, there are a few simple principles worth knowing, and you don't have to contort your body into some supposedly magic pose that always does the trick. Trying to force some alien body language onto your natural style will feel awkward and wrong.

But do be aware of some key nonverbal indicators and of any bad habits that can do real damage.

- **Eyes:** Eye contact is important, but it's another one of those things that can't be reduced to a formula. There's no set amount of eye contact that's somehow correct, but you can go wrong if you go to extremes, either by avoiding eye contact completely or gracing your interviewer with an unwavering stare. Make eye contact when you greet people. Don't avoid all eye contact during the interview. Look your interviewer in the eye at the scientifically determined interval of "sometimes," and you'll be fine.

- **Arms:** Ah, here we have one of the few general rules with some validity: Folding your arms across your chest will make you seem unengaged, closed, and defensive. Combining folded arms with clenched fists only adds to that impression.

- **Legs:** If you'd like to be seen as someone who is not receptive in the least, crossed arms, crossed legs, and clenched fists can't be beat. Otherwise, you can let your personal comfort tell you whether to cross your legs or not. You can find elaborate interpretations of every variation of crossed legs, but, valid or not, you don't need to consult those interpretations. Other things, especially your general posture, are more important.

- **Posture:** Sit up and lean forward slightly. That's the posture of an interviewee who is engaged, interested, and positive. You don't have to exaggerate the position, and you'll be fine as long as you're not slumped in your seat. (We reveal more details about using posture to your advantage in the next section, "Body Language in Micro.")

- **Face:** Facial expressions are a major component of non-verbal communication. We're very sensitive to each other's faces. We can tell when an expression doesn't match the spoken word. That being said, there are only a few things to remember: Smile when you meet someone. Don't hesitate to smile during the interview when appropriate. When you're listening, the occasional nod is another demonstration of a positive attitude.

- **Hands, Part One:** Hands can also be very expressive, but that's not always a good thing. Gestures are fine in moderation. Nervous mannerisms—touching your face or hair, scratching your nose, rubbing your arm, stroking your beard in anticipation of the success of your evil plan—should be controlled. Many mannerisms are unconscious, but you'll get the chance to recognize and eliminate any problems when we talk about interview preparation.

- **Hands, Part Two:** When you meet your interviewer, you'll stand, smile, and shake hands. The handshake is an element of body language that everyone seems to consider a reliable indicator. In reality, of course, there's no evidence that the way you shake hands is much of an indication of anything except the way you shake hands. Even so, it's wise to play it safe. Avoid the crushing of bones. This is not a test of strength. Similarly, avoid the dreaded "dead fish." If you tend toward sweaty palms, bring a handkerchief and discretely solve the problem before the interviewer appears. In any event, avoid the extremes. Stick with a handshake that's moderately firm, brisk, and brief.

In summary, don't overcomplicate the issue. Lean toward your interviewer a bit, nod and smile when appropriate, don't cross your arms, don't fidget or fuss, and make eye contact. Manage those simple actions, and body language won't get in your way.

Body Language in Micro

There's no doubt that much of what we communicate—some would say the majority—takes place outside the verbal realm. And there's no question nonverbal communication can give you an edge in the job interview. The problem is separating what's real from the latest fad.

Take micro-expressions. The idea is that we're communicating through a series of fleeting expressions. Those expressions happen without our knowledge, and they affect others without *their* conscious knowledge. Perhaps if we learned to control them, we'd use them to influence others. If we learned to decipher them, we'd know what people were really thinking, and we could adjust our presentations accordingly. In the end, with the help of the right micro-expressions, we'd get the job.

This strategy has problems, however.

The idea of micro-expressions originated with the work of some family therapists in the 1970s. They filmed therapy sessions and reviewed the films afterward, examining them frame by frame. They noticed fleeting facial expressions that often seemed to contradict what the patients were saying.

A magical key to unlock the truth behind the conscious façade is a very appealing notion, one that has given this idea traction in some odd places. The Transportation Security Administration (TSA), for example, has a massive training program in place that aims to teach agents to identify suspicious travelers by their facial expressions.

Yet even a cursory analysis of research into micro-expressions reveals several reasons for skepticism. Most writing on the subject, especially in popular literature, is purely theoretical, and there's been very little empirical research.

When real research has been done, results have been equivocal. People don't distinguish between real and fake expressions at a level much better than chance. They can't reliably falsify expressions, especially if they're trying to replace one expression with its opposite, faking a sad face when they have no reason to be sad, for example. We *do* seem able to mask an emotional state with an unemotional, neutral expression, so a frightened interviewee may be able to convincingly assume a blank expression. That's a lot different than the ability to replace a frightened look with the appearance of enthusiastic confidence. In the interview, the ability to assume a look of bland indifference is, shall we say, of questionable value.

We're not very good at judging facial expressions or faking them, so working on micro-expressions shouldn't be a priority in interview preparation, but there are other kinds of body language that do seem to have an impact. What's most interesting is they affect both parties in a communication, in this case the interviewer and the interviewee.

The Power of Posture

Posture is particularly significant. Experts distinguish between two different postures—high-power and low-power—and they apply to humans and our primate relatives.

A high-power posture is open and expansive. It's relaxed and takes up more space. A low-power posture is the opposite. It's closed and constricted. Someone who is hunched over his phone and shrinking into a chair has a closed posture.

When people find themselves in a situation where the stakes are high and the power dynamic unequal, as in a job interview, many of us tend to retreat into low-power postures. Sadly, it's the natural thing to do when you're feeling relatively powerless.

People respond to those postures, albeit unconsciously, and they do so regardless of whether the posture is genuine and natural or artificially adopted. In other words, it doesn't matter that you're feeling powerless. Putting yourself into a high-power posture, even if it feels completely artificial, will have positive effects on how you're evaluated.

The benefits of the high-power posture don't end there. According to a recent Harvard Business School study, there's more: "Not only do these postures reflect power, they also *produce* it; in contrast to adopting low-power poses, adopting high-power poses increases explicit and implicit feelings of power and dominance, risk-taking behavior, action orientation, pain tolerance, and testosterone, while reducing stress, anxiety, and cortisol (the stress hormone)."

The Harvard researchers took things a step further. They had people adopt poses *before* giving an interview-like presentation. Some were instructed to adopt high-power poses, others to take the opposite approach. Next, they delivered presentations to a group of "interviewers," and they were left to their own devices when it came to postures during the presentations. Regardless of how they prepared, subjects were equally likely to assume high- or low-power postures while presenting, but the style of preparation affected the interviewers' evaluations nonetheless. Participants who practiced high-power poses beforehand scored much higher in terms of their likelihood of being hired, regardless of the postures they assumed in the "interview" or of the quality of their deliveries. In other words, the effects of a few minutes of high-power posing before the presentation carried over into the presentation itself, and it was utterly independent of anything else they were doing.

The researchers hypothesized that *feeling* more prepared, accurately or not, boosted confidence. Increased confidence, in turn, made a better impression on the audience, doing so independently of speech quality, something we'd think matters a great deal.

There are lessons here for interviewees. Studying micro-expressions is not a good use of your time and energy in interview preparation. On the other hand, body language has real effects, and the way to put those to use is remarkably simple. When you arrive at the interview location, remind yourself about your posture. Don't shrink into your chair or retreat into your phone. Relax, take up space, and keep your posture open and expansive—nothing too dramatic, though. You don't need private space for exaggerated posing.

Carry those same high-power postures into the interview. Again, you need nothing dramatic or unnatural. A high-power posture isn't a caricature. It is, however, something you may need to consciously assume, especially if you tend to slip into low-power postures in stressful situations.

In the end, these simple steps can boost your confidence and change the way you're seen—giving you the edge you need.

Key Lessons

+ Appearance matters in a job interview and has a significant effect on the way you're seen and judged.

+ The clothes you wear influence your feelings about yourself, and the right outfit can actually enhance your performance based on the meaning you attach to it.

+ Dress for the interview, not the job, and even in a casual workplace, err on the side of formality.

+ Men will never go wrong with the traditional office uniform of a dark suit that fits well, a solid-color shirt in white or blue, a simple tie, and black shoes and socks.

+ Women should also stick to the corporate uniform: dark suits, a simple sweater or classic blouse, and flat shoes or moderate heels with closed toes.

+ When faced with a choice, women should choose the outfit that seems more masculine, as research indicates better interview outcomes for more masculine outfits.

+ The right clothing will help people see and remember you as a competent professional who fits in, and it will do this, in part, by making you feel like that competent professional who fits in.

+ Just like the clothes you choose, your body language can influence your state of mind and have a profound effect on the messages you give and receive.

+ Remember these simple body language tips for interviews: Sit up and lean forward a bit, nod and smile when appropriate, make eye contact, and don't cross your arms or fidget.

+ People don't distinguish between real and fake expressions at a level much better than chance, but certain types of body language absolutely affect both parties in a communication.

+ Remember that while fear may send you slumping into low-power posture during an interview, assuming high-power posture will not only make an interviewer believe you're confident, but it will make you feel confident.

Chapter 14

Information Station: *How to Make Informational Interviews Work for You*

"Judge a man by his questions rather than by his answers."
—Voltaire

So far, the job search has been all about getting ready: looking at your career choices, getting your paperwork in order, finding the companies that suit your needs—and vice versa—and identifying the people you can approach.

It's finally time to ramp up your activity level and head out into the world. Whether that prospect puts a smile on your face or sends chills down your spine, you should know that, at this stage, our goal is nothing too intimidating. All we want right now is for a few of the right people in a few of the right places to give us a few minutes of their time. We don't want to ask them to hire us. We don't expect them to be so astonished by our remarkable talent that they'll put us on the payroll. We only hope that they'll be generous enough to give us an informational interview.

What is an informational interview?

The best place to start is by being very clear about what an informational interview is not. An informational interview is *not* a job interview. That sentiment applies to every single informational interview at every time, in every place, and in every field.

Perhaps you're skeptical about that part of the definition. Why would I want to set up this kind of meeting if I weren't looking for a job? Doesn't the other person know full well that I have an ulterior motive? Isn't it obvious that jobs are on my mind?

Your skepticism is justified. Everyone *does* understand those things. Call it a polite fiction, but, with one small exception, you'll get nowhere if you make it explicit that you're looking to get hired. So you have to be disingenuous.

If you can manage that, an informational interview is a chance to meet briefly with someone in your field and talk about that person's company, her career, and the industry as a whole. It's as simple as that.

If the stars are properly aligned, you may even be able to venture into areas specific to your job search, but you can't start with that expectation. If anything, operate under the assumption that your personal situation will never be a topic of discussion. There are rare exceptions, as we'll see, when talk turns to your job search naturally. Otherwise, it's off the table.

In fact, here is a rule that will stand you in good stead in any informational interview: If you have even the slightest doubt about the appropriateness of bringing up your search, don't.

HOW TO ASK FOR THE INTERVIEW
The Setup
For every interview request, you must consider the medium, the message, and if any exceptions apply.

The Medium
Before considering the content of an interview request, there's a threshold question: What's the best medium?

You can call. You can write a letter. You can text. You can hire a skywriting plane or rent a billboard. But do none of those things. Use email. It's a medium that makes few demands on the recipient. She can ignore your message and get to it when she has a few spare minutes. She doesn't have to drop everything and respond. Everyone, even the most grizzled eminence, can do email. Email automatically includes a way to reply to the sender, no further information required. Email allows you to keep things short and sweet while still letting you say everything you need to.

The only other plausible medium is the phone, but that's much more intrusive. Either I take your call right now, or you go to voicemail, where I have to extract your contact information in order to reply. With email, I can start a reply, put it aside as needed, and return to it when my schedule allows. A phone call is an imposition on a stranger's time—a small imposition, perhaps, but an imposition nonetheless.

The Message

Now that we've settled on the medium, we can establish some guidelines for the message:

- *Keep it short.* You may be tempted to include all sorts of biographical information on the theory that it will persuade the recipient that you really deserve some of their time. Resist! When you keep it short, it increases the odds of your message being read, and you've provided empirical evidence of the fact that you value the recipient's time. A limit of 150 words should be more than enough to cover all the points you want to make.

- *Keep it formal.* Address the recipient by title and last name, as if you were writing a business letter. "Dear Mr. Buffett" works. "Hi Warren!" doesn't. Sign off in the same formal way: "Sincerely" or "Thank you for your time."

- *Make no mistakes.* Proofread your letter to make sure your grammar is perfect, there are no typos, and you've spelled everything—especially the recipient's name—correctly.

- *Put your subject line to work.* Let your subject line get right to the point. If you have an introduction from Bill Clinton, your subject line should be "Referral from Bill Clinton." If you don't, be explicit about your connection to the recipient and your purpose: "Tufts chemistry major seeking your advice."

- *Mention your referral right away.* Your message should start with the name of your referral and the briefest of biographies: "Bill Clinton suggested I contact you about your experience in the pharmaceutical industry. I am a chemistry major at Tufts and expect to graduate in 2016."

- *With no referral, make your connection clear.* "I am a senior at Tufts with a major in marketing, and I found your information in the university's online database."

- *Be even more specific if you can.* "I am particularly interested in the use of Twitter for marketing to infants and toddlers, and I see that you have done a great deal of work in that area."

- *Ask your question.* Let your recipient know what you want and why you want it. "I would love to learn about your experience in marketing and at Company X. Would you be willing to meet with me for 20 minutes, at your convenience, to discuss that experience?"

- *Promise to follow up.* There's every chance that your recipient has more than enough on their plate already, and your email is likely to sink slowly into the abyss of their inbox, never to be seen again. Acknowledge that they must be busy and that the two of you may not connect this time around, but let them know that you'll follow up in a week or two to find a more convenient time. It's a meaningless deadline, of course, but it is a deadline. It may be just enough to earn a reply.

The Exceptions

With every rule, of course, there are exceptions:

- *There's a job posted.* This is the one time when it's acceptable to use the word "job." Mention that your contact's company has advertised an open position and that you're applying for the job. One school of thought holds that contacts may be reluctant to meet because they fear you'll be asking about openings, and they don't know if any exist. At the very least, the presence of an opening removes that anxiety.

- *You saw an article.* If you've chosen this contact because of something that's been published by them or about them, mention that fact in your email. Provide a very brief summary of what interested you. Let your contact know that you'd love to discuss the subject further.

Intermission: The No-Waiting Game

As the noted moral philosopher Tom Petty famously said, "The waiting is the hardest part."

Like fledglings leaving the nest, your emails have taken wing and traveled far and wide. They're on their own, out of your control, and doing what they can on your behalf. Is it enough now to sit back and anxiously wait for the replies to start rolling in?

You could, but you'll want to take action. For one, there's no better source of free-floating anxiety than the utterly passive routine of doing nothing while hoping for the best. And here's another reason: Remember, you've actually made a small commitment; you promised your contacts that you'd follow up in a week or two. Now is the time to make good on that threat.

As usual in this step-by-step process, you don't have to do anything heroic to get through the next step. Using the same list you compiled to identify the companies and people you've written to, you should be tracking any responses. Set your own deadline for follow-up, but don't make it longer than two weeks. When that deadline rolls around, give your contacts another nudge.

This time, you can send another email or you can pick up the phone. Email is still less intrusive. A call is something of an escalation, and that can have one of two effects: Your contact may see it as an annoyance, or your contact may see it as evidence of your serious commitment.

Whether you use phone or email, however, your message is the same. You'd sent an email recently asking if it would be possible to meet. You'd still be very interested in doing that.

What if your contact answers the call, live and in person? The scenario is the same. Remind them of who you are and why you're calling, and ask if they'd be willing to spare a few minutes of their time in the near future.

Of course, things can play out differently. What if this happens?

- *You:* Hello, Ms. Contact. My name is Walter White. I sent you an email a few days ago asking if you'd be willing to . . .

- *Contact:* Yes, Walter. I remember that. You're the chemistry major. I haven't had time to get back to you yet, but I'd be happy to talk. I'm free now, in fact. What would you like to ask?

- *You (panicking):* Mmmm . . . rrr . . . *(drops phone, knocks coffee onto laptop, decides to escape to desert)*

If you're going to call, be prepared. Be ready to launch the interview if invited. It can feel awkward, but it's not that difficult if you have a plan, and that plan is very much on the agenda.

There's also the possibility that your contact will respond without giving you what you want. They are just too busy now, or it turns out they don't think they can help. All is not lost. If they can't or won't help, perhaps they know someone who can. Can they recommend someone else who might be willing to take the time? If so, ask if they'll let you use their name when you contact that other person. You now have a very good lead.

For contacts who are never heard from, even after you've followed up, set another deadline, again no more than two weeks after your second connection attempt. If there's still no word, cross them off the list. You've spent enough energy. If the contact in question was at a company that you still want to pursue, it's time to start digging for information about an alternative.

Don't Give Up the Ship

If you're still waiting for your first positive response, you'll need to backtrack, either by approaching other contacts at your preferred companies or by adding to your company list. Remember that it's by no means fatal to the plan if you expand your list of companies. You still have the chance to gain a foothold in your preferred industry, and an employee of Company X, the place that was never very high on your list, may still help you connect with the right person at Company Y, the place that's really in your crosshairs. In other words, there's no reason to throw in the towel.

What about those blessed souls who give you what you want? Obviously, you want to respond quickly. Thank them for getting back to you and for being willing to meet. If they suggest a time, you'll be there.

If they don't suggest a time, the ball is in your court, but here's where it gets interesting. An abundance of choices is not necessarily a good thing. According to Columbia Business School professor of management Sheena Iyengar, whose expertise is the psychology of choice, "People might find more and more choice to actually be debilitating." In other words, don't leave things too open-ended. Offer a few possibilities: any time Monday and Wednesday, or Tuesday and Thursday mornings. If you leave the scheduling wide open, that may actually make things harder for your contact. We want to make it easier.

Once you've set the time and date, confirm your agreement, thank your contact again, and let him know you're looking forward to meeting.

YOUR WISH IS GRANTED—NOW WHAT?

If you've gotten this far, we can assume that at least one of your contacts has agreed to spend a little time with you.

Unlike a job interview, the informational interview lacks a predetermined structure. In most job interviews, you can expect to be asked a series of questions, many of them predictable, and you can rehearse your performance, somewhat secure in the knowledge that you've covered most of the bases. You'll get a chance to ask your own questions, and you'll rehearse those as well. You'll be aware of different interviewing styles. You'll know if you're likely to be asked to solve a problem.

Compared to that, an informational interview is a formless void, but that's not a bad thing—it's just like any social interaction. When you're meeting some friends for a couple of drinks after work, you don't have to arrive with a prepared conversational agenda. It's wide open. If you wanted to, however, you could set an agenda, and your friends would comply because they would have no reason to resist.

That's exactly the situation of the informational interview. You set the agenda.

Defining Success

That freedom can leave people feeling even more at sea than they would if faced with an actual job interview. The idea that you're free to talk about anything puts a lot of responsibility on your shoulders. Unlike a job interview, where a bad interviewer is quite capable of sabotaging what could have been a good experience, you're the one who determines if the informational interview will be a success.

The key to a successful informational interview is to give it some structure, and we can use that structure to manage this interview with the same systematic, step-by-step method we've used in every part of the job search. Before we get to those steps, though, we'd better ask a basic question: In the informational interview, what do we mean by "success"?

There are two ways to answer that question. The easy answer is that an informational interview that yields a referral is a success. That's the right result, the one that benefits us the most. Ask the question another way, however, and things are not so clear. Why would our contact be willing to give us the kind of referral we need? Contacts will help you in your job search because they like you.

If you can build rapport with your contact, that's half the battle, and you can help the process along by being prepared.

Getting Current

Start with research. When you walk into an informational interview, you should know a good deal about three things:

1. The Industry: You should know something about the industry from the very start. This is, after all, the field that interests you.

Even if you have a solid grounding in the basics, be sure to catch up with the latest news. People on the front lines of a given field tend to stay on top of current events that have industry-wide implications, and those events tend to be the topic of conversation. Know about important trends. Take the time to understand new opportunities and new obstacles that are likely to be on people's minds. It's nice to know some history. It's crucial to know what's new.

This kind of research doesn't have to be at all complicated. A simple web search, looking for industry trends, will do the trick. For best results, include a separate search of the "news" category, an option that can turn up big stories that may be otherwise buried. Industry publications are another option. Every industry has its own magazines and newsletters, all providing a more "inside" perspective than the general outlets.

2. The Company: You should also already know something about your contact's company, if only because it ended up on your list of desirable employers. This is another situation in which what's new trumps deep historical background. Has the company undertaken any new initiatives? Launched new products? Made news?

You can use the same research tools to learn about the company, but you cannot, under any circumstances, ignore the single best news source: the company's own website. That's where you'll find all the things the company *wants* to talk about. If the company itself is devoting space to some new development, it's a safe bet that your contact knows all about it, and you've discovered a natural topic of conversation.

3. The Contact: So far, we're three for three. You know something about your contact. But you can probably find out more, perhaps a lot more. The danger, though, is that you can cross the line that separates a bright, interested recruit from an overly personal, intrusive, and boundary-violating stalker. To make matters worse, you can cross that line without even knowing it. We all have different tolerances for mixing business with personal matters, and you don't know where your contact fits in that continuum. Always approach personal information with caution.

There are three sources of information you can safely use to learn more about your contact. First, there's the company website and any biographical information published there. Second, there's the interview, article, or posting that led you to this contact to begin with, if that was the case. Third, there's LinkedIn. No one will be shocked to learn that you took the time to consult a professional network in preparation for an informational interview.

While there's no reason to turn your research into a dissertation-level project, it's worth some real effort. You worked hard enough to get to this point. You'll be more comfortable in the interview if you feel you've familiarized yourself with the topics that are likely to come up in conversation. Besides, much of what you learn will be useful as you go forward. So there's no reason to shortchange this part of the process.

THE MAIN EVENT

Now we're getting somewhere! We have an appointment with a contact we really want to meet.

We know what we'd like to accomplish in that meeting. Our goal is to establish rapport, to use this interaction to elicit all the positive feelings we can. We want this contact to like us, and to like us so much that he's willing to do something on our behalf.

We've done our homework. We know what's happening in the industry and what's new at this company. We know something about our contact. As you'll see, all that knowledge will come in handy very soon.

On the day of the interview, we arrive at our destination. We make our presence known. Our contact is ready for us. The door opens. We stand, smile, and shake hands. We follow him into his office. We take a seat.

Now what?

Small Talk

Some people dread it. For them, it's a painful ordeal. Some love it. They take to it naturally. Regardless of where you fit on the dread-love scale, small talk is a necessity. It breaks the ice and starts the ball rolling.

If you don't have the gift of gab and can't imagine getting through this part of the interview, rest easy. This interview has just enough structure to make it an easy task for even the worst conversationalist. This is not a cocktail party, where your small talk, once it begins, may never end. You're even blessed with an easy place to start. Open things by saying thanks: "Thank you very much for meeting with me today."

That's pretty simple, but what's next? Strangely enough, your contact may respond immediately to your brilliant opening—"You're welcome"—and he may even go on from there. If he does, you're off and running. If he doesn't, the ball is back in your court, but take heart. One secret of good small talk is the ability to put the focus on the other person, and that's a very natural next topic here. What's more, you can keep things moving by asking an implicit question: "I hope this time worked out in terms of your schedule today and that it's not too much of a disruption." You're inviting a response, and you're likely to get one. A contact who was willing to meet with you is not likely to tell you that the timing is terrible and he wishes you'd just go away.

In this context, you won't need much more in the way of small talk, but follow your host's lead. If he wants to get down to cases, start right in. If he opts for a more informal chat, go with the flow. You do have an agenda, though, so be aware of the passage of time. You don't want to let the entire interview slip away in idle chatter, but you can't press too hard if things are going well. Remember that rapport is the essential outcome. Small talk can enhance rapport, but it will take more to actually get your contact on your side in a meaningful way.

Big Talk

Once past small talk, managing an informational interview is greatly simplified if you rely on a structure, the same one you can apply to any informational interview, regardless of industry or company. It's an all-purpose approach that does the job regardless of the particular position or experience of your contact. You can remember the steps that make up the structure with the help of a handy acronym, ICAN: Industry, Career, Advice, and Next Steps. You can cover each area in turn if time permits or, if pressed for time, you can omit an area or two, with one strict exception: Never omit "Next Steps." The reason for this rule will become clear as we look at each step.

Industry

In general, the best questions about your contact's industry are open-ended inquiries into the industry's past, present, and future. How have things changed? What developments are having the greatest effect on the industry today? How do you see those trends playing out in the future? How have businesses been responding to those changes? Where do you see the industry in five years?

These are questions that encourage thoughtful responses. They don't call for simple, one-word answers. You'll find that they often lead to questions that naturally follow what you're hearing, and, when that happens, the interview can feel like a conversation. That, by the way, is a good thing.

Career

Next, you can engineer a subtle shift in perspective. Instead of asking about general trends, ask about what it has all meant to your contact. What was your job like when you first started? How have things changed? What qualities have you found most important to your success here? What lessons have you learned? What's taken you by surprise?

You started out with general questions that could have been answered by someone observing the industry from the outside. This new perspective asks your contact to consider his own career, and that's a step in the right direction. We want the conversation to turn as naturally as possible to questions of career. It doesn't matter, at this point, whose career we're discussing. The fact that careers are on the agenda is enough.

Advice

With "Advice," we change the focus one more time. We started with relatively impersonal questions about the industry. We moved on to more personal inquiries about our contact's experience in that industry and in his job. We want to add one more career-focused ingredient, your own situation, and we'd like some advice. If you were starting out now, what would you do to give yourself the best chance to succeed? What should I be doing to maximize my chances? What's the best way for me to stay on top of developments in this field?

The point here is not so much to get the best possible advice, although that would be nice. The real point is to encourage our contact to act as, and see himself as, an advisor. We'd like him to take on the role of mentor, someone who is invested, even slightly, in the outcome of our job search. That kind of investment can result from the simple fact that he has given you advice.

The mechanism behind this transformation is simple, but it's not obvious. Most of us, when put in the position of advisor, want our advice to be sound. We want to think that we're competent. We want our advice to work. Ultimately, some part of our self-image is tied up in that outcome. If the advice doesn't work, our self-image suffers, and, psychologically speaking, that's not something we enjoy. Cognitive dissonance comes into play (see "Making Psychology Work for You," below).

Making Psychology Work for You

In 1841, Ralph Waldo Emerson published *Self-Reliance,* a book of essays that included what is, perhaps, his most famous remark: "A foolish consistency is the hobgoblin of little minds." As generally remembered today, we've somehow managed to omit the word "foolish" from the quotation, and we assume that Emerson disdained consistency without qualification.

Foolish or not, though, modern psychology doesn't really buy what Emerson is selling. Consistency doesn't just poison "little minds." It motivates minds of all sizes. Consistency is something we seek, because, as a rule, we're not comfortable holding two opposing thoughts at the same time. In modern terms, we experience "cognitive dissonance." And we'll alter our opinions, and even our behavior, to achieve some degree of psychological consistency.

The "Ben Franklin Effect" is one example of cognitive dissonance in action. In 1736, when he was appointed clerk of the Massachusetts General Assembly, Franklin had a political opponent who favored another candidate for the position. Franklin liked being clerk and the "very profitable" opportunity it gave him to be the government's printer. Naturally, he wanted to turn his opponent into an ally.

Conventional wisdom would hold that the rival would be more kindly disposed if Franklin did him favors. Franklin did the opposite. *He asked his foe for a favor*—he borrowed a book—and found that his former enemy was suddenly much more of a friend. As Franklin saw it, "He that has once done you a kindness will be more ready to do you another, than he whom you yourself have obliged." In short, Franklin used cognitive dissonance to his advantage.

In other words, doing a favor for someone you don't even like creates an uncomfortable dissonance. To relieve the psychological tension, something has to give, and it's usually the attitude: "Since I did this guy a favor, I must like him, because I wouldn't do a favor for someone I didn't like." Note that it's never a question of persuasion. The mechanism works because it involves taking an action that conflicts with a person's state of mind.

In the informational interview, we'd like to see a similar process take shape. Once you've elicited advice from your contact, they become an advisor. They didn't start out in that role. When you walked in the door, you were merely a brief, possibly pleasant, interlude. Once you elicited advice, they start to have an investment in its quality. Ultimately, that investment can extend to the results if you follow that advice. In the best case, they start to act as a mentor.

The bottom line: Anything that encourages your contact to take on the advisory role is something that is worth pursuing.

As we'll see, whatever the advice is, it's your job to follow up. We want to be able to return to this contact for further ideas if his initial ones don't yield results. That can be crucial, but you can't be passive. Whatever the advice is, give it a try. If it goes nowhere, so be it, but put yourself in a position to report back. If you can't explain how you acted on the initial advice, it's impossible to come back for more help.

Next Steps

You may have noticed that the last set of questions were hypothetical in nature. We will now leave the world of hypotheticals behind, though, because we're about to tackle something very real and very important.

In this stage, questions are all about what's next. For someone in my position, what would be the best thing to do next? What resources would be most valuable to someone like me at this point? What should I investigate next given my particular background?

You get the idea. These are all questions designed to prevent this interview from turning into a dead end. If things have gone especially well, you can ask who you might speak with next and, if your contact seems enthusiastic, ask if you can use his name.

There are areas you can omit from the "big talk" part of the interview. This is not one of them. Questions about the industry and about your contact's career are not irrelevant or unimportant, but they're not critical. Questions that deal with next steps are the ones that get your contact thinking about where you go from here, and that's what gets your job search moving.

 7 Informational Interview Success Tips

1. *Dress for the occasion.* Dress as you would for a real job interview. If in any doubt, err on the side of formality.

2. *Be prompt.* In fact, there's no harm in getting to the interview 15 minutes early. Make allowances for delays and, if you really want to be sure of things, take a trip to the site in advance. You don't want to show up after a frantic search for a location you had trouble finding.

3. *Prepare questions.* You don't need to do full-blown rehearsals for an informational interview, although it can't hurt, but do prepare some questions in advance.

4. *Take notes.* Ask your contact first, but notes can be useful reminders of what happened when it comes time to follow up. Don't, however, use your laptop. Pen and paper are much less intrusive.

5. *Turn off your phone.* Please!

6. *Don't overstay your welcome.* Stay conscious of the amount of time your contact has committed, and be sure to get your "next steps" questions in before it's time to go. Follow your contact's lead, though. If they're in no rush, there's no need to race to the door.

7. *Be nice to everyone.* Be courteous to everyone you meet, whether it's the CEO or the receptionist. Remember, you never know who might be helpful down the road.

Bonus Tip!

Prepare, at least in one respect, as if this were a real interview. The reason is simple. Early on, your contact may make a very typical interview request: Tell me about yourself. It's a natural inquiry, so don't leave it to chance. Arm yourself with a two-minute answer, and, in this case, rehearse instead of trusting on-the-spot improvisational skills.

There's More Where That Came From

If you're in need of inspiration, here are some additional industry and career questions, all adaptable to your specific situation.

Industry

- What do you see as the major trends affecting the industry? How has that changed from previous years?

- What challenges does the industry face? How are companies meeting those challenges? Are there clear distinctions between organizational approaches?

- What kind of educational background is most valuable in the industry? Has that always been the case? Are there new developments in terms of training?

- What skills are most valued? Has that changed over the years? What skills do you think will be valuable in the future?

- What informational resources are most popular in the field? Is there a publication or a website, for example, that's mandatory?

- What's the most common way for people to enter the field? What's the best way?

- How would you characterize the outlook for employment in the industry?

- What qualities distinguish companies in this industry? What sets the successful ones apart?

Career

- What first interested you about this field and about your position?

- What's a typical day like? Has that changed over time?

- Was your path to this position typical? Was it unusual? In either case, in what ways has this been true?

- Has your career been more centered on individual work or on functioning as part of a team?

- What were your expectations when you started out? Have those expectations been met? Have they changed? What would your expectations be if you were starting today?

- What are the best and worst parts of your job? How would you change things?

- Knowing what you know today, would you have approached your career differently? What do you wish you had known when you were starting out?

- What parts of your background contributed most to your success? What was the most important part of your education? What was the most valuable part of your experience?

- What parts of your career have you found most challenging? How did you handle those challenges? Are they the challenges you expected to face earlier in your career? How are they the same or different?

- What parts of your career have been most rewarding? What is it about those parts that put them in that category? Have those rewards come as a surprise? How do they compare with your expectations earlier in your career?

- What parts of your career do you expect to be most rewarding in the future? Where do you expect to encounter challenges?

- What sort of background would you see as ideal for someone entering the field? Has that changed? How close was your background to that ideal? What would the ideal background look like today?

FOLLOWING UP

Regardless of how your informational interview turned out, your work is not done when you leave the room.

At the very least, even for an informational interview that went nowhere, you are going to thank all contacts for their time. The best way to express your thanks is by email, and the best time—in fact, the only time—is within a day of your appointment. Don't let this task linger.

Writing your thank you note shouldn't be a difficult job, especially because this is another example of the virtue of keeping things short and sweet. You don't need to use more than three sentences: one to offer your thanks; a second, optional sentence to mention a highlight; and a third to cover the future.

You don't need to recap the whole interview. You don't need to elaborate on anything or to supply additional background, unless you were asked. You don't need to attach a resume—again, unless asked. You need to get to the point, hit a highlight, look to the future, and sign off.

Subject: Thank you

Dear Mr. Trump:
Thank you very much for taking the time to meet with me yesterday. I found your advice very helpful, especially your thoughts on hairstyles for the budding megalomaniac.

If you have any additional advice, I would certainly appreciate it. In any case, I'll try to update you on my progress going forward.

Thank you again,
Barack

 ### Don't Put the Cart Before the Horse

For job seekers, it can be a little worrisome when companies in every field proudly extol their commitment to the idea of hiring only superstars. Take it from us, hiring managers won't readily admit it, but the fact is that "good enough" is often good enough to get you hired. That's why past performance is such an important indicator. They have neither the time nor the tools to comb through towering stacks of applications in search of the best, and, even if they had endless time and every tool known to man, they can't guarantee that only the best would be identified.

Whatever the reason, don't let it worry you—*because you don't want to be hired.*

If that sounds strange, it shouldn't, because it makes perfect sense as part of the systematic, step-by-step job search we're advocating. Getting hired is a goal, of course, but it's a goal for another day. Today's goal is smaller. Today, we're enlisting the aid of contacts who can better your odds.

What does this have to do with you? For many of us, it becomes too easy to be distracted by the perfect outcome—in this case, the offer of a job—and the pursuit of that outcome can be paralyzing. Looking only at the best possible outcome can lead us to neglect the little things that move us in the right direction, even if they don't immediately get us to the ultimate goal.

Voltaire, in a poem he included among his "moral stories," said, "The best is the enemy of the good," a sentiment that has since been repeated in many contexts. It's there, for instance, in the Pareto Principle, the 80/20 Rule that tells us to put our efforts into the things that are likely to pay off. If we wait for perfection before we act, we'll be waiting a long time—or we may never act at all.

So don't get distracted by the best outcome. Just get first downs. Keep moving forward, understanding that not every play has to end in a touchdown.

At this point in your search, you can extend your forward progress by following up with contacts, and that is what matters most.

At this point, only a day after your meeting, you won't have had time to act on any recommendations you received in the interview, but your email accomplishes three things:

- First, it supports whatever positive impression you were able to make.

- Second, it commits you to further action with respect to this contact.

- Third, it keeps your name in front of your contact.

That third item is very important. Don't forget that your contact is much less interested in your job search than you are. They won't, as a matter of course, remember that they have a candidate out there who may be a decent fit for a job opening, and they certainly won't be actively seeking openings on your behalf.

On the other hand, they may hear of openings in a casual way. Ordinarily, they may pay that information no mind. When their reminded that you're out there, however, they may pay a little more attention. So when they hear of something, they may think of you. If the stars are properly aligned, they may just pass your name along to a colleague or a hiring manager.

Take a moment to put yourself in the position of the hiring manager faced with a stack of 100 resumes, 99 of which came in response to a posting on the web. There's one, though, that's slightly different; it's the one that reached you via Fred in marketing. Guess which one you'll look at first.

Anything that gives you the slightest edge is valuable, and an application with a familiar name attached has a head start. When your contact hears of an opening, you want your name to come to mind, and you want to increase the odds of that happening. That's the purpose of doing additional post-interview follow-up on a regular basis. Your job search is not at the top of your contact's to-do list, so they may need an occasional nudge to keep you in mind.

How frequent should those nudges be? A monthly email is enough. Weekly is too much. If you're too persistent, you risk being remembered in a bad light. "Here's another message from that kid I met with two weeks ago. I feel like I've subscribed to his newsletter. If I'd seen this coming, I never would have met with him in the first place." The "spam" folder awaits the overly persistent. That is not the place you want to be.

What about content? What should you be saying in those monthly nudges to get the best results? Again, simplicity rules the day. Your email should be short and to the point. Again, you want to thank your contact for meeting with you. Again, you'll refer to whatever advice you received in your initial meeting.

The Art of the Nudge

The similarity to the initial follow-up email ends there. Your path now changes direction. This time, you're going to report back with results. Your exact report will depend on the advice you received in the informational interview.

- *If your contact advised you to consult a source of information that is not a person:* In other words, your contact didn't suggest that you make an additional contact with someone else in the industry. In this case, you're no less grateful for the recommendation than you would have been if they'd given you a name. Mention something about your meeting. Thank them for whatever advice you received. Let them know that you acted on that advice and that you found it helpful—even if that's a stretch—and let them know, perhaps, how it was helpful. Ask if they have any additional advice, and tell them you'll be back in touch to keep them posted.

Dear The Donald:
Thank you again for meeting with me last month. I was especially interested in what you had to say about delusional behavior in public life, and your personal analysis of that situation was uniquely informative.

I've followed your suggestion to make American Pompadour a part of my regular reading, and that's been enormously helpful in keeping abreast of the hidden trends that drive the business world. I'm now much more in tune with cutting-edge tonsorial research.

If you have any additional advice, I'd be very grateful, and I'll keep you informed of any developments.

- *If your contact advised you to contact another person, and that person didn't respond:* The same rules apply. You're still grateful for the advice. You'll still refer to something from the original conversation. Let him know that you acted on their advice without success, but do so without saying anything negative about the advice or about the person you tried to reach. Only the second paragraph needs to change, and it doesn't need to be at all complicated.

    I followed your suggestion that I approach Mr. Romney, who I'm sure would be a wonderful resource, but we haven't been able to make contact quite yet. Do you have any other suggestions of whom I might contact if I don't succeed with Mr. Romney?

- *If your contact advised you to contact another person and you've had a response:* The message stays much the same, again with only the second paragraph changing. Here, you want to acknowledge the referral and report on the results.

    I followed your recommendation that I approach Mr. Romney, and I'm happy to report that we've spoken by phone and he has offered to meet with me next week. I'm enormously excited to have this opportunity, and I want to thank you again for your suggestion.

Notice that nothing much changes from message to message. In each case, you'll continue asking for advice and promising the occasional update. The only difference is the specific report you're delivering about a particular piece of advice you received.

Once you have one email written, it can serve as a template for the rest. The job does not have to be arduous unless you continually reinvent the wheel. Remember, only the names and details change. In fact, as time goes on, your messages get simpler. You don't have to refer to your first meeting and the incredible insight you obtained. If nothing specific has happened, stick to generalities. You're continuing to follow through on your contact's suggestions, and you'd welcome additional advice if they have any. If this sounds superfluous, never forget that a large part of our purpose is simply to remind your busy and distracted contact that you're still out there.

Some contacts will not respond. First of all, let's not make too much of this. When you start contacting people, be prepared for a good deal of failure. Assume that you will not make great progress with most of the people you approach. You'll find that, even after agreeing to an interview, some contacts won't stay in touch. For them, the interview was no more than an obligation. Having discharged that obligation, they're not really interested in joining your team. That's the very predictable nature of the beast, and it's why your list of potential contacts is not limited to one or two names. Understand that it's nothing personal, so there is no reason to add pressure to an already stressful experience by seeing any of this as a reflection of your shortcomings. That is absolutely, unequivocally, and inarguably *not* what's happening here.

Should you write off unresponsive contacts at some point? Certainly a reasonable argument can be made that you should conserve your energy for the contacts who seem more invested in your situation. It harks back to the 80/20 Rule: Save your energy for the contacts who are most likely worth your time. The problem with that argument, however, is twofold: First, you can't really tell who will be most helpful in the end; second, with a systematic approach, the expenditure of energy is hardly prohibitive. The fact that you've sent an email and received no reply really tells you very little. Is your contact on vacation? Swamped with work? Distracted by something else? If you don't have a hotline to your contact's psyche, you just don't know. Take 10 minutes and send a short, simple email based on your template. If nothing else, remind your contact of your existence. You have nothing at all to lose.

An Organized Job Seeker Is an Effective Job Seeker

If you keep working your contact list, you may find yourself corresponding with more than one of your contacts. That is, in fact, the goal. You want to have a lot of irons in the fire, but managing all those irons can make things confusing. With multiple contacts in the works, each one may be in a different stage of the follow-up process. Keeping it all straight is not a challenge if you're organized. Decide on a schedule that works for you—monthly is always an option—and add each event to your calendar. If you met on September 1, send your thank you email the next day, and schedule future emails for October 2, November 2, and so on. Be systematic.

If you have more than one contact in the works, your systematic approach can help keep track of scheduling your emails, but you can still lose track of who said what. Here, though, you'll get help from the way you handled the informational interview itself. You'll be able to keep things straight because you took notes during your informational interview. Refer to those notes and you'll never be lost. You did take notes, didn't you? Now you know why.

What if the stars do align, as we said earlier—and you strike gold? Your contact gave you a name or got you to a hiring manager, and you made it through three rounds of interviews and got the job. Congratulations! But don't forget about that contact who started the ball rolling. They deserve your thanks and to know what happened. You don't want to run into them at an industry event six months from now and have them realize that you didn't think enough of them to report back. Be sure to thank them profusely for their role in your success. Then you can celebrate.

Key Lessons

✦ An informational interview is a chance to meet briefly with someone in your field to talk about that person's company, career, and the industry as a whole.

✦ Use email to request the interview, mention your referral or connection, state why you want to meet, and promise to follow up.

✦ Send a follow-up email or call if you don't receive a response by your deadline, but if you call, be prepared to launch the interview right then.

✦ An informational interview that yields a referral is a success, and you will be more likely to achieve this if your contact likes you.

✦ Prepare for your interview by researching current trends in the industry, the latest developments at your contact's company, and your contact's professional life.

✦ Structure your interview around questions related to each of these categories: industry, career, advice, and next steps.

✦ The goal isn't to get the best possible advice, but to encourage your contact to see himself as a mentor who is invested in the outcome of your job search.

✦ Don't skip the "next steps" category because these are questions that will get your contact to think about where you go from here and get your job search moving.

✦ Send a thank you email within a day of your appointment, then send monthly updates on your progress to stay at the top of your contact's mind.

Chapter 15

Interview Skills, Part 1: *In the Mind of the Interviewer*

"Death will be a relief. No more interviews."
—Katharine Hepburn

It doesn't matter what the position is, the job interview is the final step in the job search. If you've been nominated to the Supreme Court, the inquisitors ensconced in the Senate chamber want to spend some quality time with you. If you've applied to your local McDonald's, the store manager insists on having a word.

Job interviews make a lot of sense. The Senate wants to know how good you are at giving platitudinous answers that, while closely resembling actual sentences, are as lacking in substance as possible. The store manager wants to know that you can follow simple instructions and answer a few questions without leaping over the counter and beating your customer.

Why does it all come down to the interview? They want to have a look at you, of course. In one study, a 1965 survey of 852 organizations, 99 percent believed in the power of the interview. Interviews have "an intuitive appeal" for hiring managers, whether they're being conducted in 1965, in 2013 or, it's pretty safe to say, in 2065.

The interview may not be going away, but, on another level, it does start to look a little odd. Does a good interview translate to a good employee? Is there any reason to think it would? Conversely, does a bad interview mean a hire you'll regret?

To researchers, validity and reliability are two different measures of how well a particular method gets its results. Reliability is the measure of how similarly two different interviewers rate the same interview. Validity is the measure of how well the interview predicts future job performance. Suffice it to say, interviews are far from perfect on either measure.

How bad are they? One study found that they're a whopping 3 percent better than simply picking a name out of a hat. When prospective colleagues are doing the selecting, they operate at a level 2 percent worse than random chance. On the whole, interview assessments manage to predict only 2 percent of ultimate performance.

Be all that as it may, we're stuck with them, and, even though there is evidence that some types of interviews—the highly structured ones, for example—are better than others, you're in no position to neglect any of the highly imperfect possibilities that may come your way.

To do that, it makes a great deal of sense to treat the process systematically and to emphasize one underlying theme. Here, that theme is simple, and it stems from an assessment of the one field in which job skills are analogous to interview skills: sales. To have a successful career in sales, you have to be good at selling. To have a successful interview for a sales position, you have to be good at selling yourself. After all, if you can't sell yourself, how likely is it that you'll be good at selling anything else?

And that's the theme that underlies the interview. It's about selling yourself as the right candidate for the job. In fact, it's the same theme that has applied to the job search over and over again. The search is a marketing campaign in which you use all the tactics at your disposal to convince prospective buyers that they should make an investment in you.

Is this a cynical view? Perhaps, but the alternative is a "purer" approach characterized by total honesty and forthrightness. With that approach, you're committed to putting the most honest version of yourself on display, warts and all, rather than showing off the best possible version of that same self. If honesty compels you to tell the interviewer that his questions are moronic, do so by all means, and you may be canonized among applicants who refuse to bow to the reality of the marketplace. You won't, however, find yourself a job.

Take it as a given, then, that all job interviews are invalid and unreliable to some significant degree, and we just have to make the best of a bad situation.

Faced with this mess of a hiring tool, there's no reason to look askance at the idea of "gaming" this very broken system. Even people who admit that interviews are deeply flawed show no signs of giving them up. Many of those same people, while acknowledging the general flaws, are quite convinced that they are the exceptions to the rule. "Everyone else may be doing it wrong, but my interviews are a different story. I'll stop doing them when you pry my clipboard from my cold, dead hands."

INTERVIEW PRIMER

Troubled as it is, the interview is, after all, the inevitable culmination of the job search. As such, an invitation should be cause for celebration, but that's often not the case. Interviews are the cause of great trepidation for many. How could it be otherwise, when it's such an arbitrary and unreliable process?

In fact, though, interviews themselves are hardly random. They follow predictable patterns. Questions adhere to a few different styles. There are bad answers, good answers, and better answers, and once you understand how interviews work, they become much more manageable. Nervousness may never disappear completely, but it no longer has to rule the day.

To get to that point, however, you have to learn all you can about interviews—how to prepare for them and how to handle them. You have to know how to operate no matter what interviewers throw at you. In short, you must learn to play the game in all its grisly variations.

To do that, there's a lot of ground to cover. But don't worry, that's what we'll be doing in this chapter and the next two.

- What are interviewers thinking?

- What are they looking for, and why?

- What styles of interviews will you encounter?

- What happens when you're operating by phone or video?

- What's hot this year? What's not?

- What questions will they ask? What answers should I give?

- What can you do to prepare? What should you do?

- And, of course, what should you do in the interview itself, and what should you avoid at all costs?

Pay no further attention to the question of whether an interview is worth the time it takes. It is what it is. We're stuck with it, for better or worse. All you can do is take it as it comes, and be the better interviewee no matter what's happening across the desk.

WHAT DO INTERVIEWERS WANT?

The best way to start analyzing the job interview is by looking into the minds of the people doing the interviewing, and the best place to start that psychoanalysis is by asking what the interview is trying to accomplish. What's the goal? Why are you conducting an interview in the first place?

If we can answer that question, we can look at the ways interviewers determine whether a given interview has met that goal. Some interviewers make that analysis difficult. They can't articulate actual reasons. They "go with their guts." They can "just tell" when someone is right. Still, we can look a bit deeper and get beyond that line of unscientific thought, ultimately painting a more complete picture.

To begin at the beginning, what's the goal of an interview? The goal is simply *to select the best possible candidate from among a set of interviewees.*

It's worth noting that the set of interviewees is not necessarily equal to the set made up of the very best applicants. You've gone to great lengths to secure some slight advantage—in this case, a personal connection—that would place you among the interviewees.

What do we mean by "best possible candidate?" The answer gets us to an important point, one that was central to earlier stages in the search that involved things like crafting effective resumes and cover letters. The best possible candidate is the one who is seen as bringing the most benefit to the employer. It's as simple as that.

In other words, the selection process takes place in a very specific context. You are selling yourself to the employer, and your sales proposition is based on the benefits they will receive if you are hired. Ask not what the employer can do for you; ask what you can do for the employer. Keep that thought in mind.

We now have two principles to apply to the interview, but they're awfully general. We haven't really gotten inside the heads of interviewers, and we need to give those principles life to make them useful.

One shortcut to the interviewer's psyche is to put yourself in their shoes. Picture this: You're running a business that has one employee, one product, and only one goal. In this exercise, you're the employee. You're also the product, and the sole goal of the business is to mount a job search that ends in an offer.

So far, then, we're talking about a situation that's not hypothetical in the least, but we'll add one further circumstance. After some efforts at searching on your own, you've decided to get some help. You're going to hire someone to take charge of this operation.

You've advertised, describing the job and asking for resumes. You've narrowed the field to three, and you're going to meet with each one before making a decision.

On Equal Footing?

We're assuming that your three candidates are, at this point, relatively equal. Imagine, though, if you got one name from a friend, or from a friend of a friend, or from one of your uncle's colleagues. Is there some chance that recommendation helped place this candidate among the finalists? Do the three interviewees still occupy a level playing field, or does one of them have a bit of a head start? Do you have the slightest doubt about the value of a helpful contact?

Well, Mr. Interviewer, what do you want to know? Obviously, you want to hire the person most likely to give you the most help. They all look good on paper. How will you decide?

Here are a few things you, the interviewer, may want to know:

- *Where, if at all, do paper and reality diverge?* This person looks very successful on paper, but he's probably making himself look as good as possible and leaving out his less successful moments. How does he cope when things aren't going well?

- *Regardless of the success this person has had on behalf of others, how do I know he'll do the job for me?* My one-man company is a special company. It's not like the others. It has its own culture. Will this candidate's success translate to this unique environment?

- *What if the search drags on?* Will he be there for the long haul, or will he ditch me in a heartbeat if a better offer comes along?

- *Does this person seem to have the knowledge I need?* Does he know what makes a good resume? Is he well-versed in the different styles of interviews? Does he understand what aspects of my background I should emphasize in the search?

- *Does he seem to get the idea that the point of all this is to get me hired?* Is he looking hard at helping me reach my goals? Has he come prepared with workable strategies?

- *What would it be like working with him on a project of such great personal importance?*

They Like Me; They Really Like Me!

It's not hard to compile a long list of questions, but the ultimate issue in all this is often reduced to the simplest possible terms: Do I find this applicant likable? Put another way, the question sounds like this: Is this a person I want to work with? Despite its vagueness, that question frequently trumps all others.

"Likability" is not a scientifically measurable characteristic, but it probably works well enough in a personal hiring effort in which you expect to be working one-on-one as you navigate the job market. However, transposed into a more typical hiring environment, one in which you're evaluating multiple candidates for multiple positions on a regular basis, it becomes increasingly difficult to base hiring decisions on the likability factor. Smaller organizations may still have interviews conducted by repurposed managers with no particular expertise in hiring, but larger organizations are much more likely to systematize the interview process. Even with multiple interviewers, they may stick to a standard script throughout. They may implement scoring systems that give at least the illusion of objectivity. They may proceed in stages, with different interviewers responsible for different phases of the process.

Don't be misled. Likability, as an acknowledged factor or not, is always going to play a part in the decision.

Happily, interviewees can take steps to make themselves as likable as possible—or, at least, they can take steps to ensure that they're not terribly unlikable. Those steps are specific, practical things that will make a difference. There are similar steps that help throughout the process, with good interviewers and bad, in structured interviews, unstructured interviews, behavioral interviews, group interviews, video interviews, and every other interview permutation. Too often, candidates are told to show up on time and look confident. Be focused and positive, intelligent and knowledgeable, bright-eyed and bushy-tailed, but there's nary a hint of how, exactly, to make all those wonderful qualities shine through.

For a first small step, start here: Again, put yourself in the shoes of the interviewer. What questions would you ask? Why is this interviewer asking that particular question? What does she hope to learn? What answers would you be looking for? What would the best applicant look like given the characteristics of this particular job? What qualities would convince you that this person would be great for the organization?

Always keep the employer's perspective in mind as we look more closely at the interview in the following chapter.

Key Lessons

+ An interview is all about selling yourself as the right candidate for the job and convincing a prospective employer to make an investment in you.

+ The interviewer's goal is to select the best possible candidate from among the interviewees, meaning the person who appears to bring the most benefit to the employer.

+ Likability will always play a part in the hiring decision.

+ Always keep the employer's perspective in mind during interviews.

Chapter 16

Interview Skills, Part 2: *What to Know Before You Go*

"Luck, that's when preparation and opportunity meet."

—Pierre Trudeau

Even before they consider the kinds of questions interviewers are likely to ask, applicants can use the view from across the desk as a guide to effective preparation. What does the interviewer expect you to know? What do they want you to know?

Think back to your hypothetical efforts to hire someone to help you in your search. You'd expect your candidate to be, at a minimum, familiar with their own abilities and experience. You'd want them to know something about the kind of position you want. You'd hope they know something about the field in which you want to work and about the companies operating in that field.

This is not rocket science. You should arrive at the interview armed with basic knowledge of four very relevant areas.

1. You

You'd think that applicants would have this one covered. What could be more basic than knowing the details of your own background? Doesn't that go without saying?

It's almost that simple, but there's a catch, one frequently overlooked in interview preparation. The "you" that's open to inspection in the interview is the person who embodies all the information contained in your resume. There's every chance that you haven't actually read over that resume recently. You prepared it last year, and you've had no reason to revisit the document. It's no longer fresh in your mind.

Do, please, review your resume before the interview. Assume that your interviewer will have reviewed it as well. Sadly, this isn't always the case, but we'll be generous and assume some minimal level of interviewer competence. Go over your resume with an eye toward questions that an interviewer might ask. Perhaps there's a job description that's rather vague. Maybe your college major isn't an obvious fit for your career. Or you spent only six months at one of your former jobs. Details like these can attract an interviewer's attention.

When you prepare a resume, it's always a good idea to get a second opinion on its effectiveness, and that advice applies again. Have a friend take a look. Is there something she doesn't understand? Does she wonder about something you said? An interviewer is likely to have the same response, so take those reactions to heart.

2. The Job

Take time to think about the position you've applied for and the qualities that matter in that job. If you're applying for a back-office bookkeeping position, organization and attention to detail mean a lot. Superior customer service skills matter less. In the interview, focus on the things that matter in your desired role, even if you are the very model of versatility.

Be sure to review the job description. When a company posts its requirements, it generally, if not always, means what it says. The exception, of course, is the posting that asks for "bright, energetic team players" or something similarly generic. When that's no help, a bit of sleuthing within your own resume is in order. What was it that got you the interview? What skills did your resume showcase that would have attracted this employer's interest?

In other words, we're still trying to see things through the interviewer's eyes. There's something about you that got you here. Whatever that "something" is, a successful interview will reinforce the idea that you're blessed with that quality.

3. The Company

Hard as it may be to believe, the job market battlefield is littered with the corpses of applicants who weren't quite sure what the interviewing company did. If they knew what it did, they didn't know what it was doing lately.

Given that one of our interview themes is your ability to benefit this employer, ignorance can be fatal. Learn what you can about the company before the interview. Visit its website. Check the latest news. See what you can glean from Facebook and LinkedIn. Visit the company's Twitter feed. The more you know, the better you'll be able to synchronize your skills and experience with the company's needs. First, though, you need to have a sense of those needs.

If nothing else, it gives you ammunition when you're asked to explain your interest in working for this company.

4. The Industry

The job you're applying for exists within a company, and that company exists within an industry. We don't have to go beyond that. Interviewers won't pose existential dilemmas for you to contemplate, but you should know something about the field in which you want to work.

This may seem like another obvious area of knowledge that must be part of your repertoire already—you want to work in this field, after all—but it's worth refreshing your industry-specific recollection, especially as it pertains to the company. What are the latest industry trends? What issues are likely to be on people's minds? How have those trends and issues affected this company?

Your interviewer is probably well aware of all these trends and issues. They may well figure into the company's hiring decisions. They may have something to do with your possible role with this employer at this point in time. Especially if there's big recent news, you don't want to be caught short if the subject comes up.

Investigate industry news through any source you can find. Take an Internet tour of competitors' sites. Are there industry-shaking product announcements? Is there a blockbuster management change? Has a company been bought out? Does another seem to be going under? You don't necessarily need to learn a lot about these things, but you do need to make yourself aware.

When Time Is Short

Sometimes, you won't have the luxury of sufficient time to make a detailed study of all four areas. Your phone rings. They want to see you tomorrow. When that happens, hit the highlights:

- ☐ Review your resume.

- ☐ Review the job description.

- ☐ Think about the ways in which the resume and description match.

- ☐ Visit the company's website.

- ☐ Pay attention to its mission statement, and consider that statement in light of your background.

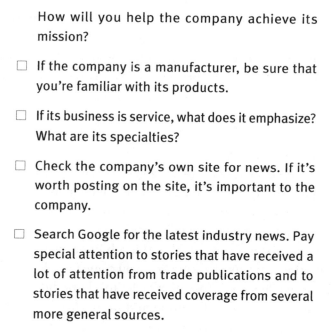

How will you help the company achieve its mission?

☐ If the company is a manufacturer, be sure that you're familiar with its products.

☐ If its business is service, what does it emphasize? What are its specialties?

☐ Check the company's own site for news. If it's worth posting on the site, it's important to the company.

☐ Search Google for the latest industry news. Pay special attention to stories that have received a lot of attention from trade publications and to stories that have received coverage from several more general sources.

Even if you only have an evening at your disposal, you can accomplish all this in a couple of hours.

Your investigation has another important benefit: It provides you with a basis for your own interview questions, something to say when the interviewer asks if there's anything you'd like to know. They will ask, and that can be a golden moment for you. Before we tackle that opportunity, one that typically comes late in the interview, we'd better spend some time with the other side of the coin, the questions you're likely to be asked.

THE USUAL SUSPECTS

Interview questions come in many different varieties. Some good, some bad, some indifferent, and some simply weird—you never know what an interviewer is likely to ask.

Despite that uncertainty, there are some questions for which you must prepare. It's not that they're the best questions. To the contrary, they're often the ones asked by an interviewer who doesn't know any better. The problem for you is there are a lot of those interviewers out there. As a result, you cannot afford to ignore the usual suspects.

Tell Me About Yourself

This is hardly one of the more egregious examples. It's an open-ended inquiry that can make for a good introduction to the interview and a good jumping-off point for further questions, but it's not another way of asking for your autobiography. Limit your answer to things relevant to your career and to this job in particular. Think of the question as a way of asking how you came to be here today. What have you done in the past that's relevant? How did it lead you here? What is the source of your interest in this field and, especially, in this position with this company?

Why Do You Want This Job?

It's a fair question. The problem is that many truthful answers won't get you hired. You need the money. You need a job, period. There aren't many openings out there, but you saw this one posted.

In the job interview, honesty is almost never the best policy. Surely, a practical-minded employer should respect a forthright, practical-minded answer, but that's not the way the game is played.

And it is a game, with its own customs and rules, so you're not encouraged, or even expected, to be brutally honest. You do, however, have to be credible. In addition, remember, your answer shouldn't focus on the ways you'll benefit, but on the benefit you'll bring to the employer. There's no harm in saying it's a job you'd enjoy and one you'd be awfully good at, but it's not hard to tie those qualities into an employer-focused response.

Since you've done your research, you should have a handle on what's been happening lately at this organization. Whatever the news may be, it's worth considering ways to relate that news to this answer. Perhaps the company has some new products in the works. You'd like to be part of the launch, and you're especially enthusiastic because you've been through something similar, you found yourself right at home with the complicated logistics involved, and you want to put those skills to work at a moment that's bound to be exciting. You also know how challenging that moment can be, but you've risen to that challenge before and you're even better prepared to meet it now—ready and willing to bring your abilities to bear wherever they might be useful.

Take note: "Why should we hire you?" is a similar question that calls for a similar approach. You should hire me, not because I could really use one of those free massages your company provides, but because I have knowledge, experience, and skills that perfectly match the position. They will be great for the organization, especially at a time when you're bringing that new gizmo—a gizmo I know all about, by the way—to market.

What Are Your Greatest Strengths?

It may be excessive to call this question the last refuge of the interviewing scoundrel, but only because its continued presence is not clear evidence of scoundrel-like behavior. Sometimes, interviewers don't know what else to ask, so they resort to this and its sibling, the "greatest weaknesses" question. Everyone prepares for this one. Every answer is less than spontaneous.

Even so, interviewers are unfazed, and the question continues to plague interviewees everywhere. To deal with it, take inventory of your strengths. You can probably arrive at a decent list if you think back to the questions related to career decisions and the accomplishments you included in your resume. The key here, though, is to take that global list and narrow it down. Look back at the job description or, if that's lacking, look at job descriptions from other companies for this same position. If none of that helps, think about the job-related strengths an employer would likely value.

The goal, after you've done all that inventorying, looking, and thinking, is a set of strengths that's relevant to the specific position. Those are the ones to emphasize. If you're applying for a back-office accounting job, customer service skills are probably not highly valued. Meticulous attention to detail is.

What Are Your Greatest Weaknesses?
There are four options here. Only one of them works.

- Option 1: *You have no weaknesses.* After a great deal of reflection and analysis, an extended period of soul-searching and intense meditation, you've finally had to admit that you're weakness-free. Godspeed to you, perfect being. You'll have to find another place where people will appreciate your perfection, because you won't be working here.

- Option 2: *You have a landslide of weaknesses.* After that same period of reflection, you've come to realize that you're just a mess. If you're at all tempted to go with this approach, first make sure that your trust fund is still there for you. Next, go back to the beginning and start over.

The "Real" Questions
We're looking at a range of questions, but it's only a slight exaggeration to say that they don't really mean a thing. It's not that you can ignore them. You need to know the questions you're likely to hear so they don't take you by surprise. Time spent thinking about your answers beforehand is time well spent, especially if

you're like most of us and the best answers don't always roll off the tongue.

Despite that, there are just two questions that matter. Everything else is camouflage for what every interviewer is really asking:

1. *Can you do the job?*

2. *Can we work with you?*

It's not always immediately apparent that those are the questions on the table, but everything always comes back to the not-so-hidden agenda of those two questions.

There can certainly be complications, since a simple yes or no answer doesn't always tell the whole story. Yes, you can do the job, but, then again, another candidate can do it better. Yes, we think we can work with him, but we'd really like to work with her. Despite those less absolute answers, even other questions that seem basic—Will you stick around if we hire you?—are really extensions of the big two. For example, an employer who wonders if you'll stick around is not posing a separate question. He's simply defining longevity as part of what goes into doing the job.

Can he do the job . . . even if he'll only be here for a month?

Can we work with him . . . if he's left other jobs within a year?

Both questions also pose the ultimate question, the one to which we always return: Will the company benefit from hiring this person?

The two hidden questions give that ultimate question a more practical slant, and it leaves you with something you can use in the moment. When in doubt about what to say, let the hidden questions guide your approach. Not sure how to describe your strengths? Choose the strengths that show you can do the job at hand.

- Option 3: *My weaknesses are really strengths.* I'm a perfectionist! I work too hard! I care too much! It's been tried many times before. Nobody's buying it. It's an answer that can leave an interviewer wondering if you heard the questions and, if you had, if you'd given your work any thought at all.

- Option 4: *We come at last to a viable option.* Before spelling it out, take a minute to look at things through the employer's eyes again. If you were doing the hiring, would you want someone with real weaknesses? Probably not, but, at the same time, you'd be forced to acknowledge that we all have our weaknesses and that anyone you hire will be imperfect.

Given those competing notions, how will you find someone worth hiring? You wouldn't want someone riddled with weaknesses, but you wouldn't want someone so unaware that he fails to see any weaknesses at all.

You might be willing to go with someone with a flaw or two, provided:

- The flaw is not mission-critical.

- The applicant is aware of that flaw.

- The applicant has taken steps to deal with it, even if it's still a bit of a work in progress.

That's the blueprint for answering a question about your weaknesses. You don't have to provide a litany of all your flaws. Pick one that's at least slightly peripheral. Don't say your phone skills are poor if you're interviewing at a call center. "I've had problems prioritizing in the past, but over the past couple of years I've developed a system of project tracking that combines my calendar and an ordered task list. That way, I can relate every project I'm involved in to deadlines and next steps."

No matter what you say, understand that the last option is the best option. It acknowledges a real weakness and describes a credible method you've used to overcome that weakness or, at least, come to grips with it.

Where Do You See Yourself in Five Years?

Where, indeed? There are many things you just can't say in response to this:

- I hope to be somewhere else.

- I'd like to be working for one of your competitors.

- I don't see much changing.

- In five years, I'll be sitting where you are, and you'll be in charge of getting me coffee.

- Hang on a minute while I get out my deck of tarot cards.

Those are the very obvious "don'ts" when it comes to your future plans. The right thing to say is not terribly exciting. It's another instance of harping on employer benefit, although the specifics vary according to context.

The general idea is that you want to get better at what you do so that you can contribute more. If you're a programmer, you want to become fluent in a new language, one that has some application to this position, or you want to become even better at a language you know. If you're in sales, you want to become the company's best closer, the one who is exceeding his targets year after year. In any field, you want to hone your skills so that you become truly expert, the person who makes every team better.

Depending on how you answered the "weaknesses" question, if it was asked, you can build on that answer. In five years, you'd like to see that you've made a strength out of something that was once a weakness.

Do You Have Any Questions?

Finally, we get a question that's asked by good and bad interviewers alike, sometimes as a matter of simple courtesy, but we don't care about its motivation. If space creatures are interviewing applicants in the neighborhood of Alpha Centauri, they're closing the interview with this social nicety. Of the entire universe of standard, timeworn, hackneyed, and unimaginative questions interviewers ask, however, this is one you should be delighted to hear.

This question is a golden opportunity, which you can take advantage of in several ways, but the important point is that you always have questions:

1. *You can ask questions about the workplace, both in general and with reference to the position.* What sort of training do you offer? How do you handle promotions? How are evaluations managed? How did you come to work for this organization? How do you see the company's culture? Why is this position open right now?

2. *You can ask questions about the company and the industry.* How is the company responding to the latest trends? What consequences will the latest bit of news have for the industry? What are the company's short- and long-term goals?

3. *If you're willing to try something a little different, you can ask questions about your candidacy.* Is there anything missing

from my qualifications? Is there some weakness in my education or experience that I need to deal with? Have I said anything today that's led you to see me as someone who's not a great candidate for the job? Now that we've talked, do you have any reservations about hiring me?

Each series of questions has its own value. The first set shows that you're focused on meaningful workplace issues specific to this position; the second, that you're a knowledgeable candidate who pays attention to broader, industry-wide concerns. The third option is the least comfortable of the three, in some sense turning the tables on the interviewer, but it has value even if the answers are not the ones you want to hear.

If your interviewer has nothing but good things to say, perhaps that will cement your value in his estimation. If, on the other hand, he's expressing doubts, at least you've gotten some feedback—something more valuable than most interviewees take from the many interviews that don't lead to offers.

When Questions Come to the Rescue

When an interviewer resorts to canned questions like most of these, he invites canned answers. Nine out of 10 interviewees will have rehearsed each of the usual suspects. They are, after all, the usual suspects.

That's not the worst consequence of using a series of utterly predictable questions. That distinction is reserved for a side effect that's as predictable as the questions themselves: When an interviewer sticks to this routine, he forecloses any possibility that the interview becomes a conversation. For interviewer and interviewee alike, a conversation is a much more valuable—and potentially illuminating—phenomenon than an interrogation.

While both sides are hurt, it's the interviewee who suffers the most. Think about it. Who are you more likely to see as a potential colleague? Is it the candidate who's been grilled for an hour in a one-sided interaction, or a candidate with whom you've had an interesting and engaging conversation about work?

When an interviewee gets little opportunity to have real communication with the interviewer, he's at a distinct disadvantage. The one thing that stands a chance of rescuing the experience is the possibility that the interviewee takes control, and the one time an interviewee can accomplish that is when he's asked if he has questions of his own. Those questions can lead to a conversation. That's all the more reason to be sure that you've given your own questions a good deal of thought.

AND NOW FOR SOMETHING REALLY DIFFERENT

With the usual-suspects approach open to all sorts of criticism, and with the high cost of hiring always on their minds, hiring managers have spent decades looking for something better, especially something with a basis in science. Today's psychological literature is filled to overflowing with studies of interview techniques, interviewer biases, and nonverbal influencers.

Despite all the study, the perfect interview remains stubbornly elusive. Perhaps it always will, but we don't need to be overly concerned with the frustrations of researchers. For our purposes, the only thing that matters is the influence of the research on the real-world experience. Hiring practices, like those in any field, are subject to trends. Styles come and go. You don't need to know the rational underpinnings, if any, for a given change. If there's a hot new trend, however, you'd better know about it.

What Interviews Are in Vogue Today

At the moment, the trend favors "situational" and "behavioral" questions. To get an idea of what that means, we can return to your own attempt to hire the person best able to help you in your job search.

You could, of course, ask your candidates about their strengths and weaknesses. In response, you'll probably get some vague answers that don't get you very far. People will tell you what they think you want to hear. But what does that mean as a practical matter?

On the other hand, you could try something like this: "Have you had clients who were hearing absolutely nothing after sending out 200 resumes? Were you able to help them at that point? What did you do?" That, in essence, is a behavioral question. Behavioral questions often start with the phrase "Tell me about a time when . . ."

Situational questions are simply hypotheticals called by a different name. Instead of asking you to recount some moment in your working past, they ask you to imagine a situation and describe your response. The key phrase here is "What would you do if . . . ?"

If you wanted to put this same question in situational terms, ask: "If I end up sending out 200 resumes, and I'm getting nowhere, how will you handle that situation?"

Rather than asking for generalities, these questions ask for specifics. The theory, at least, is that interviewers can predict how you'll perform in the future on the basis of your performance in the past. Note, though, that it's not quite so straightforward. The prediction isn't really grounded in past performance. It's grounded in the interviewee's report of that past performance. There's another layer of uncertainty interposed.

As you can see, there's not much difference between situational and behavioral, although the latter requires some relevant past experience on the part of the interviewee.

What if you're asked a behavioral question and don't have that relevant experience in your background? Make it situational: "I haven't had that particular experience, but if it were to happen, here's what I'd do."

The Google-Question Question

Once upon a time, in an enchanted land known for its mountain views, lived a company with very deep pockets. As a tech company, it wanted to fill its offices with the best and brightest of the world's engineers, and it could afford to do just that. But the company's rulers were not satisfied with the usual suspects that every other company asked its job-seeking supplicants. This company, in addition to forswearing evil, had a better idea.

It would administer tests. Those tests, however, would have no obvious connection to the position. Instead, they would be riddles, questions no applicant would anticipate. By answering these riddles, applicants would reveal the innermost workings of their minds. The company didn't care if the answers were right or wrong. In fact, there may be no "right" answer at all—the truth was to be found in the process, not the result.

Our magical company posed questions like:

- How many piano tuners are in New York City?

- Why are manhole covers round?

- How many marbles will it take to fill Google co-founder Sergey Brin's head?

- Devise an evacuation plan for the city of San Francisco.

This new style was a hit. "If this powerhouse of a company is doing it," other companies said, "it must be good."

Hence, the day of the "Google question" came to pass. Other companies—big and small—instructed their hiring wizards to join the bandwagon, even if they didn't quite get the point.

Did it work? Not so much. Google's own wizard, Laszlo Bock, graced with the title SVP of People Operations, was later interviewed in *The New York Times* and had this to say:

". . . we found that brainteasers are a complete waste of time. They don't predict anything. They serve primarily to make the interviewer feel smart." Bock went on to say that, after studying tens of thousands of Google interviews, the company concluded there was "zero relationship" between interview performance and job performance.

Bock, in fact, has serious doubts about applying systems to the hiring process, since human judgment seems to be an irreplaceable part of the equation, but applicants shouldn't ignore Google questions completely. There are plenty of companies still using brainteasers, misguided though they may be.

Interviewees can't prepare for every possible riddle, but the situation can be managed by focusing on the way in which you get to whatever answer you choose. Right answers are not the point. The thought process is what matters. Give interviewers an idea of how you're trying to find a solution, every step of the way. Think out loud and walk them through it. If you can manage that, even the worst answer won't sabotage the entire interview.

Answering Situational and Behavioral Questions

The turn to situational and behavioral questions represents an attempt to systematize the hiring process.

Behavioral Questions

It makes sense, then, that interviewees should look to systematic strategies themselves, and, for behavioral interviews, the best known method is the "STAR" system. The STAR system breaks the response into four components.

1. **Situation:** You can't deal in generalities here. You've already been given a topic—a time when you had to persuade someone to accept your approach, or a time when you dealt with a difficult customer—so you have to get down to cases. Talk about the very specific situation you faced.

2. **Task:** Tell the interviewer what goal you were trying to achieve.

3. **Actions:** What actions did you take?

4. **Result:** What did you achieve? What did you learn?

That's the standard elaboration of the STAR approach, and it's a fine structure, but there are several pitfalls, often overlooked, that deserve your attention.

- **Situation:** With some questions, there's almost an invitation to say negative things. If, for example, you're asked to recount a time when you had to convince your manager that his approach was flawed, you can end up saying all sorts of bad things about that manager. His approach was always flawed. He was an incompetent who slept his way to the top, and you constantly had to rescue him from his terrible decisions. Despite the way some questions seem to invite negativity, stay positive about former colleagues and managers. Negativity is not a quality that's highly valued in the interview room.

- **Task:** Treat this part of your answer similarly. If your goal was to correct the horrible mistakes your supervisor was making, you may be tempted to underline the negatives. Instead, put the emphasis on the positive results you were trying to achieve.

- **Actions:** Here, the pitfall lies in the failure to take the question literally. What did you do? A good answer should not put the emphasis on the actions of others. It's not about what you did as one of many members of a team. Instead, focus on your personal actions. If you're inclined to be modest, and you firmly believe in giving credit where credit is due, you're probably a pleasure to work with. Here, though, you need to give every possible bit of credit to yourself. Otherwise, you're missing an opportunity to sell yourself, and that's what matters in this context.

- **Result:** When talking about what you learned, try to come up with more than one lesson. If you can, think of several ways in which the experience contributed to your growth, enhanced your skills, and increased your competence.

The STAR of the Show

Interviewing is an inexact science. So much is subjective and depends on the interviewer's mood or even the outfit you were wearing, and research has generally failed to correlate good interview performance with good job performance. In response, one format has gained an enduring place in the hearts of hiring managers: the behavioral approach. What is a behavioral interview?

Behind that fancy name is a simple concept. In a behavioral interview, the interviewer asks structured questions about what the interviewee has done in the past. Its hallmark is a six-word introductory phrase: "Tell me about a time when . . ."

- You dealt with a difficult customer.
- You had to meet a very tight deadline.
- You disagreed with a supervisor's approach to a problem.
- You had to deal with a stressful situation.

Interviewers like the behavioral approach because it focuses on actual events. There's little room to give yourself vague credit for doing things you've never actually done, and there's room to probe further into the details of your story.

Like any story, a behavioral response requires structure, and is where the STAR technique comes in.

- Situation or Task: Once you've thought of a relevant story, the answer begins with a description of the situation you faced or task you managed.

- Action: From there, talk about the actions you took in response to that situation.

- Result or Relevance: Finally, describe the result of those actions.

It's a simple approach, but it works. In fact, it's useful even when the questions aren't strictly behavioral. Storytelling is an effective way to draw the listener in, and tying answers to specifics makes those answers more convincing.

Simple or not, though, there are a few strategies that make STAR work well:

- *Arm yourself with stories in advance.* This is no time to improvise and certainly no time to draw a blank.

- *Tailor the stories to the job.* Do your research. What qualities is the employer hoping to find? Those are what your stories should exemplify.

- *Make your stories about you.* They shouldn't focus on the team, your manager, or the company. They have to show what you've done personally.

- *Be specific.* Avoid talking about what you "usually" do. Talk about what you did in a particular situation.

- *Remember, the questions won't all be positive.* They'll be about challenges and problems you faced. Equip yourself with tales of achievement and success, but be prepared with examples that involved making the best of a bad situation.

Situational Questions

Advocates of the situational alternative see it as a way to overcome some of the weaknesses inherent in behavioral interviews. First, the situational question doesn't discriminate against interviewees who haven't had the specific experience at issue. Second, it allows for complete standardization. Interviewers can all ask the same hypothetical questions and rate answers on a scale that, at least in theory, is completely consistent between interviewers. Thus, the interview becomes a more reliable tool.

That's the ideal, but it's not always the reality, and most of the literature in support of the situational approach presupposes very tight control of interviewers and ratings. Outside the laboratory, it's quite common for a situational question to be part of a freewheeling approach to the interview, one that doesn't have room for rating scales and scoring sheets.

Situational answers are, of course, different from behavioral answers. You don't have to cast your mind back to a time when something actually happened, and you don't have to concern yourself with what you learned from the experience.

On the other hand, it helps to elaborate on your answer in two ways. First, talk about not just the action itself, but your rationale for taking whatever action you describe. Employers want someone who thinks about what they're doing. Second, and very much in keeping with the "benefit to the employer" theme, make it clear that your rationale is based on considerations beyond the merely personal. Your choices should be made because they're the ones that do the most good for the organization.

How Did We Get Here?

In the world of hiring, everyone conducts interviews and sees them as the final step in the decision-making process, even though the best candidate is not necessarily the one who gives the best interview.

The interview-performance correlation has been the subject of study for decades. Situational and behavioral interviews were direct responses to hiring managers' doubts about their own longstanding practices.

Theoretical justifications for the interview have never been in short supply. Researchers still cite a 1968 paper by psychologist E.A. Locke and his view of goal-setting. Locke makes the point that intentions and behavior are related, a point that seems patently obvious, and that idea is frequently used in the interview context. "If what people say correlates highly with what they do, the advantage of using the interview for making selection decisions is obvious," according to "The Situational Interview," a paper published in 1980 by Gary Latham and Lise Saari, both of the University of Washington.

That's an awfully big "if," though, and it's the kind of assumption that becomes increasingly suspect as the stakes get higher. Those stakes are especially high for a nation at war, and, for the United States, World War II provided more than enough reason to try to get personnel decisions right.

One project in particular, the Aviation Psychology Program, had far-reaching effects on employment practices in both military and civilian settings, but it all started with combat pilots. Flight instructors were charged with identifying trainees who had the potential to advance, but their judgments were often based on clichés, generalizations, and stereotypes. According to instructors, however, students were simply making insufficient progress, or they lacked inherent flying ability, or they had poor judgment.

Beginning in 1941 and extending well beyond the end of the war, the Army Air Forces conducted a series of studies aimed at identifying better ways to find better pilots. Led by Colonel John C. Flanagan, the researchers devised a method called the Critical Incident Technique (CIT).

In essence, CIT called for direct observation of behaviors in the field and the identification of those behaviors that were most and least effective. Having identified the things that mattered, both good and bad, flight instructors could tie the behaviors of their students to the objective criteria that were associated with success and failure. No longer would they have to resort to gut feelings about student performance. Instead, they could point to specific attributes that separated the good pilots from the bad.

The same principles apply to situational interviews: Find the situations that matter, identify the best responses to those situations, and select the interviewees who give those responses. The assumption, of course, is that those situations are indeed the critical ones and that those responses are indeed correct. The assumptions are not always borne out in reality, but there's enough research evidence to support the situational interview as the equal of the behavioral approach. That's why situational interviews are firmly entrenched in current hiring practices. You're likely to run into them even if you're not hoping to make your career as a fighter pilot.

LISTEN UP

Communication is one thing that makes us human. It's universally understood as something that defines us and is intrinsic to the way we live our personal and professional lives.

The kind of communication we value, however, tends to be limited to that which involves *delivering* a message. Clearly, delivery matters, but it undervalues the other side of the communication equation, listening. Listening is often treated as an afterthought among communication skills.

It's a big mistake, though, to view communication skills solely in terms of the way we present ourselves, or develop our skills as transmitters if that means neglecting our roles as receivers. The way we listen can be just as influential as the way we speak.

We tend to treat listening simplistically when we consider it at all. We distinguish between "good listeners" and "bad listeners," but that's not much of a distinction. By our low standards, a good listener could just be someone who lets you get a word in edgewise.

Listening deserves a closer look. Good listening should be seen as something more than silence or sheer passivity. In reality, there are many ways to listen, and some are more effective than others.

The premise, then, is that the listener's contribution to communication can be as important as the speaker's. Among many other environments, this applies to the workplace, and it's no stretch to say that the way you listen can make a difference to your career and, by extension, to the job search, especially in the highly charged setting of the job interview. In other words, learning to listen is not just an abstract virtue. It can pay off in practical ways.

Listening styles have been studied extensively in psychotherapy, where the rather dogmatic framework of Freudian psychoanalysis seemed inadequate to many practitioners. Influential American psychologist Carl Rogers, among the founders of the humanistic, "client-centered" approach, recommended a listening style in which the listener paid careful attention to the speaker, embraced his perspective, and responded with a restatement of the speaker's points in the listener's own words. It's similar to "active listening," but it avoids paraphrasing the speaker's words, instead using completely different words to express the same thoughts.

Whether paraphrasing or using your own words, the emphasis should be on building rapport and on what the speaker is saying. That can take some sensitivity on the part of the listener, since we don't always receive the message the speaker is trying to send, whether that's the fault of the speaker or our own lack of complete attention. Active listening takes work. Ultimately, it should leave the speaker with the feeling that they're truly understood, especially within their personal frame of reference.

Most of us aren't heading for careers in psychotherapy, where active listening is of obvious benefit, but the same skills can make us better colleagues, supervisors, and employees in any field.

In the workplace, active listening lets you respond to what's truly important to the other person, not to your own potentially flawed interpretation of what you're hearing. It allows you to confirm that *this* is what the person really means. If you're uncertain, it allows you to ask questions to ensure you're hearing what you think you're hearing.

Active listening doesn't mean taking over the conversation or inserting long-winded explanations that shift the focus to the listener, and it doesn't have a place in every conversation. If someone asks you the time, tell them what time it is. Don't ask if they're troubled by the inexorable ticking of the clock.

In a job interview, active listening works in similar ways. It can help you identify what the interviewer's questions are really getting at, and it can establish and cement rapport. Getting to the point where two parties in the conversation feel like they understand each other is a major interview victory. Let's say an interviewer suggests that you seem overqualified for the job. Instead of responding defensively, ask the interviewer to explain or clarify this comment. Then you will be able to address the concerns directly.

That's not all: The active mindset has benefits all its own. Not all of us give clear signals that we're fully engaged, completely attentive, and enthusiastic participants in a conversation, yet those signals are critical to making a positive impression. Active listening forces you to be as attentive as you can. As a result, everything about you, from the words you're consciously saying to the more subtle, unconscious cues of body language, reinforces your appearance as an applicant who is wholeheartedly present, the kind of candidate interviewers like to see.

If the goal of the interview is to be seen as someone who understands what the job requires and what the employer is looking for, and who seems like someone worth working with, active listening is a skill worth cultivating.

Key Lessons

+ Prepare for your interview by evaluating how your resume and the job description match, researching the company and industry news, and developing answers to common questions.

+ Always place your answers in the context of how your strengths or experiences will benefit the company and help you do the job at hand.

+ If asked about your greatest weaknesses, pick a flaw that is not critical to the job duties and explain what you are doing to overcome it.

+ Keep in mind that the hidden questions every interviewer is really asking are: "Can you do the job?" "Can we work with you?" and "Will the company benefit from hiring you?"

+ Asking your own questions is your opportunity to show you're focused on issues specific to the position and the broader industry, to receive feedback, and to transition into a real conversation.

+ If asked to recount your reaction to a past challenge, be specific about the situation you faced, the goal you wanted to achieve, the actions you personally took, and how the experience contributed to your growth.

+ If asked about an imagined scenario, make sure to describe the reasoning behind your chosen action and explain that you based it on what would most benefit the company.

✦ When faced with a behavioral interview, remember the STAR technique: Describe a situation you faced or a task you managed, discuss the actions you took in response to the situation, and describe the result of those actions.

✦ Engage in active listening to help you be as attentive as possible, identify the intent of the interview questions, and establish and cement rapport with the interviewer.

Chapter 17

Interview Skills, Part 3: *Ready, Set, Practice . . . Close*

"When you go in for a job interview, I think it's a good idea to ask if they press charges."
—Jack Handey

W E'VE LOOKED AT WHAT interviewers are looking for and how, consciously or not, they make their decisions. We've looked at what interviewees need to know about themselves, the job, and the company. We've considered the usual questions, the ones that you have to be prepared for no matter how useless they may be. We've introduced the newfangled behavioral and situational questions. We've also considered the impact of nonverbal factors on the experience.

There's only one thing left to do, but it's crucial. Armed with a great deal of information and some insight into the process, it's time to sit down and have the interview, but not at the office of your employer-to-be—not yet.

For this interview, you don't have to leave the comfort of your home. What we need is a rehearsal, but not just a quick walk-through. We need a full-blown dress rehearsal. You can even do it in business-suit attire. Anything that gets you closer to the real thing is worth a try.

The best approach involves a partner, some friendly volunteer who can play the part of the interviewer. The only qualifications for the job are that your partner is willing to pay attention and tell you the truth about your performance.

Here's the plan:

- Prepare a list of questions that include representatives from different categories, including situational and behavioral questions.

- Encourage your partner to add questions of their own to the list. If some questions come as a surprise, that's even better. If your partner can review your resume, encourage them to ask any questions that arise from that review.

- Set the stage. The best setup is something that duplicates the interview setting as much as possible, but do what you can. Sitting in a chair, for example, is preferable to reclining on the couch.

- Set a time limit of 30 minutes.

- Go!

- Let your partner start wherever they want, and encourage them to ask follow-up questions as the "interview" proceeds. Again, it's better if you don't know what's coming.

- Answer the questions as if this were the real thing.

- When time is up, stop.

At this point, it's time for debriefing. It's important to assess your own performance, but it's even more so to get feedback. Listen to what your partner has to say, not only about your answers but about the way you came across. Were there distracting manner-isms? Did you seem engaged? Did you seem to be uncomfortable with any questions? What seemed genuine and heartfelt? What seemed false and unconvincing? Don't forget the positives. Did some things go really well? Were there questions you knocked out of the park? Where did you shine? This exercise may not be for the thin-skinned—after all, it's a very personal performance in a very artificial situation—but it's invaluable.

Once you've been thoroughly debriefed, you'd be forgiven if you thought your work was done, but we're not quite home yet. There's a twist at the end, and it goes like this:

Change places.

Act the part of the interviewer, and ask questions from the same list your partner used. Don't expect much from her answers. Just go through as many questions as you like.

Why do this, especially when you can't expect much from your partner's answers? The point is to get a taste of the perspective that's only available from the other side of the desk. What did you make of the questions? Were there better options that occurred to you? What would you be expecting from an interviewee? What kind of answers would have impressed you? What answers would have done the opposite?

You can't expect this role reversal to put you fully in the inter-viewer's shoes, but it's a surprisingly effective way to get an inkling of the view from the other side. Looking at things through the interviewer's eyes can help you understand how and why some answers work and others fall flat.

Although a two-person rehearsal is the best option, it's not the only one. A video recording can accomplish something similar. It can't offer the feedback provided by a second pair of eyes and ears, but seeing and hearing yourself on camera is a very different experience from simply running through projected answers in your mind. If video isn't an option, the very least you should do is give your answers voice. Speak them aloud. Get used to putting the words and sentences together. Even here, you're likely to find that some answers, even the ones that seemed like gems when you thought of them, don't work when they're actually said. This is your chance to edit and revise.

VARIATIONS ON THE STANDARD INTERVIEW

Although the template for the typical interview is well known—two people sitting in chairs and talking, desk optional—there are important variations, some of which are increasing in popularity along with the global increase in connectivity. You don't need to explore each variation in minute detail, but you should have a basic understanding of alternative forms to serve as a starting point should you be the target of one.

Phone Interviews

Phone interviews are generally used for initial screenings. They're rarely used for making final decisions. Given their limited function, phone interviews are often left to lower-level employees or contracted out to third parties. In other words, the bar is not set terribly high.

In most cases it's enough to be able to string a few sentences together and sound reasonably professional. However, employers will also use phone interviews to identify candidates with specific skills or experience, especially if those qualities are not immediately obvious in your resume. Remember, there's no room for subtlety. You're dealing with a checklist, and the answers are either "yes" or "no." Don't lie, but, for example, if you're asked if you know Java and you have a slight familiarity with the programming language, err on the side of "yes." This is yet another step in the step-by-step approach. The goal here is not to get the job; it's to stay in the pool of candidates worthy of further review. You can explain further at an in-person interview, but you first have to make that interview happen.

Obviously, a phone interviewer can't see you, but do whatever you can physically to put yourself in the best possible interviewing frame of mind. Find a quiet spot for the call, with no interruptions or distractions. Smile when you speak—somehow, it comes through—and stand for the duration. Consider dressing up. It may help to reinforce the professional attitude you want to convey.

Video Interviews

Video is booming. The technology is finally up to the challenge, and replacing in-person interviews with online video interviews helps employers save time and money. There are two distinct styles:

1. **Synchronous:** You and the interviewer are speaking to each other via computer. If video weren't the medium, it would be exactly like a traditional interview.

2. **Asynchronous:** It's just you, your webcam, and the on-screen interview questions. There's no conversation. You may—or, more likely, may not—get the questions in advance, and you'll have a limited time to answer them.

Before you even start to think about the interview itself, there's one thing that you should do as soon as you sense there's a video interview in the wind. Check your Internet connection and the program you'll rely on for the interview. Get it all up and running. Don't assume everything will work smoothly when the time comes. You do not want to be troubleshooting software or hardware glitches midinterview. You want that to be the least of your worries, and only a thorough trial under real-world conditions can assure you of that. Fix what needs fixing now.

Some video tips:

- Check your surroundings, and make sure that the camera sees only what you want it to see.

- Tidy up. If your desk is a mess, now is the time for a major cleaning. Adjust the lighting if necessary.

- Make sure that you'll have a spot where you won't be interrupted.

- Turn off your phone.

- Dress up. This is a real interview, and they can see you.

- Look at the camera, not at the screen. There's no eye contact per se, but you can achieve something similar if you direct your gaze to the camera.

- Keep a copy of your resume handy.

- If there's something useful online—a company's website, for example—leave it open on your computer for quick reference.

- Make a dry run. Record yourself answering a few questions before the actual event. You may pick up on mannerisms and habits that don't show you in your best light.

Group Interviews

If you find that the two-person interview is not stressful enough, the group interview may be just what you need to get your adrenaline flowing. Employers sometimes use group or panel interviews as an alternative to a more time-consuming succession of individual meetings. The panel often consists of interviewers in different company roles, with an HR representative included.

The fact that it's a group doesn't make it profoundly different. The usual advice applies. Be careful, though, to address your answers to all members. Make eye contact with each of them, even if one panelist is doing most of the talking. There's no way to know who's really calling the shots, and the person in charge may well be the woman on the end who seems distracted and, by the look of things, bored by the proceedings.

Tests

Every interview is a test in a sense, but the test is sometimes a literal one. Technology companies will sometimes give candidates problems to solve, especially when the work involves programming. You'll have to show your work as you proceed, and it doesn't hurt to think out loud in the process. Tests are common in creative fields, like writing and editing, where applicants are tasked with writing a sample article or blog post, or are given an error-filled piece to see how many mistakes they can spot.

Tests are also favored by big management consulting operations, companies like Bain and McKinsey & Company. As part of the normal interviewing procedure, they ask candidates to work through case studies on the spot. You'll find examples online, especially for McKinsey itself, which provides applicants with a multitude of sample questions, tips, and guidelines on its site. You'll even find what McKinsey views as good answers for its sample cases. It's an excellent resource for anyone interested in the field. Even if a consultancy is nowhere in your future, it's worth a visit for the insight it can give you into the way a big, sophisticated employer thinks, and McKinsey, for one, has given the hiring process a lot of thought.

FOLLOWING UP

A job seeker's work, it seems, is never done. You may have left the interview with a weary sigh, no matter how things went, and you'd like to put the whole thing behind you. But, once again, you're not quite finished.

The first order of business is the thank-you note, something you should get to within 24 hours of the interview. Don't put it off.

In the fairly recent past, there was a strong case to be made for the handwritten note, sent by mail. It was the personal touch, and it stood a chance of setting you apart from the competition. Especially if you interviewed for a job in a traditional field, like banking, a handwritten note is appropriate. In all cases, email works fine, and you should send an email even if you're also sending a traditional note. If you do take that double-barreled approach, don't send the exact same note in both media. Find something different to say.

The same rules that applied when sending messages related to informational interviews apply here. Keep the message short and to the point. Proofread relentlessly. Make it personal, addressed to a person's name and not to a title. Try to include something specific—no more than a sentence or two—that refers to some highlight of the interview or a specific aspect of the job and your perfectly matching qualifications.

Beyond the Thank You Note: Other Post-Interview Tips

- *Follow up when told.* In the interview, you may have asked about the company's plans with regard to next steps, or your interviewer may have volunteered that information. In either case, take it literally. If your interviewer said that a decision would be made in about a week, don't jump the gun and start calling before the time is up.

- *Don't be a pest.* If you still haven't heard anything, you shouldn't take that silence as license to start calling on a daily basis. You may see that behavior as evidence of enthusiastic commitment, but you will be alone in that view. To everyone else, you become the dreaded daily call that no one wants to take. Don't be surprised if the person you're trying to reach seems to be constantly out of the office.

- *Don't burn bridges.* You are hereby prohibited from saying anything negative about the company, its personnel, its offices, its location, its parking lot, its landscaping, and every single thing that pertains to the company in any way. If your interviewer was a leering homunculus who spent the time guzzling whiskey straight from the bottle, keep it to yourself—even if it's the absolute truth—and, especially, don't head directly to social media and turn the experience into an amusing post. It's not a question of whether you're right. No potential employer wants to see negative comments about anyone, even his worst enemy, no matter how justified. Those employers will wonder what you'll say about them, and you don't want them to be wondering anything of the kind.

If you didn't get the job, so be it. You'll have to pick yourself up and keep right on going. You'll wonder, of course, what influenced the decision. Employers won't tell you, but you may be able to learn something by going back over your interview and reviewing your performance. If there were obvious missteps, you'll put that knowledge to work next time. It's tougher if you thought everything went well and you left the interview feeling like you'd earned a standing ovation. Still, it's one more experience that helps to make you more comfortable with the whole process.

If you got as far as you did with the help of a contact who was kind enough to meet with you, someone who starred in Chapter 14, be sure to touch base. You've kept them informed of your progress, and it's simple courtesy to keep them posted. Let them know where you stand. If they seem receptive, share some details. They may offer you some words of wisdom, but, more than that, they now know you're still looking and may be willing to offer additional help.

The Sound of Silence

It's at least somewhat understandable why employers don't always tell you that you weren't hired. If you've delivered a resume that's just one out of a thousand submissions, silence doesn't come as a great shock. According to a CareerBuilder survey, 75 percent of applicants never hear a word.

You'd think, though, that a company that took the trouble to interview you would advise you of its decision. According to that same survey, you'd be wrong most of the time. Some 60 percent of the 3,991 respondents said they heard nothing further once the interview was done. Even after they'd been identified as the most promising people out there, they were left, as they say, to twist slowly in the wind.

Why the silence?

- *It's no skin off our backs.* Employers leave you hanging because they can. The attitude results from a job market with no shortage of applicants, one in which employers have nothing to gain by being "nice." Their behavior won't dissuade other applicants from knocking on their doors.

- *Who has the time?* The silence is partly the result of employer time constraints. Processing the throngs of applicants takes enough time as it is. Adding another step, however small, is a horrifying imposition on already tight schedules.

- *Why take the risk?* Employers are notoriously risk-averse. If they start telling people they weren't hired, they might even start telling them the reasons behind the decision. Then come the lawsuits.

We can't change employers' minds, but at least we can acknowledge how hard the typical situation is for applicants who are left to stew over their chances in the face of utter indifference. You worked hard to make it through the multiple screenings. You dealt with uncertainty and rejection, but you persisted. You got to the very last stage, a moment worth celebrating. It's hard not to take things personally when you put so much into the search, but take what comfort you can from this: It's not you, it's them.

INTERVIEW ESSENTIALS: 8 QUICK TIPS

In Chapters 14 through 17, we've covered the spectrum of the interview process, from informational interviews, how to dress, question practice, and more. As a final summation of the interview process, here are eight practical tips to remember.

1. **Be on time.** For an interview, "on time" doesn't mean arriving at the last possible second, nor does it mean arriving an hour early. The ideal time of arrival is about 10 minutes before you're scheduled to begin. You'll have enough time to collect yourself and get the lay of the land. If you can manage it, especially if you're going someplace unfamiliar, make a dry run to the interview location a day or two in advance. Confirm your route and take note of any potential delays. If you've gone down the road before, you'll be a lot more relaxed when the actual day arrives.

2. **Dress the part.** This means formal, professional attire for both men and women. If you're absolutely positive that this office operates at the height of informality, you can consider a "business casual" look. If there's any doubt, err on the side of formality. Avoid excess, whether in scent, makeup,

or an overly revealing outfit. Save fashion statements for after you've got the job. For now, go with "candidate for Senate, probably Republican."

3. **Treat everyone well.** You never know who you'll meet on-site, and you don't know who the gatekeepers really are. It's not so much the case that that shabbily dressed hobo wandering the lobby could actually be the company's billionaire CEO. It *is* the case that your interviewer may ask a receptionist or security guard what they thought of you. In fact, many employers enlist the aid of a receptionist as part of the routine. Always assume that the interviewer will solicit post-interview feedback from anyone whose path you cross. In short, don't make a negative impression on anyone.

4. **Pay attention.** You should look alert and interested throughout, not just for the sake of the impression you make, but also for the information you can gather. What's the atmosphere like? Are people engaging with one another, or do they seem isolated and remote? What about equipment? Are people using the latest devices, or are they chained to vintage computers running Windows XP?

5. **Don't carry too much.** Travel light. If you arrive at the office with coat, hat, scarf, briefcase, umbrella, and whatever else you might pack for a cross-country expedition, you'll have to deal with all those accoutrements when you've taken a seat and are waiting for the interviewer to appear. When you stand to greet your interviewer and shake his hand, it's hard to do so gracefully while managing all that equipment. That's not your most direct route to a good first impression.

6. **Do bring your resume.** Throw a few copies of your resume into your briefcase, along with anything else—a portfolio, for example—that may be relevant.

7. **Check yourself.** If you can get thee to a mirror, give yourself a final once-over before the interview begins.

8. **Turn off your phone.** Please.

Key Lessons

✦ Conduct a practice interview with the help of a friend who is willing to give you honest feedback on your performance, and then change places to get a perspective from the other side of the desk.

✦ Phone interviews are used for initial screenings, so when asked if you have a skill you are slightly familiar with, err on the side of "yes."

✦ A video interview can be conducted like a traditional two-person interview, or with just you, your webcam, and on-screen interview questions.

✦ Troubleshoot your Internet connection and software prior to the video interview, tidy up the area the camera will see, and dress as you would for a traditional interview.

✦ In group interviews, address your answers to all members and make eye contact with everyone, because you never know who's really in charge.

✦ Some companies will give candidates tests, problems to solve, or case studies to work through during the interview.

+ Send a thank you email within one day of the interview, but beyond that, do not follow up before the date the interviewer gave you.

+ If you don't get the job, the employer won't tell you why, but you may be able to learn something by going back over your interview and evaluating your performance.

+ Remember these practical interview tips: Be on time, treat everyone you meet well, pay attention, don't carry too much, bring your resume, and turn off your phone.

Chapter 18
Make Me an Offer:
Negotiating Successfully

*"You wiggle to the left, you wiggle to the right,
you do the Ooby Dooby with all your might."*
—Roy Orbison

Y OUR RESUME PASSED MUSTER, your cover letter
knocked them dead, and your interview was stellar. After the long
grind of the job search, with all its anxiety, uncertainty, and stress,
with all the hoops you've jumped through, it's a little dizzying, but
you didn't just survive—you succeeded. Someone wants to hire
you. So what now?

One last task remains. There's an offer on the table, but it's a
little vague, especially in terms of compensation. You think you
have a ballpark idea of what's in store, but you don't have specifics.
You'll meet with the employer and work out the details. It won't be
"take it or leave it." There's always a little wiggle room on both sides.
The size of that room will be determined once you get the chance
to talk things over. Negotiation, in other words, is in the wings.

Let's take a small step backward, though, before considering
the details of negotiating an offer. The scenario above assumes that

the offer happens at the very end of the process. As part of that assumption, all details of the offer fit into one neat package that's revealed, in all its glory, like a present opened Christmas morning. In reality, though, negotiations often happen earlier on, especially if you've sat through multiple interviews.

When there's more than one interview, negotiation often happens from the start, whether it's part of the first interview or included in what follows. For example, you've aced that first meeting, and you're delighted to get that fateful call inviting you for a second. That call may touch on practicalities: When are you free for another meeting? If we're interested, are you willing to relocate? What's the earliest you can start? On the whole, those matters are simple enough. They're probably the very things you've thought about since you started the search.

You may also find yourself dealing with salary, a more complicated topic, so don't be surprised if money is part of the conversation before you've even received an offer. There's unlikely to be much talk of other things that make up an overall compensation package. Benefits and the like, important as they are, can wait. If you and the employer are worlds apart when talking salary, one of you may decide there's not much point in going further. Everyone wants to know if this will work, and they want to know sooner rather than later. As a result, salary can be part of the discussion early on.

PRINCIPLES OF EFFECTIVE NEGOTIATION

The principles of effective negotiation don't really change according to the stage at which the question arises. Good strategies work all the time. Bad ones never improve.

Early Is Better

If looking for a job is your hobby and you just can't get enough of the job search, postpone discussions of money for as long as you can and, if you have the time, consider an intensive course of psycho-therapy. Otherwise, get to the question sooner, not later. Even—or especially—if an employer loves you to death, the company wants to know if it can afford you. It's a question you'd like answered, too. If your salary expectations are dramatically different from what's possible, it's better to know that before subjecting yourself to additional interviews.

Know Your Stuff

We've harped on the value of research at every step along the way, whether it's choosing a career, writing a cover letter, handling an informational interview, or drafting a resume. Knowledge is power, regardless of the situation. Know your market. What are employers paying comparable employees? Understand that the numbers change according to several variables. Pay scales are different in different cities. They're different in the city and the country. Big companies pay differently than small. Take those factors into account, and head for the Internet. Several sites, including Glassdoor, Payscale, and Monster, give numbers for many fields, and specialized sites, like tech-focused InformationWeek, cover particular industries. Robert Half offers salary guides for technology, finance, law, and several other areas.

Use the Internet, but don't limit your inquiry to what's available on the web. Ask around. You may know someone in a similar position, even if she's at a different company, or someone at the target company, even if he's in a different position. Money is one of those things we just don't talk about, but you're not asking for personal information. You just want a general idea of what's happening out there. In the process, you may get additional information that can help. Perhaps one company is known for its generous bonuses. Another may be notoriously tightfisted. A third balances lower pay with fabulous benefits. All this can be useful.

The information is out there. Don't start talking salary unless and until you know the ballpark figures that apply. Employers know these numbers very well. If you don't, your ignorance will put you at a disadvantage.

Keep Within Range

Recruiters and hiring managers frequently ask for your current or most recent salary. On the whole, this is a question best left unanswered, especially if the salary you're seeking is significantly above what you've made in the past.

If you're asked a direct question, try to deflect it. Let's say you've had one interview and a company recruiter calls. They'd like to see you again next Thursday. The recruiter asks if that will work.

- *You:* I think so. Let me check my schedule for next week, but can I speak with you about compensation first?

- *Recruiter:* Yes, of course. Let's get a sense of whether we're in the right ballpark here. What's your salary at Satanic Mills?

- *You:* I'm considering jobs in the range of $90,000 to $100,000. If that sounds like it can work for you, let me pull up my schedule here and see what I have for Thursday.

Since you've done your homework, you know that the range you're naming is realistic for the position. If you provide your current salary, you may be locking yourself into a range that's much lower than this employer is willing to pay.

Who Goes First?

The old negotiating adage was simplicity itself: Never go first! The idea was that you'd go too low and miss out on the lavish compensation package, or you'd go too high and price yourself out of the job.

Those were the good old days. Fabulous offers still exist, but they're only relevant if you're getting a partnership offer from the likes of Goldman Sachs. For the rest of us, employers are not wildly throwing money around. If anything, they'll opt for the lowball offer and hope you rise to the bait. By letting the employer know your range, you'll know whether that next interview is worth your time. You know the going rate. You're asking for something realistic. Don't hesitate to be the first one to talk numbers.

- **Counterpoint:** There are still many people who believe the old ways are best. These people are not stupid. There's no denying that it's a mistake to be the first to speak in some situations, but most of the arguments for keeping your mouth shut about salary take that position because they want you to make sure you got the job before doing anything else. Save all talk of pay until you know they want you. Don't speak first lest you (a) price yourself too low and miss out on a much better offer, or (b) price yourself too high, missing out entirely because you're too expensive.

- **Counter-counterpoint:** If you're picking numbers out of thin air, that advice makes sense, but that's not what you're doing here. You know what people like you in places like this are making. In addition, we're talking about a situation in which you have clear evidence that the company is interested. Here, we've used the example of an invitation for a second interview, a clear indication if there ever was one, but the advice holds true even if there's only one interview. Trust us: Salary won't be on the table, even in a single interview, if the company is not interested.

When You Have to Include a Salary

One of the more delicate questions for job applicants and one that attracts the most conflicted opinions from experts is the one posed by job postings that require applicants to specify their desired salaries.

In this situation, the applicant's dilemma is all too clear. Of the three choices available, not one is obviously correct:

- Aim too low, and you're liable to leave money on the table. Alternatively, employers might conclude that your low expectations mean you're not at the level of the job in question.

- Ask for too much, on the other hand, and you'll price yourself out of the job entirely.

- Refuse to answer, and it will be held against you. If the posting made salary expectations an explicit requirement, you've proved yourself incapable of following instructions. That's reason enough to toss your application without a second thought, especially for hiring managers who are looking for ways to cut the applicant pool to a manageable size. Don't make that job easier for them.

There's no ideal solution, no approach that's right for everyone in every job, so the decision comes down to an assessment of your individual situation and this particular job opening.

If there's anything that applies across the board, however, it's that it's never wise to ignore the employer's request entirely. At the very least, the decision to withhold the information should be made in the full knowledge that it may disqualify your application. If you balk at including dollars and cents, consider a line that shows you read the instructions: "My salary range is flexible, depending on total compensation and specific job responsibilities." That won't solve the problem, but it's better than nothing.

If you're willing to delve into the world of numbers, use a range instead of a specific salary. At the low end, use the salary that you'd reasonably need to take the job should an offer be made. At the other end, list the salary that's the maximum typically paid for the position.

Don't just throw out numbers; some research is in order here. You can find salary information from the Bureau of Labor Statistics, from job postings, and from sites like Glassdoor and Salary.com. You can get more personal information from people you know in the industry. They may not be willing to divulge their own salaries, but they'll probably be willing to talk salary in a general way.

Remember that geography can play a surprisingly large role, and salaries for the same job may be very different in California than in Nebraska. For example, your current salary is $150,000. You're not about to take a cut in pay, and you're applying to a larger organization for a job with slightly more responsibility. A 30 percent increase would be reasonable, and it's consistent with what you've learned about the market. All you need to do is include a simple statement, perhaps with an indication of your willingness to adapt to circumstances: "My salary range is from $150,000 to $195,000, depending on the particular scope and responsibilities of the position."

You don't have to make your flexibility explicit, just as you don't need to mention that references are available upon request. Everyone knows you'll deliver those references when called upon, and everyone understands that there may be further talk about pay.

It should go without saying that there's no need to broach the salary question unless the employer insists. Don't make it part of your cover letter as a matter of routine. When the employer asks, though, you can stand in silence on principle, knowing the risks, or you can give your best possible answer, knowing that all you can do is make the best of a bad situation.

Don't Sell Yourself Short

Your thoughts may run along the following lines: The job market has been horrible for years. Employers hold all the cards. You're lucky to be hired at any price. There are ten equally qualified people ready to take your place at a moment's notice, and they'll work for less. You'd better grovel before prospective employers, or you won't have a chance.

No! For far too many people, the job market has indeed been a swamp of misery and pain, but that doesn't necessarily define your individual place within that market. That place, after all, is the only one that matters right now.

If you and your prospective employer are talking salary, that means something. The subject would not be on the table if they'd decided you were a terrible fit. In fact, they have a certain investment, both financial and psychological, in hiring you. The best outcome, for both of you, would be a job offer that you accept, on terms that satisfy both parties. This is not the time to lose the positive, professional, enthusiastic, and competent persona you've displayed thus far. Hold your head high, look for realistic compensation, and don't feel that you have to accept less than the going rate. You're going to do good things for this employer—they apparently think so, too—and that makes you valuable.

This is not to say that employers aren't above putting lowball offers to the test. They know about desperate job seekers, and that's one of the arguments in favor of being the first to speak. Don't give them the chance to start that low, and don't forget that an offer far below the going rate may be a sign of bad things to come if and when you're on the job.

IS THE OFFER WORTHWHILE?

Not every offer is a dream offer. Sometimes, you have to take what's there because you're at the end of your rope. At that point, any offer seems dreamy enough. For many candidates, though, those not driven by desperation, there are offers that, while they don't live up to your highest expectations, are still worth considering.

How can you decide if an offer is worth a serious look? Start by asking yourself some questions.

- *What are you giving up?* Let's leave compensation out of the equation for the moment. We'll get there soon enough, but first take a look at what's being asked of you. Start with the "small" things. Does this job force you to make unwelcome changes? Do you have to relocate and leave friends and family behind? Does it require you to work disruptive hours? Does commuting become an issue? Next, look at the big picture. Does the job have a place in your career as a whole? Does it fit in with your plans? Does it derail your career goals? If the job won't cause a major upheaval in your life and it has a place in the trajectory of your career, it hasn't disqualified itself yet.

- *How well does it meet your needs?* Take inventory. What are all the things you'd like to get out of a job right now? Some will turn out to be more important than others. For example, the job may be short on vacation time but long on benefits like health insurance. Each of us weighs those criteria differently. If you have a family, good health insurance may be more important than an allotment of vacation time even the French would envy.

    By creating a weighted inventory, you'll know which aspects of the job are deal-killers and which are tolerable in the grand scheme of things. Focus on the deal-killers.

- *What's in it for your skills?* If it's not a dream job, questions of personal growth become especially important. What can you learn on the job? Will you be able to develop new skills? Are they the skills that will get you closer to your dream job? Is there a formal route to those skills by way of on-the-job training? Will you have the chance to attend conferences and seminars?

  Think about this in specific terms. Any job will give you experience. It's the nature of the beast, and you can make a very good case that all experience is valuable. However, some types of experience are more valuable than others. Some jobs encourage—even require—you to stretch, and, for the sake of your career, those jobs deserve a serious look.

- *What about the big picture?* Every job you have, whether it's a dream job or something approaching a nightmare, occupies a place in your career. Where does this job fit? Does it move you any closer to your ultimate goals? Is it the kind of position that fits naturally into the working history of someone with those goals in mind? Can you build on it? Can you point to this job and put it in the context of your career? Is it in any way, shape, or form a stepping-stone?

  Picture yourself in the future, when you're looking for a better job. When you're discussing your history with an interviewer, where do you think this job will fit? Granted, any job offers experience, and that is valuable, but what about this particular job? Is it irrelevant to your larger goals? Is it an aberration, or a move others will understand and appreciate? Is there more going on than "I really needed a job, and this was where I found one?" If there *is* more, the offer deserves at least a second look. If not, and you have the luxury of forgoing the paycheck that comes with the offer, it may be time to move on.

What About the Culture?

Quite naturally, most offers are judged on the basis of pay, and if not pay, then on perks and benefits. One thing that's never on the table is the company's culture. But the importance of workplace culture cannot be overstated. At the extremes, it's less of an issue. An enormous paycheck can make a difficult workplace tolerable, but a terrific culture won't make up for horribly inadequate compensation. Between those extremes, company culture is a big issue that deserves a great deal of weight in your decision.

Ask yourself a few simple, if unscientific, questions, and start with the absolute basics. Do you think you'll enjoy the job? Does it seem like a good place to work? Do you think you'll look forward to getting there each morning? Do you like the people you've met? Can you picture yourself spending a lot of time with them? Is the atmosphere positive and energetic? Did the people you've met make you feel welcome?

This is a real "go with your gut" moment. You can't be certain that your predictions will be borne out. Perhaps that lovely interviewer who made you feel right at home is, in reality, the office harridan who can hardly wait to make you utterly miserable. Anything's possible. Generally, though, your experience so far will give you a basic sense of what this place is like and how you'll fit in. Trust your instincts, even if you can't explain the conclusions you've drawn. Company culture deserves your full attention. Money makes the world go round, but being happy in your work and in your workplace is, as the commercial says, priceless.

LEAN IN—SPEAK UP!

Of course, these negotiation principles don't mean anything if you're not going to use them. You need to stand up for yourself to get what you want and need. In other words, you need to speak up!

The most recent data from the Bureau of Labor Statistics show that for every dollar earned by men, women in the United States made 78 cents. This problem is true across occupations. Male middle school teachers earn a median of $1,096 per week compared to $956 for women. In retail sales, the gap is 70 cents to the dollar, and for lawyers it's 83 cents.

The reasons for this discrepancy are many, and they're well beyond the scope of a single chapter devoted to job offers. Culture, psychology, and history all play their parts, and institutional sexism is hardly a thing of the past, but there seems to be growing agreement that women's approach to negotiation plays a role, perhaps a large one, in keeping the discrepancy alive.

In the book *Women Don't Ask*, authors Linda Babcock and Sara Lashever, noting that male MBAs were making 7.6 percent more than their female counterparts, asked a simple question of men and women: Did you try to negotiate your compensation? The majority of men, some 57 percent, did. Among women, only 7 percent tried to get themselves a better deal.

At the same time, however, research has shown that women are equally willing to participate in, and are equally adept at "representational negotiating." In this case, you're not acting as a principal in the negotiation. You're negotiating on behalf of others. Why is this?

Facebook COO Sheryl Sandberg stirred some controversy in her book *Lean In*, when she argued that it's not all sexism, institutional or otherwise, that holds women back, but that there's a powerful internal component as well. To oversimplify a bit, women suffer from their desire to be liked. Negotiation, especially when the subject is a "selfish" one like compensation, can too easily become adversarial. By definition, an adversarial relationship does not make people like us. It follows, then, that women will sacrifice their earnings on the altar of likability.

According to Sandberg, that was one of her problems as Facebook's COO. As part of a performance review six months into her tenure, Mark Zuckerberg made it plain that her need to be liked was making her a less effective leader. She had to stop trying to please everyone.

To be sure, these are vast generalizations. We all sit somewhere between the two extremes, and the basic lessons that apply to negotiations apply to everyone. We should all strive for a win-win outcome, we should be aware of the other party's needs, and we should try to focus on benefits to the organization, that last being a variation on the idea that women do best if they can frame the negotiation as a "communal" negotiation. In addition, negotiating on a point-by-point basis may make for a more adversarial environment, something you can mitigate by adopting a packaged approach that doesn't make each point its own subject for argument.

Those ideas are all worth bearing in mind, but they don't really speak to something fundamental if the real problem is your unwillingness to negotiate at all.

If that's the true obstacle, here's one way to increase the chance that you won't just accept the first offer: Prepare. Preparation has many virtues. It puts you in a position of strength. You know what you're talking about when it comes to compensation. You'll know whether that first offer is realistic or fair.

Those are all good reasons to prepare, but preparation has another virtue that can make all the difference. In effect, preparation adjusts your expectations.

By preparing, aren't you acknowledging that there's something to prepare for? Doesn't your preparation mean that you're expecting to negotiate? Expectations, after all, drive outcomes. Once you've gone so far as to prepare, it only makes sense to put that work to use. Why else would you have spent all that time getting ready? The only possible answer is that you were planning to speak up.

Now follow that preparation to its logical outcome and, in the nicest possible way, ask for what you're really worth.

DOWN TO BRASS TACKS

We now know that you're not going to be Mr. or Ms. Milquetoast; you're going to speak up in the negotiation phase. This is where things get personal. There are no hard-and-fast rules for what trade-offs are acceptable, and there are no compensation packages that work well for every candidate. Only you know the cost of living your particular lifestyle. Only you know the relative importance of an extra week of vacation or the relative value of a flexible schedule. No one can measure those things for you, but, personal as it all is, here are some essentials to bear in mind when negotiating:

- *Underline your enthusiasm.* No matter how far apart you are, always preface your statements in negotiations with the message that you're delighted to get the offer, excited by your prospects, and anxious to start making a contribution.

- *Don't take things personally.* Let's say you've put your numbers on the table and you're not offered what you want. You're a few thousand dollars apart. Don't take this as a slight. You don't negotiate your compensation very often. Employers do it all the time. They expect there to be some give and take in the process, even if they're beside themselves with glee at the very idea of bringing you on board. In other words, it's business as usual. It's nothing personal.

- *Always ask for a range.* Don't ask for one specific number. That can sound too much like an ultimatum, and it doesn't communicate flexibility or a willingness to negotiate. Remember to do your salary homework and "Keep Within Range" (refer back to page 308).

- *Think carefully about bonuses.* A signing bonus is a lovely thing, and it can sometimes bridge the gap between what you want and what the company is willing to offer. It can be of benefit to the employer, too, since it's not a recurring cost that needs to be part of the annual budget, but that same benefit can be a disadvantage to the employee. For example, if raises are made as a percentage of current salary, a higher starting salary may have consequences far into the future.

- *But don't dismiss bonuses entirely.* Bonus structures can also be worth considering when you're getting close to an agreement. Perhaps the bonus schedule can be accelerated or the amount increased. Since it's likely to be performance-based, employers may find it an easier cost to justify.

- *Beyond bonuses.* Bonuses are one place where there's a significant difference between one-time and recurring payments, but they're not the only place. Relocation expenses are another, and tuition reimbursement can fall into the one-time category as well.

- *Look through the employer's eyes.* The employer's salary agenda is a little different from yours. To an employer, compensation can be divided into two columns. In one column are the hard numbers, things like the salary itself, bonuses, and the cost of many benefits. These expenses are itemized in the organization's budget. The other column holds "soft" costs, things like vacation time or the ability to work from home. Even soft costs are true costs, but you may find more flexibility in that column. When the employer tells you that your salary is the amount that's in the budget, that may be true, and there may be little maneuvering room. But you may be willing to give a little on salary in exchange for another week of vacation or a more flexible schedule, and the employer may have more room to accommodate those softer requests.

- *Look through the employer's eyes again.* Bonuses are one place where there's a significant difference between one-time and recurring payments, but they're not the only place. Relocation expenses are another, and tuition reimbursement can fall into the one-time category as well. It's often easier for an employer to agree to a limited expenditure than to a continuing cost.

- *Know what matters.* If nothing else, dealing with the job search is a wonderful opportunity to resurrect the Boy Scout motto: Be prepared. You've done the research that enabled you to give your salary negotiation some context. Now, look within. Ignore salary for the moment and list all the benefits that might come along with that salary. Which matter the most? What would you trade for an extra week of vacation if the offer is $5,000 below the low end of your range? What about two weeks? Would the ability to work from home make a difference? If so, how much of a difference would it make? Is maternity leave important? What about tuition reimbursement? Don't walk into the negotiation without knowing what you'd like to have when you walk out.

- *Look for help from the other side.* If you're not quite coming to an agreement, you don't have to do all the work yourself. Ask the employer for suggestions in an open-ended way: "Do you have any other ideas about what we can do to bring us closer together?" As a psychological matter, a question like that puts the two of you on the same side. Even in a negotiation, the other side doesn't have to be the enemy. Here, the "enemy" is the gap between you. You're looking for creative solutions, and you're working together to bridge that gap. There may be options you hadn't thought of, and you may be pleasantly surprised by what you hear.

- *Get it in writing.* You've worked through all the differences. You've come to an agreement, and everyone is smiling and shaking hands and talking about great plans for the day you start. Congratulations are just around the corner, but you're not done yet. Until that agreement is written down and signed, there's no real agreement. Review the written version carefully. Make sure it covers everything. Make sure there's nothing unexpected. Once you've all signed, that's when you open the champagne, and not a minute sooner. Congratulations!

WHAT YOU SHOULD EXPECT IN A JOB OFFER

You've run the gauntlet of the job search and come out in one piece. In fact, everything has gone so well that an offer is on the way. All that's needed is the quick finalization of a few details, and you'll have the offer in hand. What should you expect to see?

The first and most important answer to that question is contained in the question itself. What should you expect to *see*? A job offer shouldn't come in the form of a conversation, although offers are frequently promised over the phone or in person. For it to be real—something to rely on and on which you can base your plans—an offer has to be in writing. Nothing else will do.

Employers should understand this. A written offer is just as important to them as it is to you, and they should recognize your legitimate need to have something you can rely on before committing to a big change. Of course, this doesn't translate to a 12-page illuminated manuscript, delivered by bonded messenger and presented with great ceremony on a velvet cushion. A simple email will do, provided it spells out the offer's terms.

Before you get to the written offer, however, there are other issues to address, and they can often be handled when you're told that an offer is coming your way:

- *What's the time frame for a response?* Presumably, you're happy about receiving an offer. You may be downright thrilled. Still, the offer may determine what your working life will be like for years to come. It deserves a thorough look, which doesn't imply second thoughts about the job. Rather, it's a sign that you take it seriously.

- *Is the offer self-contained?* In other words, does it make reference to documents—details of a benefits package, for instance—without actually including them? If it does, you'll need to decide if you can accept regardless.

- *Who's your point of contact?* Different companies handle the hiring process in different ways, and the person handling things now may be a completely new face. Find out who you should reach out to for further discussion or for answers to your questions.

With those preliminaries out of the way, what should you expect? Given the variability of company offerings, it's impossible to specify every question that might apply to a given offer, but here are some highlights:

Compensation

This one's obvious, but there are still wrinkles:

- If you're salaried, base compensation may be straightforward, but is a provision for bonuses spelled out? Are there performance-based variables?

- If you're hourly, when does overtime kick in?

- If you're commissioned, how are commissions structured? When are they paid? Is there a draw against commissions? Is there a base salary?

- For every type of compensation, other than those inescapable taxes, are there deductions? How often are you paid?

Benefits

Benefits come in two varieties, but both are enormously valuable. Some benefits, like health insurance and retirement plans, have clear monetary value, and the more information the offer contains, the better. In some cases, benefits may be subject to a vesting period—a time before they become truly yours—and that variable can have important consequences.

Other benefits, like vacation time, telecommuting options, holidays, sick days, maternity leave, and paternity leave, may be harder to valuate, but they're equally important. In terms of quality of life, they may even be more important. Again, you want as much information as possible.

Companies will often leave the details until later, but it may be worth asking some questions and getting a copy of the benefits handbook.

Responsibilities

The ideal offer would contain a complete job description, but most fall short, with many of them simply detailing the job title you're going to assume. If you haven't already seen it, a look at the official job description can help avoid any misunderstandings.

Timing

Once the offer is made, the clock starts ticking. First, there's the deadline for accepting the offer. Next, there's the start date. There should be some indication of your expected schedule once you're on board, along with the specification of any probationary period.

Conditions

Finally, not every offer, even a written one, is unconditional. There may be contingencies, like background checks or drug tests, to be satisfied before your start date. They're mere "formalities," of course, at least according to whoever is keeping things contingent, but they're quite real. Make sure you know what still needs to be done, and ask about timing. Contingencies are only formalities, until you meet one that trips you up. At that point, even a small detail can ruin your day.

Key Lessons

+ Salary negotiation often starts before you've even received an offer.

+ Know your market and what employers are paying comparable employees, look for realistic compensation, and don't feel you have to accept less than the going rate.

+ Don't hesitate to be the first one to talk numbers; by letting the employer know your range, you'll know whether that next interview is worth your time.

+ Avoid providing your current salary to recruiters, or you may be locking yourself into a lower rate than you want.

+ Offers that don't live up to your expectations are still worth considering, based on how well the job meets your needs, what you could learn, and what you'd have to give up.

✦ Consider company culture when evaluating a job offer, and don't undervalue the importance of being happy in your workplace.

✦ Negotiation principles don't mean anything if you don't use them, but preparation can make you more likely to follow through on asking for what you're really worth.

✦ Always ask for a range instead of a specific number because it communicates flexibility and a willingness to negotiate.

✦ Consider whether you're willing to give a little on salary in exchange for more vacation time or a flexible schedule, and don't walk into the negotiation without knowing what you'd like to have when you walk out.

✦ Your agreement isn't real until you've received it in writing, carefully reviewed it to make sure it covers everything, and you've all signed it—then you can celebrate.

Afterword:
Doing Well by Doing Good

"We all need somebody to lean on."
—Bill Withers

IN THE JOB SEARCH, getting someone's help is often the biggest determinant of success or failure. If you had a productive informational interview, received some advice that led you to change your job-hunting strategy for the better, or were introduced to the right person at the right time, you probably know how important help can be.

You would certainly have returned the favor if you could, but that's not always possible. You have the option, though, of offering to help someone else—a sort of favor-once-removed. You know how much that can mean.

Maybe help is something you wish you'd had but never received. Perhaps that makes you more empathetic when a job seeker comes to you for advice. Or maybe it has the opposite effect, and you're convinced that everyone should navigate the job market on their own. It builds character, after all.

Regardless of your personal story, there are good reasons to help others. As it turns out, helping works in mysterious ways, and the results of giving are not the ones we'd necessarily expect. Helping does at least as much for the giver as for the recipient, and that fact should mean something, even to the most hard-hearted and self-interested of Ayn Rand's disciples. Helping doesn't have to be a matter of doing good deeds for their own sake. The truth is that the helper has a lot to gain. That doesn't mean you will find your reward in heaven or that virtue is its own reward. It means that helping rewards you in ways that are meaningful, practical, and even measurable.

Around the turn of the last century, the phrase "pay it forward" entered the public consciousness, gaining popularity because of a best-selling novel that suggested an unusual way of changing the world for the better. The central idea was that we should repay a kindness done for us by doing something good for someone other than the person who'd helped us. We wouldn't pay a favor *back*. We'd pay it *forward*, and, one person at a time, the world would be made better.

At first glance, however, there seems to be something unnatural about paying it forward. Human nature seems more attuned to a transactional perspective. Favors should be repaid. There's a quid pro quo, a feeling that help comes with an implied obligation to repay the debt. Selfless helping is a job reserved for saints. Mere mortals expect something in return.

The transactional perspective is part of our makeup, but a closer look shows that the psychology of giving and receiving is more complicated. The transaction isn't always what it seems to be.

If someone helped you in the job search, you're probably grateful. You may have sent a thank you note. You may feel that you owe that person something. If she ever needed a favor, you'd be first in line.

Here's where it gets interesting. You may not have a favor to offer, at least right now, and that creates a psychological imbalance. Receiving help, regardless of specific circumstances, puts the receiver in a dependent role. It lowers self-esteem and damages what psychologists call "self-competence." Researchers in social psychology have identified a host of negative consequences for recipients, including global consequences like "negative affect" and "distress," and more specific ones like negative feelings about the helper.

There's more than one kind of help, however—the kind that makes a difference. Those same researchers draw a distinction between "autonomy-oriented" and "dependency-oriented" approaches. In the former, help comes in the form of tools or hints that aid in problem-solving. In the latter, a complete solution is dropped into the recipient's lap. The distinction mirrors the well-known proverb variously attributed to Confucius, Maimonides, and an assortment of lesser sages: "Give a man a fish and you feed him for a day; teach a man to fish and you feed him for a lifetime."

Autonomy-oriented help is clearly the more educational option, and it lessens one problem with the helping relationship: the creation of marked inequality between the helper and the helped. Interestingly, one other factor that influences recipients' reactions is whether the helper is acting voluntarily or not. For recipients, self-esteem and feelings of well-being fare better when help isn't compelled.

If you received help during your job search, fine distinctions between autonomy and dependency probably didn't cross your mind. Presumably, you would have had no objection to the sudden appearance of a job offer on the spot, dependency be damned. In that respect, the job search has something in common with a natural disaster. In a disaster, the need is urgent, and there's just no time for autonomy-oriented help. People need fish, not fishing rods. In the job search, any help is good help, even help that may not be the autonomy-oriented help that's psychologically optimal. Most job seekers will happily put up with a touch of inequality or a lingering concern about an unpaid debt if the help they get ends up getting them hired.

If getting help has some unexpectedly negative consequences, however tolerable they may be, giving help has very different effects on the giver. A 2014 study published in the *Journal of Applied Social Psychology* summarized some previous findings about those effects, and the psychological benefits alone are impressive:

- Increased feelings of self-worth

- Improved mental health, quality of life, and well-being

- Increased longevity

- Reduction in depressive symptoms

In addition, when someone who has gotten help has the opportunity to give it, the change in roles reduces the negative effects of having received it in the past. This happens even if the help you provide isn't directed at the person who helped you. In other words, paying it forward isn't just a chance to be altruistic. It actually helps the person doing the paying.

In the end, giving doesn't even require an altruistic mindset. Giving does the giver worlds of psychological good, but the benefits don't end with improvements to the giver's mental health. The world outside is influenced as well.

Helping does good things for your reputation; it enhances your public prestige. The fact that you're someone people come to for advice and assistance speaks well of you. If job seekers come to you for help, that means something to anyone who's aware of your role. You're a worthwhile source of help. Why else would they come to you? You're willing to carve time out of your schedule when it looks like you have nothing to gain. How noble! Your image isn't tarnished because, as we've seen, you *do* have something to gain.

Does your advice have to be good? Does your "help" actually have to help? Looked at purely in terms of how the helper is seen by the wider world, the quality of help is essentially irrelevant. Your image benefits even if your help is misguided. No one is looking over your shoulder. There's no one scrutinizing your outcomes. Viewed from a position of utter cynicism, the important point is that you're seen as a source of expertise and assistance. In the eyes of third parties, the fact that people come to you for help means you must have help to give. The poor victims of your efforts aren't likely to make a public fuss. You meant well. On the other hand, you won't reap the personal psychological benefits of playing the helping role if you know your efforts are bound to fail.

The concrete benefits don't end with improvements to your reputation. Up to this point, there has been no direct benefit as motivation for helping. And that kind of benefit is never guaranteed, but its possibility adds another reason to assume the helping role. In this case, the transactional view applies, and the quid pro quo is simple: A job seeker may not be able to return any favors now, but things change. That same person may be in a very different position in the future, and there may come a time when you need some help yourself.

Given our natural inclination to see help as something to be repaid, you don't have to emulate Don Corleone by making help contingent on the recipient's promise to be there for you in the future. You don't have to mention that you may call upon this job seeker. The expectation of reciprocity is already built into the relationship of giver and receiver. The more people you help, the more people in the world who are likely to come running when you need a hand.

The next time the opportunity presents itself, act in your own best interests, and do yourself some good by doing good for someone else. You'll be glad you did.

Acknowledgments

I WANT TO ACKNOWLEDGE my remarkable clients. They come from the world over—all the continents, major cities, and suburbs—and work in every imaginable profession. Each day I'm overwhelmed by the ingenuity of people, and I am lucky for the opportunity to help them find their dream job.

Now, about this book.

Special appreciation to Marla Markman, who helped throughout the process with editing, project management, and overall professional publishing expertise. She swooped in to ensure that this book reached the finish line, patiently managing tasks and applying creative problem-solving when needed.

Michael Neuendorff provided business expertise, a trustworthy sounding board, encouragement, and a new friendship.

Tiffany Thompson kept me organized (as much as is humanly possible), a miracle in the midst of the phantasmagoria of e-commerce.

Michelle Penn Swanson has been kind, wise, and generous from day one, willing to share her understanding of the vicissitudes of career management.

Thanks to colleagues who provided insights, assistance, and support, including the dynamic Dan Dorotik, who will one day turn a resume into a screenplary. Assistance from Rachel Akers, Amy Pedersen, and Gayle Keefer has been professional and reliable. They didn't know until now that they saved the day many times.

Sarah Crystal appeared like magic to offer thought leadership after a 40-year hiatus.

Larry Jacobson willingly shared his marketing expertise and secrets about business ideas.

Laurie Kretchmar contributed a scintillating nickname and a future IPO.

Howard Bailen was always down the block, ready to play the groundball game and provide moral support, research, and observations.

Bill Anderson and John Goodenough learned agility and angles to help me blow off steam with brutal games of table tennis.

Thanks to Bethany Brown, and Michele DeFilippo of 1106 Design who helped create a cover and pleasing interior page design.

My appreciation and love to Jeannie, Max, and Edan is unabating.

Index